The
FATEFUL
ALLIANCE

Also by George F. Kennan

American Diplomacy, 1900–1950

Realities of American Foreign Policy

Soviet-American Relations 1917–1920
Vol. I: Russia Leaves the War
Vol. II: The Decision to Intervene

Russia, the Atom, and the West

Soviet Foreign Policy, 1917–1941

Russia and the West Under Lenin and Stalin

On Dealing with the Communist World

Memoirs 1925–1950

From Prague After Munich: Diplomatic Papers 1938–1940

Democracy and the Student Left

The Marquis de Custine and His "Russia in 1839"

Memoirs 1950–1963

The Cloud of Danger: Current Realities of American Foreign Policy

Decline of Bismarck's European Order

The Nuclear Delusion: Soviet-American Relations in the Atomic Age

GEORGE F. KENNAN

The FATEFUL ALLIANCE

France, Russia, and the Coming of the First World War

PANTHEON BOOKS
New York

Library of Congress Cataloging in Publication Data

Kennan, George Frost, 1904–
    The fateful alliance.

    Includes index.
    1. World War, 1914–1918—Causes. 2. Soviet Union—
Foreign relations—France. 3. France—Foreign relations—
Soviet Union. 4. France—Foreign relations—1870–1940.
5. Russia—Foreign relations—1894–1917. 6. Triple Alliance,
1882. I. Title.
D511.K34   1984   940.3'11   84-42709
ISBN 0-394-53494-8

Manufactured in the United States of America

3456789

Contents

Illustrations

AUTHOR'S NOTE

The number of institutions and persons to whom I am indebted for help in the preparation of this study is so great that I despair of trying to mention them all in a note of this nature. But the following, I think, deserve special mention.

First of all: the research for this work involved much travel as well as secretarial and research assistance. For help in meeting the costs of this assistance I am deeply indebted to three institutions.

The Institute for Advanced Study at Princeton, which has been my academic home for so many years, has continued, even in these years of my retirement, to give generous support for my scholarly work and much understanding for the unusual conditions under which that work has had to be pursued.

The Buffett Foundation has been exceptionally helpful in making it possible for historical scholarship to proceed hand in hand with efforts to take a useful, if restrained, part in the discussions of the great problems of American foreign policy in the nuclear age.

A research grant from the National Endowment for the Humanities has been of prime importance in covering the various costs of travel and research in a number of foreign capitals.

The study has required recourse to government archives in several capitals: among them, the Archives des affaires étrangères at the Quai d'Orsay in Paris; the Haus-, Hof-, und Staatsarchiv in Vienna; the Arkhiv Vneshnei Politiki in Moscow; the Public Record Office in London; and the Overhofmarskallatetsarkiv as well as the Danish foreign office archives in Copenhagen. In all of these places I was met with unfailing courtesy and helpfulness; and I regret only that limitations of space prevent me from mentioning individually the archivists and curators in whose debt I find myself.

Among the many other individuals who have contributed helpfully to this study I must mention:

M. and Mme. Eugène Simoneau-Ribot, of Paris, who kindly gave me not only access to the personal papers of Mme. Ribot's grandfather, Alexandre Ribot, but also the benefit of the many personal memories that have come down in the Ribot family. I shall not soon forget their charming and generous hospitality.

Ms. Lyte M. Fozard of Washington, D.C., who kindly let me see the exhaustive work she is preparing on the official career and activity of Charles de Freycinet, and told me much about the latter's personality that could scarcely have been learned from any other source.

Professor Martin Schmidt of the University of Wisconsin, who is the author of the only scholarly work done to date (to my knowledge) on the political career of Alexandre Ribot, and who allowed me to tap his special knowledge of Ribot's life and personality.

Professor P. A. Zaionchkovski, of Moscow, distinguished authority on the history of nineteenth-century Russia, who kindly shared with me his impressions of Alexander III and other leading Russian personalities of the period.

I must record my deep gratitude to Mrs. Chantal Hunt for the devoted and effective help she gave me as a research assistant for part of the time that the book was in preparation. Particularly, but not only, for the work in Paris, where the foreign scholar has special needs for guidance and tactful intercession, her help was of exceptional value.

I recall with deep appreciation the interest so kindly taken in this volume by M. Francis Ley, formerly of the Banque Worms of Paris, himself a fine scholar in the great tradition of dilettante historians.

My thanks are also due, in this connection, to my brother Kent Kennan, professor emeritus in the field of music theory at the University of Texas at Austin, who ran his incomparable editorial eye over this entire volume and called attention, with the benevolent relentlessness only a brother could bring to the task, to its all too many blemishes.

Mrs. Ilene Cohen deserves my sincere thanks for her conscientious checking and editing of the hundred fifty–odd reference notes the volume contains—a service all the more appreciated because of my own deficiencies when it comes to such matters of detail.

I have saved for the last the expression of my thanks to the two secretaries, Mrs. Constance Goodman and Mrs. Elizabeth Stenard, who have held my official life together during all (or, in Mrs. Stenard's case,

AUTHOR'S NOTE

much) of the time this volume was under preparation. Few will ever know what strains this effort involved, for them as for me; and the patience, devotion, and skill with which they have met these strains have been a lesson to their employer.

. . .

Permission to use the long passage, in Chapter 1, from the Gerard Hopkins translation of Proust's *Jean Santeuil* was graciously granted by the publisher of that work, Weidenfeld and Nicolson, of London.

. . .

The reference notes to this volume are to be found at the end of the book. Abbreviations have been used, throughout the text as well as in the reference notes, for titles frequently referred to. A list of these abbreviations appears on page xii.

Abbreviations

Austrian archives	Haus-, Hof-, und Staatsarchiv, Vienna.
DDF	*Documents diplomatiques français*, First Series (1871–1900).
French archives, vol. 30	"Russie: Politique étrangère: Relations avec la France: Négociations franco-russes. Août, 1890–juin, 1892," vol. 30, Archives des affaires étrangères, Paris.
French archives, vol. 31	"Russie: Politique étrangère: Relations avec la France: Négociations franco-russes. Août, 1890–juin, 1892," vol. 31, Archives des affaires étrangères, Paris.
French military archives	Archives de l'armée française, Vincennes.
Grosse Politik	*Die grosse Politik der Europäischen Kabinette*
Kennan, *Bismarck's European Order*	George F. Kennan, *The Decline of Bismarck's European Order* (Princeton: Princeton University Press, 1979).
Lamsdorf diary	V. N. Lamsdorf, *Dnevnik, 1891–1892* (Moscow: Akademia, 1934).
Ribot mss., French archives	Ribot mss., Archives des affaires étrangères, Paris.
Russian archives	Arkhiv vneshnei politiki Rossii [Archive of the foreign policy of Russia], Moscow, file Sekretny arkhiv 1891–1894.

INTRODUCTION

The volume these words will introduce represents the second part of what was conceived as a study, in depth, of the relationship of alliance that linked Russia and France in the period from 1894 to its breakdown in 1917–1918.

The first part of this study, published in 1979 by the Princeton University Press under the title *The Decline of Bismarck's European Order*, was addressed to the gradual dissolution of the earlier close relationship—not quite a defensive alliance but not far from it—that had prevailed between Russia and Germany during the 1880s. Attention to that subject was unavoidable, for the decline of the special Russo-German relationship was the prerequisite for the establishment of any significant political and military intimacy between Russia and France.

The present volume, picking up the story in 1890 with Bismarck's retirement and the failure of the Germans to renew their last treaty bond with Russia, is addressed to the process of negotiation by means of which the French and Russian governments arrived at what came to be known as the Franco-Russian Alliance of 1894.

A third part, still to be written, should carry the tale from 1894 down to the total collapse of the Alliance in the turmoil of the Russian Revolution and of the resulting withdrawal of Russia from the First World War, in 1917–1918.

The attention of the author was initially drawn to this subject by certain of the appreciations borne in upon him by his earlier studies of the first months of the Soviet-American relationship in 1917 and 1918. Central to these appreciations was the recognition of how endlessly unfortunate, primarily for Russia but scarcely less so for France and the remainder of Western Europe, turned out to be this involvement of Russia, through her ties to France, in the great Western European conflicts of the first years of this century. It was largely this involvement that caused what had begun in 1914 as a Balkan quarrel to grow into the dimensions of a general European war. And it was Russia's participation in this great war, coming as it did on the heels of her costly and unsuccessful conflict with Japan in 1904–1905, that fatally interrupted the adjustment of her social and political system to the demands of the modern age and thus played a leading part in bringing on the Revolution, with all its fateful consequences for both Russia and the world at large.

For France, too, what a dismal ending—these events of 1917–1918 —to a political arrangement, namely, the Alliance, once conceived in such high hopes of victory and glory: abandonment by the intended ally at the moment of maximum difficulty in a great military conflict; the subsequent shattering (because Russia was no longer available as a participant) of the entire effort to construct a durable European peace in the wake of that conflict; and then, fifteen years later, the necessity for France of facing alone, initially without any effective ally, the hydra of an embittered, hysterically governed, and immensely powerful Germany!

To note these things—to note the extreme disparity between the high hopes and expectations that had entered into the creation of the Alliance in the first place and the disasters with which it ended—was to ask oneself what it was, then, that had gone wrong, what it was that had not been expected, why such a denouement had not been foreseen, what were the faults of vision that had produced so drastic a miscalculation, and what had caused those faults. It seemed that a careful scrutiny of the steps that led to the conclusion of the Alliance in the first place and inspired its cultivation over the course of some twenty-three years might just tell us something about the pitfalls that lie in wait for statesmen who try to look too far into the future and to meet distant and imagined contingencies by the devices of military alliance.

Whether the contents of this present volume, intended only as a reasonably full and factual account of the processes by which the documents comprising the Alliance were actually negotiated, serves this purpose, is something the reader will have to judge. It is, of course, not the whole story. There was the preceding account, itself in many ways instructive, of the stages by which the earlier Russian-German relationship broke down. And there should eventually be, good fortune and strength permitting, the further account, referred to above, of how the Alliance was developed, and clung to, in the decades just following its conclusion. But it is the author's hope that out of the totality of these investigations there will emerge a clearer understanding of at least a few of those many missteps and misconceptions by which a forward-looking and confident nineteenth-century Europe brought itself, through two world wars, to the dreadful bewilderments and dangers of the nuclear age.

. . .

Are there things of which the casual reader might usefully be reminded before he tries to picture in his mind's eye the people and places that go to make up the particular segment of diplomatic history covered by this book? Would it be useful, for example, to remember that these years of the early 1890s were, in many physical and technological respects, an age of rapid change, and particularly of incipient change? —an age of candles and gaslights, about to yield to the greater but less colorful brilliance of the electric globe? —an age of handwritten notes and messengers and unannounced visits, about to yield to the more hectic rigors of the telephone? —an age of quill pens, sand blotting, and wax seals, about to make place for the typewriter (the first typed diplomatic documents were beginning to appear precisely at the time the Alliance was concluded)? —an age of horse-drawn carriages and far-flung railway networks, soon to be invaded by the internal combustion engine of the automobile and the airplane, revolutionizing wartime mobility along with a host of other things? —an age of the bourgeois frock coat of nineteenth-century official and diplomatic society, now about to yield to the short jacket and derby hat of the early twentieth? Is it helpful to try to picture how things looked and sounded and were felt in that day, and how all this affected the actors in the drama? These connections are hard to demonstrate; but surely, they had their significance.

And even more significant were the personal characteristics of those actors themselves—the traits, in particular, that set them off from the statesmen and officials of earlier and later periods. The years of the early 1890s were witnessing the disappearance from active political life of the last of those men (Bismarck, Lord Palmerston, and the old German Emperor William I were among them) over whose personalities and activities there still hovered something of the atmosphere of the respective *anciens régimes* in which they had been reared. In many respects these were primarily eighteenth-century personalities. Those who were now succeeding them were different in subtle, yet striking, ways. Most of them, even the non-English ones, were in some respects Victorians, in the sense that they were less secure in their values, more self-conscious, more imitative, more given to enacting a role, than their predecessors. These qualities were reflected in their political judgments and reactions, marked as they were by a love for the intricate, the indirect, the oversubtle, the allusive, and above all for the pretentious, in place of the blunt, sometimes brutal, but usually elegant and impressive facility of their predecessors for going to the heart of things. Whereas the members of the older generation had been governed in their social and official conduct by the manners of the eighteenth century—clear, schooled, unapologetic, a law unto themselves—the conduct of these late-nineteenth-century people seemed, by comparison, uncertain, histrionic, overacted—always with an anxious eye to the spectators. The healthy self-confidence that had enabled their fathers and grandfathers to come to terms, fatalistically and good-humoredly, with the persistent weaknesses of the human flesh was yielding now to forms of hypocrisy in which the appearance of virtue was given more importance than its reality, and the lapses from it, sexual or financial, were more anxiously concealed, hence more morbid and more painful. It was an age of frequent and pathetic failures in both of these respects—an age of helpless, tragically ending clandestine liaisons, à la Anna Karenina, and excruciating financial embarrassments, all silhouetted against the pretenses of insecure men and women, lonely, vulnerable, and sometimes desperate, in their private worlds of sin or financial embarrassment, yet most of them unmercifully critical of others who found themselves in just these very predicaments. And all of this was superimposed, so to speak, upon the overelaborate social pretensions of the day. Precisely because the old firm class structures were now disintegrating under the impact of the industrial revolution, the poorly formed new ones, based predominantly on affluence rather than birth—and often sudden, unstable, insecure affluence at that—were clung to with anxious desperation, the external showiness betraying at every point the inner uncertainties. Many of the diplomats and statesmen (though less in Russia than elsewhere) suffered from these compulsions, feeling it necessary to display a style of living they could not really afford, caught between the relaxed largesse of a land-owning nobility to which they did not belong and the pretensions of wealthy new bourgeoisie whose ostentation they could not rival.

This was not really a very healthy age, especially for the upper-class people who populate the scenes of this book. They were, for the most part, overfed, oversexed, and underexercised. Too often, their bulging bodies were enveloped in garments too tight for either comfort or health. The cigarette was now coming into its own as the fashionable public vice; a great many people, up to and including royalty, smoked most fearfully—and paid the price. Tuberculosis, no respecter of wealth or class, was rampant among them; and its ravages, like those of the other infectious diseases (to which there was as yet no significant medical answer), struck the young even more cruelly than the old. Death was a ubiquitous phenomenon, and not just among the aged. Health, in these circumstances, was a prominent subject of conversation and of correspondence. It was widely believed that the state of one's well-being depended importantly on the qualities of the air one breathed, the waters one imbibed, and the medicinal baths one took. Spas, with their various corrective regimes, were accordingly looked to to counteract the vicissitudes of life in other places, and visits to them preempted a great deal of time, attention, and expenditure on the part of those who had the means for this form of indulgence.

. . .

Is it also necessary, the author wonders, for the reader to remember, before undertaking the contemplation of the following story, that the two capitals in which so much of it took place—Paris and St. Petersburg— were at that time the scenes of a tremendous outpouring of artistic, literary, not to mention technological and scientific, activity—an outpouring beside which the written records of the dealings among statesmen, in the shadows of their heavily guarded chanceries, appear obscure, colorless, and dreary, like dust-covered legal documents?

Paris was at that time, of course, a veritable caldron of aesthetic and intellectual impulses—emerging, flaming, seething, declining, yielding to others, but each leaving its mark on ensuing periods. What was happening there in the visual arts alone—"la grande bourrasque des environs de 1890," as the French painter-theoretician Maurice Denis described it— surely represented one of the greatest outpourings of creative activity ever to take place at one time and in one place in the modern Western world. It would be pretentious on the part of this writer to attempt to describe it.

Much of the same could be said, though on a lower scale, of literature and music. Balzac was dead; and Maupassant, publishing in 1890 the last volume of his stories, was about to fade, embittered and desperate, into his final miserable decline. But Zola, Pierre Loti, and Maurice Barrès were at the height of their powers. And new names—Claudel, Proust, Anatole France—were in the wings.

Saint-Saëns was just then at the peak of his popularity. Wagner was banned, to be sure, from the stage of the Paris Opéra; but his music could be heard, and was heard—with intense interest—elsewhere in the capital.

There was also a veritable vogue for Russian music at just this time, reflecting the growing enthusiasm of the Paris public for all things Russian. Rimski-Korsakov and Tchaikovsky had both recently conducted at the great 1889 Paris Centennial Exposition: the former presenting the works of a whole series of Russian composers—Glinka, Moussorgsky, Borodin; the latter, several of his own. And before the year 1890 was out, Tchaikovsky's *Sleeping Beauty* ballet score and his freshly composed *Queen of Spades* could be heard on the Paris stages.

Petersburg was of course not Paris; but here, too, especially if one includes the second Russian capital of Moscow, it was an exciting time. Literature, as always, remained the leading Russian art form. Tolstoi, the great artist, was fading away; but Tolstoi, the moralist, was now coming into his own—captive of a new dedication that was to hold him in bondage to his death. In 1890, the first of his moralistic plays, *The Power of Darkness*, had just appeared (arousing, incidentally, the disgust and ire of Alexander III). He was now working on *The Fruits of Enlightenment.*

Anton Chekhov, weary of his life as a humorist, a short-story writer, and a rather unwilling participant in the social life of the Russian literary community, was just then embarking on that strange penitential journey across Siberia to the remote island of Sakhalin that was to mark a dividing point in his life; and one may be sure that there were already ripening in that exquisitely perceptive and sensitive spirit the seeds that were about to come to fruition in the great plays of the 1895–1904 period—plays that, interpreted by the fresh young talents of Stanislavski and the Moscow Art Theater, would revolutionize dramaturgy and the stage not only in Russia but to some extent in Western Europe as well.

Music, too, in the Russia of 1890, had reached a point of great vitality. Anton Rubinstein, in addition to conducting and performing all over the Petersburg area, was functioning once again, and for the last time, as director of the great Petersburg conservatory he himself had founded. Tchaikovsky was now at the acme of his creative powers. With four years to go before his premature death, he was producing some of his finest and most mature music. *The Sleeping Beauty* had had its Russian premiere just the year before (in a private dress rehearsal attended by the imperial couple in the palace theater at Tsarskoye Selo). The opera *Pique-Dame*, then undergoing completion by the composer in Rome, was about to make its appearance. Moussorgsky and Borodin were dead; but their work was only now coming fully into its own in the appreciation for it among the Russian public. In that very year of 1890, Rimski-Korsakov and Glazunov were completing the score of the late Borodin's unfinished opera, *Prince Igor.*

Secular art was a relatively new feature of Russian life; but there was by this time, both in Petersburg and in Moscow, a galaxy of modern painters, of differing and rapidly changing schools, who, with the support of their remarkable merchant patrons, were giving to Russian art its greatest age since that of the great icon painters of earlier centuries.

In general, it is fair to say that Petersburg, in those years of the early 1890s, stood on the threshold of that wild explosion of artistic and intellectual activity that was to mark its life over the few remaining years of the tsarist epoch—an explosion so brilliant and startling that it now shines out for the historian like some inexplicable celestial object, suddenly flashing across the otherwise somber sky of Russian history.

It is hard to establish the relevance of all this to the tale to be unfolded in this volume. The documents do not, as a rule, reveal it. But relevance there must have been, however hard to identify. The lonely actors in this diplomatic drama were, after all, men of their time. They lived in these same capital cities. They could not have been entirely unaware of, or indifferent to, all that was happening around them. But they were busy men. Their diplomatic responsibilities sometimes represented full-time jobs. The responsibilities were important ones; and someone had to bear them. So they struggled along, as we shall see, in another world from that of the artists, the writers, and the musicians. It was their professional world—a world of duty. And if they were moved, or disturbed, by the cultural frenzy of the time, there was nothing they could do about it. All that was their private life. They were obliged to keep it aloof from their official duties.

.   .   .

To many among the cultural intelligentsia, and particularly the younger ones, these great flowerings of genius in the arts presented themselves as endlessly hopeful beginnings—openings to a new world of wonder and promise. New horizons were being extended, outworn disciplines discarded, new modes of creative self-expression discovered. It was the opening of a new age; and who knew—who could tell—to what it might all lead?

It would be comforting if the historian, looking back on the life of that time and the events of the century to follow, could regard these hopes as well placed. Obviously, he cannot. The years around 1890, historically viewed, constituted only the prelude to much tragedy. Of the 470,000 male infants born in France in the year 1890, fully half were fated either to meet an early and painful death in World War I or to emerge from that bloodbath maimed or otherwise injured. A whole generation of those who were at that time young parents would someday face the terrible bereavements and discouragements these losses would bring to them.

A comparable situation existed in Russia, with the added feature that nearly all of the persons born in the year 1890 into the educated and more privileged classes were destined not only to see destroyed the entire social framework that had made their families what they were, but themselves to suffer death, hardship, oppression, or exile in the successive horrors of world war, revolution, civil war, or thereafter in the exactions of an implacably hostile dictatorship. This applied no less to those who would one day become the artists and writers than to millions of others. And all these disasters of the 1914–1924 period would soon be followed by further miseries: the political failures of the interwar period; the rise of German Nazism, the Second World War; the division of the European continent; and the further dissolution of European society into the bewilderments of the technological revolution of the mid-twentieth century. Truly, the final years of the nineteenth century, however things may have appeared at the moment, were not a happy time to be born.

The
FATEFUL
ALLIANCE

Chapter 1

POLITICS AND PERSONALITIES, 1890

Before turning to the events to be recounted, let us consider briefly the situations that prevailed, respectively, in the two capitals as of the beginning of the year 1890.

In France, the crisis of Boulangism had now passed. The elections of 1889 had marked the end of General Boulanger's brief and stormy political career. He had himself gone into exile. It was only a matter of months before he would die by his own hand, on his mistress's grave in Belgium. But if his leadership and his person had now disappeared, the flood tide of patriotic feeling on which he had been carried had not disappeared at all. Not only was this tide still running, stronger than ever, but it was now serving as a rallying point for French political forces that had hitherto been kept apart by deep ideological divisions.

On the Republic side, the dry positivism that had marked the Opportuniste approach to France's problems throughout the 1870s and 1880s, riveting attention to such burning internal problems as the secularization of education, was giving way to a cloudy and emotional enthusiasm for the restoration of the glory of France. The militant secularism—the violent hatred of ultramontane Roman Catholic influence by which so many of the Opportuniste politicians had been driven—was now being subjected to erosion. To the younger members of the republican constituency this entire conflict was in fact losing its appeal as an issue. And correspondingly, the attitude of the Church towards the Republic was also beginning to change. It was in November 1890 that Cardinal Archbishop Lavigerie, in a speech delivered at his episcopal seat of Algiers, called upon French Catholics to abandon their principled opposition to the institution of the Republic. This was the first step towards the so-called *ralliement* —a movement of reconciliation between Church and Republic destined, over the ensuing years, to split both the monarchist and the clerical oppositions and to cause portions of both these elements to find common cause with their erstwhile Opportuniste opponents on the basis of a shared patriotic fervor, a shared enthusiasm for the demonstrative restoration of the power and greatness of France.

For these deep currents of French feeling, in which the accumulated frustrations of the two decades that had passed since the Treaty of Frankfurt (1871) were now finding their release, there was of course no focal point that held higher symbolic value than the dream of a Franco-Russian alliance. If it was the persistent and apparently successful development of the French armed forces that was beginning to provide what seemed to be a realistic basis for these yearnings, it was the concept of an alliance with Russia that supplied the necessary symbolic accompaniment to it. What finer symbol could there be than this one for the fact that France was again becoming a great power—not just in her own eyes but in those of the outside world as well? And what more eloquent confirmation that France was no longer alone, that there were others, including one of the world's greatest and most powerful empires, who coveted her friendship and her support?

For the French public of that time all this met a deeply felt need. Here was reassurance. Here was the recovery of a lost sense of identity for a France whose confidence in her very greatness had been shaken by the humiliation of 1871. What, in these circumstances, could have had a more profound emotional-political appeal than the thought of an alliance with the great and mighty Russian empire? What could have lent itself more readily to unrestrained, uncritical, open-hearted acceptance? In this thought there was not only hope, there was the shaping of a new national consciousness and consensus. Here once again, as so often in the histories of modern democratic societies, the awkward embarrassments of internal conflict, ideological and political, were to find their sublimation (or so it seemed) in the pursuit of external glory.

This, then, was the political soil out of which the most important elements of French statesmanship over the ensuing four years would grow. None of the manifestations of French policy are fully intelligible to posterity unless this background of feeling is taken into account.

. . .

In Russia, the situation was quite different. Here, there was no such things as internal politics. There was no parliament, no electorate, no prime minister, no cabinet. There was only the Tsar; and there were his principal ministers: those of finance, foreign affairs, and war. And in the personal incumbencies of these offices there reigned, in contrast with the situation in France, a great stability. Two of the incumbents—the ministers of foreign affairs and war—had been in office from the beginning of the reign of Alexander III. They would remain there until its end. The third, the finance minister, had been in office four years. As of 1890, he had, to be sure, only some two more to go; but he was at the time nonetheless firmly in office. In all of this, 1890 marked no great change.

These men were all conservative figures. Whatever their inner feelings, they formed part of a regime that was in the process of undermining most of the liberal reforms of the period of Alexander II. It was a regime marked precisely by its insensitivity to what was occurring all around it in the development of Russian society, and above all by its lack of contact with, and its estrangement of, student youth and the cultural intelligentsia generally. But this was a state of affairs that marked the entire reign of Alexander III. It was no different in 1890 than in any other year. And its profoundly unfortunate effects were ones that would not make themselves significantly felt until ten to fifteen years later. Meanwhile, Petersburg was the scene of what appeared to be a monumental political stability.

. . .

This brings us to the question of personalities. In general, these will be introduced as they appear on the scene of the tale about to be unfolded. But in the case of the Russians, the two leading figures—the Tsar Alexander III and his foreign minister, Nikolai Karlovich Giers—had been at their posts throughout most of the 1880s and would remain there down through the entire period of the negotiation and final conclusion of the Franco-Russian Alliance. They appeared, as of 1890, to be permanent fixtures at the Russian end of the relationship. A few special words about them will therefore not be out of place.

The figure of Alexander III is one familiar from a multitude of historical sources and treatises: this huge, ponderous, taciturn man, often compared to a bull or an ox—a tall, heavyset, bearded figure, of immense physical strength—a retiring, unsociable sort of a person, seldom visited by others, seldom seen in public, and when seen, then always in uniform. He was often accused of laziness, of phlegmatic temperament, of indifference to his surroundings, of a sort of bovine stubbornness. There was some truth in most of these accusations, but they were far from penetrating the complexities of this extraordinary personality.

While indeed unsociable, retiring, given to burying himself in his various palaces, and not in the habit of learning about the rest of Russia from personal observation or from wide personal contacts with other people, Alexander was not really so indifferent to what was occurring throughout his empire as was commonly supposed; he merely preferred to learn about it in the privacy of his palace, through the reports of his leading ministers. He was, of course, so far as internal matters were concerned, profoundly conservative—reactionary, if you will. He bore, throughout his reign, the scars of his reaction to the murder of his father in 1881. These scars took the form of a belief that this, and other political assassinations of that period, would not have occurred had his father and those around him not temporized with the liberal and radical political currents of the preceding decades. He was determined not to make the same mistake. He punished ruthlessly what he saw as attempts to over-throw the dynasty or to undermine the imperial system. But he took—at least up to the time when this account begins—a keen interest in foreign affairs; and wherever his personal sensitivities were not too exten-sively involved, his judgments on such matters were not devoid of percep-tion and good sense. His sensitivities, on the other hand—his likes, dislikes, his reactions to what he saw as slights to his person or to his authority—could be lively in the extreme. Once aroused, they were not easily assuaged.

Alexander III preferred to take no part personally, and above all publicly, in the execution of Russian foreign policy. He disliked public appearances. He abhorred the thought of speaking before any sort of assemblage. He never signed anything personally if he could help it. He left all that to his ministers.

He was fully aware of his power and his responsibility. His leading ministers reported to him weekly throughout most of the year. He was punctilious in receiving them, listened carefully to what they had to say, made his decisions and gave them their orders when he considered that the proper time had come; but he left to them the execution of those orders. He was in a certain sense personally diffident—a quality not to be confused with any lack of readiness to assert his own power. He simply liked to deal with familiar faces, and disliked having to confront new ones. For this reason he changed his ministers very rarely—sometimes even kept them long beyond the period of their greatest effectiveness. But he never allowed them—or even the members of his own family—to forget who was the Tsar, and what this meant. The numerous grand dukes who formed part of his family, some of them older and headstrong men, all learned to respect his authority. Yet there were certain individuals in his entourage to whose opinions he was particularly sensitive, and whom he hesitated to controvert. When these disagreed among themselves and gave him conflicting advice, he was capable (like many another absolute ruler) of vacillating, temporizing, and even acting deviously. He did not like dramatic personal confrontations, and would go out of his way to avoid them. For all his strength and his consciousness of authority, there was within him a curious streak of evasive shyness (or was it slyness?), which caused him to avoid participation in collective discussions of any sort, to deal with his ministers only individually, and to take his decisions in private and to make them known in ways that precluded objection or counterargument.

In his secluded palace life, accessible to few outsiders, Alexander was flanked by his pleasant and beautiful Danish wife, the Empress Dagmar (in Danish usage), Mariya Fyodorovna (in Russian), daughter of the Danish King Christian IX, and sister of the future Queen Alexandra of England. A much more outgoing person than her husband, she would no doubt have liked to lead a more open and sociable existence; but in this respect she, too, had no choice but to defer to the Tsar's wishes, and she made the best of it. She never interfered overtly in governmental affairs; but she had ways of making her influence felt behind the scenes; and that influence, highly colored by her personal reactions to individuals, and particularly by her bitterness against Germany, and Bismarck personally, over Denmark's sufferings in the Prussian-Danish War of 1864, was sometimes primitive and not always helpful.

Alexander's father, the Tsar Alexander II, while no great friend of Bismarck, had had high respect and affection for his own uncle, the German Kaiser William I, to whom he was related by marriage. He had accepted a reasonably close relationship to Germany as something flowing naturally from the common imperial title and the common interest in sustaining the principle of inherited monarchy as the kingpin of any proper political system. He had naturally observed with mixed feelings, as had so many others in Europe, Bismarck's stormy advancement of the position of Prussia in Central Europe and the final creation, in the wake of the Franco-Prussian War, of the new German empire. But he had no emotional prejudice against Germany as such. The French Republic, established at the same time as the German empire, was far less to his liking.

In all of this, his son, Alexander III, differed. While sharing his father's personal respect for the venerable Kaiser William I, Alexander III appears to have entertained doubts, throughout his reign, as to whether the kings of Prussia really had a legal right to the imperial title; and he viewed imperial Germany, generally speaking, with a suspicious dislike, increasingly so as his reign progressed. This was, of course, an inclination encouraged by his wife and other Danish relatives (particularly Dagmar's mother, Queen Louise of Denmark), among whom the humiliations inflicted upon that country in the Prussian-Danish War of 1864 had been by no means forgotten. Beyond this, there was jealousy of Bismarck for his various successes, military and political, and particularly resentment of his role at the Congress of Berlin. There was also, on Alexander's part, a resentment (founded in certain unhappy personal experiences) of the influence various Baltic-German officials had exercised in the political entourage of his father, and a resulting tendency to view all things German with some distaste. Finally, there was Alexander's instinctive personal distrust of, and antipathy towards, the new German Kaiser, William II—feelings destined to grow in intensity over the years of the early 1890s.

Alexander was also strongly anti-Austrian. The origins of this attitude seem to be complex. There was, certainly and perhaps most importantly, the influence of his former tutor, the formidable "Oberprokuror" of the Russian Orthodox Church, Konstantin Petrovich Pobedonostsev. The latter was strongly affected by his resentment of Vienna's support of the Catholic clergy in the Russian-occupied portion of Poland. There was also the effect of Alexander's memories of his own experiences as an officer in the Russian army during the Russo-Turkish War of 1877–1878, and notably a feeling that the Austrians, instead of supporting Russia's political purposes in that war, had contrived to exploit to their own advantage the political and military embarrassments the war had ultimately come to present for the Russians. To this was added Alexander's conviction that Austrian obstruction had contributed to the subsequent failure of Russian efforts to develop the former Turkish province of Bulgaria into a reliable Russian puppet state after the war.

Given these attitudes towards Germany and Austria, it is clear that Alexander had no enthusiasm for the "three-emperor" relationship (Germany, Austria-Hungary, and Russia) that had played so prominent a part in the diplomacy of his father. He could not be successfully appealed to, as could his father, in the name of a three-emperor solidarity against the revolutionary tendencies of the time. While he had respected the other two imperial sovereigns—Franz Joseph and William I (the latter died in

1888), he had nothing but suspicion for their respective chancellors, premiers, and foreign ministers—or, in the case of Kaiser William I, for the latter's grandson and eventual successor, William II.

The so-called Pan-Slavs, whose Balkan ambitions had had so much to do with the war with Turkey and its outcome, were by the 1890s a declining force in Russian policy; but their place, and in large part their enthusiasms, had now been taken over by people best described simply as strong Russian nationalists, jealous of the other great European powers, thirsting, like so many other nationalists of that age, for the expansion of the glory and power of their own country. This form of nationalism was less attached to the fortunes of the Romanov dynasty as such than to those of Russia as a political/cultural (and in part religious) entity. This being so, it was often alleged by German and other Western European conservatives that Russian nationalism contained, as a movement, certain revolutionary tendencies, or at least implications. In this, there was an element of truth: it was eventually to contribute, in fact, to the demise of the dynasty. But the argument appears to have made little impression on Alexander III. In general, he may be said to have shared the imperialistic aims of the Pan-Slavs and of their nationalistic successors with respect to the Balkans and Southeast Europe. These included the desire to obtain such a position at the Turkish Straits as would assure to Russia the ability to move her own naval vessels freely through the Straits in both directions while denying to the warships of other powers entrance into the Black Sea. It was this dream that had played so prominent a part in the unleashing of the war with Turkey. It had been constantly present, as a background factor, in subsequent Russian policies towards the Balkans and the Turkish empire. But here Russia had met with a long series of failures and frustrations; and one has the impression that by 1890 the Tsar's enthusiasm for this cause had been somewhat worn down, to the point where it had ceased to represent an important immediate motivation for his policies. His attachment to the dream remained unchanged; but he evidently now regarded its realization as something that was not a matter of the near future—something, rather, that would someday flow automatically from victory in the eventual armed struggle among the great European powers, the inevitability of which few then doubted.

· · ·

Nikolai Karlovich Giers, Alexander's foreign minister, who had served in this capacity since 1882, was a highly competent career diplomat, probably the most seasoned and able statesman of his time in Europe, after Bismarck. His competence was based on extensive previous experience with Russian policy in the Balkans and Western Europe, including not only service as a diplomat in those regions but later responsibility as head of the Asiatic division of the Russian foreign office, and then as deputy foreign minister in the 1870s.

Giers was a modest, quiet, scrupulously honest man. Being neither well-born nor wealthy, he had no position at court or in the higher social circles of the Russian capital. He was generally underestimated by people in those circles, some of whom were envious of his position and even took pleasure in running him down in the hopes of undermining it. But he stuck faithfully to his tasks, despite much adverse criticism and despite some very high-powered attempts to displace him. Indeed, it was probably in large measure the very modesty of his circumstances, together with his experience and ability, that moved the Tsar to keep him in the ministerial position as he did, through thick and thin, down to the end of his own reign; for Giers' aloofness from Petersburg high society held him removed from the gossip and intrigues of the capital; and his integrity and lack of political ambition gave Alexander the assurance that so long as Giers was there the important position of foreign minister would not be misused for unworthy purposes.

Much the older of the two men (he was born in 1820, Alexander III in 1845), Giers had not unnaturally come close, by 1890, to the end of his own physical powers. But Alexander's health, too, was now beginning to show the unfavorable effects of a sedentary palace life, and of much chain smoking, on so great a physical frame, for which no doubt much more in the way of outdoor exercise would have been required if it was to maintain its tone through a full normal lifetime. By 1890 both men, therefore, were showing signs of fading strength and a certain weariness with their allotted tasks. Not only were their energies, their sensitivity to outside events, their liveliness of reaction, beginning to fade, but issues that in the late 1880s had commanded their eager attention were coming to be somewhat obscured from their vision by fatigue, frustration, cynicism, and indifference. The high emotional pitch and delicate power of maneuver that had marked Russian diplomacy as little as three or four years earlier were now no longer much in evidence. On the part of the Tsar, they had given way to what one can only describe as a grumpy frame of mind, the main features of which were a continued and confirmed distrust of the Austrians and the acute dislike, just mentioned, of the new German Emperor, William II.

And as for Giers: his intimacy with his imperial master had been somewhat impaired by the strains of recent years. He no longer enjoyed quite the confidence the Tsar had once given him. Too often he had seen himself obliged to oppose or obstruct nationalistic impulses, particularly anti-German and anti-Austrian ones, that the Tsar was inclined to indulge. Giers' favored concepts of Russian foreign policy were now beginning, as we shall see shortly, to be shattered. He would continue, for the remaining years of the Tsar's life and his own, to stand formally at the helm of the ship of Russian foreign policy, but only in order to guide it unhappily, as best he could, among dangerous shoals and currents into which, left to himself, he would never have brought it. For this reason, the reader must not look to him for the same constancy and firmness of touch he had displayed in earlier years. He was now a man buffeted by the winds of contrary fate; and he sometimes swayed with those winds. He had no choice.

The year 1890, marked as it was by the great event of Bismarck's retirement, brought important changes into the international life of Europe. Alexander III and Giers would do their best to cope with these changes, according to their respective lights; and the way they did so is a large part of the story that follows. It is only fair to their memories to bear in mind that in 1890 neither of them was quite the man he had been as little as three or four years earlier. Not quite as much, then, could be expected of them.

·   ·   ·

The Tsar and Giers were not the only "permanent fixtures" of the Franco-Russian relationship. There were two others whose roles in the designing and bringing about of the Alliance were so dominant and whose names will appear so frequently in this account that they may as well be identified at the outset. These were the two generals, one French and one Russian, for whom the creation of this alliance may be said to have been a life's work: on the French side, Raoul le Mouton de Boisdeffre; and on the Russian side, Nikolai Nikolayevich Obruchev.

Boisdeffre stood, in competence, intelligence, and indeed in all the qualities that made for a successful military career, among the leading French military figures of his time. His most prominent patron during the early years of his service had been General Antoine Chanzy, who had commanded a corps in the Franco-Prussian War and had been governor of Algeria from 1873 to 1875. Boisdeffre, then in his thirties, had served on Chanzy's staff during both of those tours of duty. When Chanzy became ambassador to Russia, in 1879, he took Boisdeffre with him as assistant military attaché. From that time on, Boisdeffre, though serving in several other capacities, never lost his interest in Russia, in the Russian army, and in the possibilities for Franco-Russian military cooperation. Nor were his military superiors unaware of this interest or insensitive to the value that, given his outstanding qualities as an officer, it might have for the day when serious discussions with the Russians would begin. After Chanzy's death, in 1883, Boisdeffre's career enjoyed the strong support of General Marie-Joseph de Miribel, who had also served at one time as military attaché in Russia. When Miribel, in 1890, became the first chief of the newly created independent General Staff, it was Boisdeffre whom he selected as his deputy.* When Miribel retired in 1894, it was Boisdeffre who took his place as chief of the General Staff.

Certain of Boisdeffre's papers are reproduced in extenso in the published series of *Documents diplomatiques français* and elsewhere. Others remain in the hands of the Boisdeffre family; and this writer has kindly been permitted to examine some of them. One gains, from this material, a clear and detailed picture of Boisdeffre, the military diplomatist. It is the picture of a serious, honorable, dedicated, and highly competent officer—a man of distinguished bearing, tenacious yet tactful, excellently qualified for the highest tasks of military staff work and negotiation. France could consider herself fortunate to have at hand at this crucial time a man of such qualities.

Such is the French predilection, however, for separation of the personal from the professional that of Boisdeffre, the person, little in the way of evidence is available. The history of the later Dreyfus affair shows him dreadfully enmeshed in the entanglements of that incredible confusion and no more inclined than were certain other leading military figures to let the honor of the army be impugned for the sake of justice to a single individual. But all that was an episode that would take place some years later; nor does a single error destroy the value of an entire life. For the years before 1895 we have before us only this impressive uninformed figure: dignified, industrious, quietly persistent, everywhere respected—

*A unit called General Staff had existed since 1874 as a subordinate entity in the cabinet of the minister of war, but had had no independence and enjoyed no prestige. It was the reform of 1890 that created, for the first time, an independent general staff comparable to the one that already existed in Germany.

the waxwork model of the superior staff officer. Behind that—only a question mark.

Some idea both of the austere aloofness and the impressiveness of General de Boisdeffre can be gained from the vivid pen portrait of him painted by Proust (in his *Jean Santeuil**)—a picture of the general as he mounted the stairs, amid gaping crowds, to appear as a witness at the trial of Zola (in the Dreyfus case) in 1897:

> The most noticeable thing about him was a very high top-hat tilted at an angle. Listening apparently to the officer beside him with close attention, he moved forward slowly with a stiff motion of the legs, as though he were very tired. Every now and again he came to a halt. Though he still gave the impression of youthfulness his cheeks were covered by a delicate red and purple mottling such as one sees on garden walls in autumn when they are clothed in Virginia creeper. There was a look of concentrated attention in his eyes but from time to time they blinked with a sort of nervous tic and now and again he plucked at his moustache with an ungloved hand. . . . He seemed very calm and completely unhurried. The impression produced was that the nervous tic which set his eyes blinking, and the hand tugging at his moustache, as well as the red embroidery of his cheeks, the shabbiness of his overcoat, and the stiffness of his leg, which must often have been broken in falls from his horse, were, all of them, the special characteristics which together made up that august object known to all as "General de Boisdeffre," part and parcel of his grandeur because they were his own private property, were never separated from him. It was with those blinking eyes that he looked out upon the world: it was a result of smoking cigars and drinking brandy after long days of exacting work that his cheeks had acquired that veined and purple look. As he passed, the onlookers raised their hats and he returned the salutation politely like a man of very high rank, some Prince of the Church, who, knowing that he may excite envy, is at pains to disarm it by the perfection of his manners.

Such, as Proust observed him on that occasion, was the man who would speak for France in the negotiation of the Franco-Russian Alliance.

A wholly different sort of a person was Boisdeffre's opposite number on the Russian side: Nikolai Nikolayevich Obruchev. Born into a military family, left an orphan at the age of eight, he was at once placed in a boarding school for military orphans at Tsarskoye Selo. From that time on, until his marriage in 1860 or thereabouts, the army was his family and his home.

---

*Gallimard, 1952, pp. 122–125. Instead of making my own translation I have availed myself here of that which appears, from the pen of Gerard Hopkins, in the English-language version of *Jean Santeuil* published in 1955 by Weidenfeld and Nicolson of London.

But his was far from being the ordinary military career. In another of its branches, the Obruchev family was one of liberal—sometimes even radical—intellectuals. Nikolai's brother was a revolutionary, exiled at one time to Siberia. A niece was among the first women to be admitted, in the 1870s, to the Medical-Surgical Academy, a quasi-military institution generally regarded, at that time, as a veritable hotbed of student radicalism. She married, shortly afterward, the well-known professor of physiology of that institution, I. M. Sechenov—also no political conservative. Nikolai Obruchev himself soon developed a scholarly interest in military history, and was assigned in the late 1850s, already with the rank of colonel, to the War Academy, as professor of military statistics. Here, he founded Russia's first military-scientific journal, the *Voyenny Sbornik.* He then made the mistake of enlisting the services, as a contributor to the journal, of none other than the famous revolutionary literary figure, N. G. Chernyshevski, whose political differences with the regime were shortly to lead to his arrest and exile. This brought Obruchev into fairly serious political trouble, and made it necessary for him to leave Russia for a year or two—a device no doubt recommended by benevolent superiors as a means of keeping him out of the eye of the Russian police until the excitement over this episode could die down. The period of exile was spent in Paris, where he pursued studies of one sort or another, and where he met and married his French wife, a Mlle. Berg, proprietress (by inheritance) of a modest but lovely château near Bergerac in the Dordogne.

Following his return to Russia in the early 1860s, Obruchev continued to play a prominent part as a military scholar and educator, becoming very shortly chief of the Committee for Military Education of the Imperial General Staff. His abilities, which were clearly outstanding, were soon recognized by Alexander II's able and politically liberal minister of war, Dmitri Aleksandrovich Milyutin, who had been Obruchev's predecessor in the professorship at the War Academy, and who was one of the most interesting and impressive personalities in the official entourage of Alexander II. It was presumably Milyutin's patronage that enabled Obruchev to dispel the shadow that lay over his record after the Chernyshevski affair and to resume successfully his military career.

Obruchev served in the Russo-Turkish War, first as a commander and then as a senior staff officer on the Caucasian front. And in 1881, when Alexander III came to the throne, he was made chief of the General Staff—a position he was to retain over nearly two decades.

It is said not to have been an easy thing to persuade the highly conservative Alexander III to authorize this appointment for a man of so unusual and liberal a record as Obruchev. Particularly inauspicious must have been the Tsar's knowledge that Obruchev had for so long enjoyed the patronage of Milyutin, whom Alexander III regarded with nothing but suspicion and whom, when he succeeded to the throne in 1881, he promptly dropped as minister of war. But Milyutin's profoundly conservative successor, Pyotr Semyonovich Vannovski,* could discern no candidate for the post of Chief of the General Staff who even approached Obruchev in intelligence, in knowledge of military theory, and in general ability; and commanding, as Vannovski did, Alexander's confidence, he succeeded in persuading the skeptical monarch to give Obruchev the job.

Again, as in the case of Boisdeffre, the person of Obruchev remains for the historian an enigma. The only representation of him available to the writer (the photograph, evidently, of a drawing) shows a high forehead and cool, intelligent eyes, the mouth concealed, however, by the bushy mustache and other whiskers of the period. The Germans, who apparently knew little about him other than that he was pro-French, acknowledged his ability but suspected him of the worst. No single anecdote appears to have remained that would give color to his personality. If he had any good friends in Petersburg, the record does not reveal who they were. He obviously performed his duties faithfully and even with distinction, for he was kept in his high military office throughout the entire reign of Alexander III. His part in the negotiation of the alliance with France shows him to be a man of high intelligence and competence, skillfully guiding his ship, usually from behind the scenes, towards the port to which he wished to bring it, never inviting publicity or attention to his own person but always helpfully present and involved at the crucial moments.

Boisdeffre and Obruchev, as observed above, were in the truest sense opposite numbers. They were, within their respective military establishments, the officers with the most serious and long-standing interest in the development of Franco-Russian military relations. They had known each other since at least 1879, in which year they had, for the first time, attended each other's military maneuvers. Obruchev's French wife provided an indispensable social bond not only between the two of them but between the senior echelons of the two military establishments generally. Her home in Petersburg was hospitably open to the French officers sta-

---

*Vannovski, a venerable and blunt old soldier (just celebrating, in 1890, the completion of fifty years of official service), was one of the very few people who enjoyed in so high degree the confidence of Alexander III that he could even tell the latter, on occasion, things he did not want to hear.

tioned there. Boisdeffre visited the Obruchevs more than once—presumably many times—at their château in the Dordogne. When the two generals were separated geographically, as was normally the case, Mme. Obruchev conducted the correspondence between them on the part of her husband, presumably in view of the latter's inferior command of the French language. Without this personal bond between the two men and without the collaboration that it made possible, it is hard to imagine how the Franco-Russian Alliance could ever have been achieved.

Obruchev loved the château in the Dordogne. He normally spent his vacations there in late summer and early autumn. It was there that he eventually retired. The old house still stands today, largely deserted, in the custody of the last of the family (another Mlle. Berg, who recalls knowing the general in her childhood). The initials N and O are still visible on the stone emblems over the doorways. A full-length portrait of the great uncle still hangs in one of the drawing rooms. And among five painted panels in the dining room, decorated with Russian scenes executed in oil, there is one—a copy of a rather dreadful "court painter" representation of Alexander II, flanked by admiring but anxious courtiers, shooting a bear at a distance of about one yard—that, incongruous as this may seem, was painted by none other than the general himself. These, together with a couple of old photographs and other trivia residing in a bureau drawer, seem to be the only tangible relics in France of a man who, more than any other person except his "homologue," Boisdeffre, was the architect of that country's most celebrated and most fateful alliance.

. . .

Boisdeffre and Obruchev would stand, one must suppose, as the most likely targets of those bitter caricatures that would appear, above all in Germany and in Russia, after World War I—caricatures of the ruthless, brutal militarists who, together with the bloodsucking capitalists, supposedly led an innocent Europe into the dreadful slaughter of the war. What can be said in their defense?

These two men did not create such things as armies. They could never have persuaded their respective governments to give them up, even had they wished to do so. Once in existence, these armies had to be manned and commanded. Had these men not occupied the positions they did, others, presumably less qualified, less responsible, possibly even less humane, would have done so. Would this have been better?

Boisdeffre shared to the full the consciousness and pride of national identity that was a mark of that period. He loved his country. He believed in its prime importance, and indeed in its indispensability, as a component of European civilization. He considered its armed strength essential to the accomplishment of its historic mission. He was not aware—could not be aware, any more than could millions of other Europeans—of the preposterous damages and miseries that could flow from the colliding of the armies of great industrial powers in the modern age.

Many of the same things could be said about Obruchev. But beyond that, he was a man who had been richly exposed, through his family connections, to the full tragedy of the growing conflict between the Russian imperial establishment of the nineteenth century and the liberal intelligentsia who could find in that establishment no outlet for their idealism, their desire to be of use, their passionate determination to eradicate the social injustices on which Russian power had rested for so many centuries. One may safely assume that Obruchev, sharing with Milyutin the sad recognition that Russia was not to have in his time any parliamentary institutions through which such ideals could be pursued, also had some part in Milyutin's dream of using the Russian army as an educational force—a school of citizenship, a bridge for the overcoming of social barriers, a crucible for the welding of a new national consciousness. This was a not unworthy dream.

Both Boisdeffre and Obruchev were children of their time. Both were personally honorable and well meaning. Both deserve to be judged, if judge them one must, by the standards of their time, not of ours. The disasters that followed on their activities cannot be laid primarily at their feet. One has to dig far deeper than the professional commitments of these or any other two individuals to discover the roots of Europe's tragedies of the twentieth century.

Chapter 2

THE TURNING POINT OF 1890

Let us go back for a moment to the year 1881, when Alexander III mounted the throne upon the assassination of his father. Negotiations were already far advanced at that moment, in fact very nearly completed, for what might be called a treaty of neutrality among the three great empires of Central and Eastern Europe: the German, the Austro-Hungarian, and the Russian. Unprepared for the responsibilities so suddenly thrust upon him and not disposed to question the desirability of an arrangement so far along on the way to completion, Alexander permitted Giers (then only deputy foreign minister but already bearing the responsibilities of the ministerial position and soon to take over its title) to complete the negotiations. This Giers did, with the result that the treaty was finally signed on June 18 of that year.

This was a treaty that stipulated, in essence, that if any one of the three powers should become involved in a war with a power outside the group, the other two would observe a neutrality benevolent towards the one of the three that had gone to war. What was primarily in the minds of the statesmen who thrashed out this language was that if Russia were to become engaged in a war with England, the Germans and the Austrians would be bound to stand aside, to give no help to the British, and to shape their neutrality policies in a manner favorable to the Russians; whereas similarly, if Germany were to find herself once more at war with France, the other two—the Russians and the Austrians—would give no help to the French, and would, on the contrary, shape their neutrality in a manner favorable to the German cause. Plainly, this obligation on the Russian part precluded the very idea of a Franco-Russian alliance; for Russia could not simultaneously promise the Germans that she would give no aid to France in another Franco-German war and yet promise the French to come to their aid as an ally in just this situation.

This treaty, known subsequently as the Dreikaiserbund, or, in English, the Three Emperors' League, was concluded for a period of three

18

years but was renewed for a further three-year period in 1884. It was held strictly secret during the period of its validity and for some time thereafter. When the second three-year period expired, in June 1887, the Tsar was unwilling to have the treaty renewed for a third period. He had by this time suffered serious failures and embarrassments in his policy towards Bulgaria in 1885 and 1886. For these setbacks he had insisted (without much justification) on blaming the Germans and Austrians, particularly the latter. Under pressure from Giers, who would have preferred to renew the old arrangement as it stood, he grudgingly agreed that the obligation of neutrality might be continued with relation to the Germans; but in the case of the Austrians he would not hear of it. The result was that there was concluded in June 1887, to replace the Dreikaiserbund, a bilateral Russo-German treaty, to be known later as the Rückversicherungsvertrag (Reinsurance Treaty).* This document again bound Russia to neutrality in the face of another war between Germany and France, but with one important modification. Whereas the Dreikaiserbund had committed the parties to observe neutrality regardless of the origins of the war in which one or the other of the signatories might be involved, the Reinsurance Treaty limited this obligation to a war in which the other party was not the aggressor. This meant that if Germany were to attack France, the Russians would not be bound to observe neutrality; and the same principle was to apply if Russia were to attack Austria. If, on the other hand, France were to attack Germany, the obligation on Russia's part would apply; and the same if Austria were to attack Russia.

The Reinsurance Treaty, likewise concluded for a three-year term, came up for renewal in the spring of 1890, just at the time of Bismarck's retirement. Bismarck favored its renewal and would certainly have seen to it that this was accomplished had he remained in office. Giers similarly favored its renewal, and confidently expected that this would take place. Even the Tsar would have consented, under Giers' urging, to the renewal, albeit without enthusiasm. But in the wake of Bismarck's retirement the new German chancellor, General Georg Leo von Caprivi, under the influence of the famous éminence grise of the German foreign office, Friedrich von Holstein, and of several other senior officials, persuaded the

*The English title—Reinsurance Treaty—will be used in the remainder of this volume to designate the treaty in question. In the case of the Dreikaiserbund I have chosen to retain the German title, because the English one is easily confused with that of a personal understanding arrived at some years earlier (1873) among the three emperors. (See, in this respect, Kennan, *Bismarck's European Order*, p. 75.)

Kaiser that the treaty should not be renewed; and it was thus allowed to lapse.

Together, Bismarck's retirement and the lapse of the Reinsurance Treaty signified a fundamental change in the interrelationships of the major European powers. So far as the lapse of the treaty was concerned, the full import of this change was not apparent at the time to the public or to most of the statesmen and diplomats of the Continent, for they were unaware of the treaty's existence. But Bismarck's retirement was of course in itself a tremendous event, sending shock waves and arousing a sense of uncertainty throughout the entire Continent. And many people, even knowing nothing of the Reinsurance Treaty and its lapse, were instinctively aware that the road was now open for far-reaching changes in the entire structure of relationships among the great powers.

Let us first glance at the position of Germany herself. Holstein and his friends had urged the abandonment of this last contractual bond between Germany and Russia because they found it disturbing from the standpoint of Germany's other obligations and saw little value in it. Germany, after all, had other treaty relationships to think about. She had the Triple Alliance, which bound her—by a bundle of intricate and confusing engagements—to Austria and Italy. She had a secret bilateral defense treaty with Austria, concluded even prior to the Dreikaiserbund. She even had a defense treaty, likewise entirely secret, with Rumania. Bismarck, who had been the architect of all these engagements, knew how they fitted together and was confident of his ability to assure, in times of crisis, that the Reinsurance Treaty did not come into conflict with the others. His successors, lacking any complete understanding of the logic of his policies, were not so sure—or at least claimed not to be—that they could successfully perform this balancing act. They saw in the Reinsurance Treaty what they called a situation of "political bigamy." And if any of these treaties had to be sacrificed to restore Germany's political virtue, it was the Reinsurance Treaty that best commended itself to them as a candidate for this fate.

This was for several reasons. In the first place, the very fact that the treaty was now expiring meant that they could disembarrass themselves of it without having to denounce it. But beyond this, they did not like it or want it anyway. They had noted the growing power over the mind and behavior of the Tsar of the anti-German nationalist faction of Russian journalistic and official opinion. Given the extensive influence this faction now exercised, they regarded Russia as an undependable partner in any case. If the treaty were to be renewed, the Russians, they argued, would be able to reveal its existence at any time and thus to embarrass Germany in her relations with her other allies, as well as with Britain.

This last disturbed Holstein and his associates particularly. They placed great hopes in the development of Anglo-German relations—even dreamed of an eventual alliance between the two powers. This, they felt, would not only give them assurance against England's possible support for France in another Franco-German war, but it would help to assure that English power would continue to be brought to bear against Russia at the Straits and all along Russia's sensitive central-Asiatic border. Such pressure, they reasoned, would serve to divert Russia's attention from her western border to such an extent that there would be no inclination in Petersburg either to interfere in any future Franco-German war or to assume any formal obligations that would require them to do so. They saw in this a better assurance against the conclusion of a Franco-Russian alliance than in any formal Russian promise of neutrality, such as the Reinsurance Treaty had provided.

It is interesting to note how this outlook, which was not without its logic, differed from that of Bismarck. He was no less aware than were any of the others of those tendencies in Russian opinion that were making Russia a less reliable partner for Germany than she had been in earlier years. He knew Russia better than did any of the others. He had, after all, once served in Petersburg as a diplomat. He had observed the growing anti-German tendencies in Russian diplomacy as carefully, and with as much concern, as had anyone else. He was fully aware that there were powerful elements in Russian opinion, particularly among the military, that favored abandonment of the tie to Germany and the conclusion of an alliance with France, and this gave him great concern.

But Bismarck was wise enough and prudent enough to realize that slender, unsatisfactory, and unreliable as might be the existing tie, formalized in the Reinsurance Treaty, that bound Germany to Russia, it held important advantages and should not be abandoned before a satisfactory alternative was available. To abandon it would be to leave Russia wholly isolated and thus to compel the government of that country to search elsewhere for an alliance partner—which, in the prevailing circumstances, could be none other than France. Beyond that, Germany needed the tie with Russia to preserve her bargaining power with her own allies: Austria and Italy. Without that tie, Germany would become quite dependent on those allies; for they would then be in a position to threaten Germany, if she failed to heed their wishes, with the very sort of isolation Bismarck had himself successfully inflicted upon France over so many years. The tie with Russia was needed, in other words, both as a means of restraining that power from allying itself with France, and as a counterweight to Germany's treaty relationships with Austria and Italy, guaranteeing that these latter should not become, as relationships of alliance so frequently do, a form of enslavement of one party to the demands of the other.

In both of these calculations, the history of the ensuing years was to prove Bismarck right. The negotiations for a Franco-Russian alliance followed, as we shall see shortly, immediately upon termination of the Russo-German tie. And Germany's resulting dependence on Austria as her only ally, without whom she herself would have faced total isolation, proved to be a crucial factor in the unfolding of the events of the final days before the outbreak of war in 1914.

In connection with the high hopes placed by Holstein and others on the development of relations with Britain, it might also be well to note that Bismarck's retirement coincided closely with the final conclusion of negotiations, inaugurated in his day, between Germany and England, looking to the cession to Germany by England of the strategically important island of Helgoland, lying off the mouth of the Elbe River in the North Sea, in return for certain concessions made by Germany to England in the colonial problems of East Africa. This development naturally gave great satisfaction to Holstein and his associates, who saw in it an important step on the way to an alliance with England. It further diminished in their eyes the value of any tie to Russia. But by the same token it alarmed both the French and the Russians, appearing as it did to threaten them with the specter of an Anglo-German alliance; and it thus increased the tendency of each of those countries to look to the other for the assurance of its own security.

. . .

Bismarck's retirement also coincided closely, as it happened, with a cabinet change in France that was to be of high importance for the future of France's relations with Russia. This change involved the return to the premiership of the prominent left-liberal republican politician, Charles de Freycinet, and the assumption of the foreign affairs portfolio by the somewhat more conservative jurist and parliamentary deputy, Alexandre Ribot. There is no French biography of either of these men (the French, it seems, are not long on biographies of their republican statesmen), and in neither case is biographic information about them easy to come by; but both were, in their way, remarkable personalities, and a word about each of them is in order.

In the decade following the political demise and death of the Opportuniste political leader Léon Gambetta, in 1882, Freycinet occupied a central position in French political and parliamentary life. By 1890, he had served three times as prime minister and four times as foreign minister; in addition to which he had been, since 1888, minister of war. He would continue to hold the war ministry, combining it with the premiership, even after the 1890 reorganization of the cabinet referred to above.

Born in 1828, into a Protestant family of the south of France, Freycinet studied engineering at the famous Ecole Polytechnique in Paris and graduated there with distinction. To the end of his life he remained in many respects—in his interests, his cast of mind, and his closest collegial relations—essentially a *"polytechnicien."* As an engineer, his interests were extremely broad. They centered on railway construction and operation, but they also included a number of fields connected with public health and urban development: sanitation, water supply, and air pollution. Industrious, studious, a man of facts and figures, accustomed to doing his homework and familiarizing himself thoroughly with the factual aspects of any problem with which he was seized, he was not only a distinguished engineer in the technical sense but showed a marked talent for the organization and administration of engineering enterprises, particularly ones involving the public sector. His work in a wide variety of such fields brought him into close touch with many elements of the commercial and financial world, military circles, and the civilian state bureaucracy.

Freycinet's entry into political life did not take place until he was nearly fifty years old. He owed the inspiration and encouragement for this change largely to Gambetta, with whom he had been briefly associated during the Franco-Prussian War. With Gambetta's help, he was elected to the Senate in 1876 (he was to remain a senator until 1920). This was the beginning of his political career.

Not every engineer makes a good politician or a good bureaucratic administrator. Freycinet soon showed himself superbly competent in both these respects. To the manipulation of French parliamentary factions he applied the same cold and calculating precision he was accustomed to devoting to the problems of engineering, and the approach worked very well indeed. Within a short time he had become, as the author of the article about him in the Larousse encyclopedia put it, *"l'homme indis-*

pensable de toutes les combinaisons ministérielles. " And his success in the field of governmental administration was no smaller. He was not only a born bureaucrat but a talented master of bureaucrats, and a great connoisseur of the tortuous channels, formal and informal, through which, in the labyrinth of French governmental bureaucracy, one could get things done. As an administrator he was cold, collected, strong-willed, and ruthless— a superior whose orders were not lightly to be evaded, a formidable competitor to rivals on the same level of power.

Physically, Freycinet cut a curious figure: a thin, puny, but indestructible little man with a large head, a shock of prematurely white hair (which earned him the sobriquet of "the white mouse"), a soft voice, and steady steely eyes. He was not a warm person. After the death of his self-effacing wife in 1887, he seemed to have no significant personal life, his energies and his passions, such as they were, being consumed by his professional and official involvements, his scanty home needs being looked after by an equally self-effacing only daughter. If he had any really warm and close friends, the available record does not reveal it. He presumably had few affections, but he probably also had few real hatreds. He was a denizen of the Parisian political-bureaucratic jungle. This jungle was his habitat. He loved it, no doubt; yet he moved through it with the impersonal wariness of the experienced animal, not blaming his fellow creatures for being what they were, recognizing them as being true to their nature as he was to his, but always wary of those who could be dangerous. In every other biped active on the political scene he saw either a possible ally whose interests might occasionally coincide with his own, or a potential rival on whom a careful eye was to be kept, or, in most instances, both. In this way he survived—not only survived, but flourished, as few had survived and flourished before him.

In relation to the internal French scene, Freycinet was no doubt an asset to his country. In matters of economic development, at home as well as in the colonies, he was a useful figure, bold where boldness was in order, cautious where boldness could be dangerous. He was at home in a whole series of functions: as minister of public works, as designer of a major plan for the development of French transportation, as the architect of parliamentary combinations.

Where he was *not* at home, despite his fourfold service as foreign minister, was at the Quai d'Orsay. For the traditional intricacies of foreign policy, based as they were not on channels of established authority but on the fluid currents of personal and institutional interactions among the great powers, his talents were not effective. For the skills and devices—the charm, the tact, the intuition, the *habitude du monde*—of the still largely aristocratic members of the French diplomatic service he had as little understanding as he had respect for their persons. They lived in a world different from his and one for which he had little feeling. It was hard for him to orient himself in a system of interaction where there were no clear and established lines of authority, where one could not command but had to understand, to placate, and to make oneself personally agreeable to others in order to obtain their collaboration. And nowhere had these limitations of vision made themselves more painfully evident, in the years before 1890, than in Franco-Russian relations, where Freycinet had repeatedly applied a clumsy and self-defeating hand.

But by 1890 these deficiencies had begun to be counterbalanced in the eyes of the Russians by Freycinet's impressive performance at the War Ministry. He had already put order, steadiness, and confidence into the higher echelons of the officers' corps after the tumultuous and unsettling passage of his predecessor, General Georges Boulanger, at the War Ministry. He had created, for the first time, a proper general staff, comparable to the one the Germans already had. He had done much to raise the army to a position of numerical strength and of excellence in training and armaments, which made it a creditable competitor to that of its German neighbor. All this must have impressed the Russians—particularly the military leaders, who were well aware of the change. Not only that, but there was now taking place a significant change in Freycinet himself. When, in earlier years, he had neglected and abused Franco-Russian relations, the political climate had been a different one, and he had then been in civilian office. Now, as we have already seen, France had been overtaken by a new wave of chauvinistic enthusiasm, deriving power from the very strengthening of the French armed forces that he himself, as war minister, was doing so much to bring about. Together with the awareness that France was becoming more attractive as an ally in the eyes of other powers, there was a significant growth of interest in the possibility of an alliance with Russia; and nowhere was this interest more intense than in the senior military circles, with whom Freycinet, as war minister, was now in close contact. He, too, therefore, was now well aware of the need for mending his fences with the Russians. He recognized the political credit that was to be earned by anyone who could appear as the successful promoter of closer Franco-Russian military ties, and he was aware that his official position as premier and war minister gave him unique possibilities for playing precisely that role in the public eye. He had, therefore, every incentive and every advantage for an active engagement in the development of France's military relations with Russia in the new post-Bismarckian era.

There was, of course, a difficulty still to be overcome in the Tsar's memories of Freycinet's earlier conduct. Alexander's sensitivities had been particularly aroused by Freycinet's unceremonious and offensive yanking of the popular French ambassador General Félix Appert from his post at Petersburg in 1886.* The episode had not been forgotten, particularly by Alexander himself, who had a long memory for just that sort of thing. Those of the higher Russian officers who were most interested in the possibilities for an alliance with France were aware of this; and, regretting it, they evidently exerted themselves to overcome this aversion on the Tsar's part. They themselves had no direct access to the Tsar; but they won over to their point of view the Russian minister of war, General Vannovski, who was an old and trusted adviser to Alexander III; and Vannovski appears to have succeeded, in the course of the next year or two, in persuading the Tsar to put his rancor aside, at least to the point of permitting those under his authority to deal confidentially with Freycinet on matters concerning the military relationship between the two countries.

Of even greater importance than Freycinet's assumption of the premiership in the spring of 1890 was the selection of Alexandre Ribot for the position of foreign minister in the new cabinet.

For nearly four decades, from the late 1870s to the final year of the First World War, Ribot was a prominent and in many ways unique figure on the French political scene. Endowed with intellectual powers of a very high order, he had been brilliantly educated in the classics and the humanities generally (he had once translated much of Demosthenes; and he insisted, even at times of great turmoil in his political life, on reading Latin for an hour each morning). His professional studies, pursued with much distinction, had been in the law. Prior to entry into political life, he had served as an attorney, a judicial administrator, and a judge. Elected, in 1878, from his native district around Saint-Omer, to a seat in the National Assembly, he was to remain a parliamentary deputy for many years—even into the twentieth century, abandoning his seat, in the end, only to become a senator in 1909. He was in all respects an excellent parliamentarian; and it was here, rather than in the rough and tumble of

*See part 2, chap. 8, of Kennan, *Bismarck's European Order.*

national party politics, that he was most at home. He had outstanding ability as a parliamentary speaker, even inaugurating, in this capacity, a new style of oratory, less florid and less burdened with classical quotations, more sober, more simple, and directly addressed to the subject matter at hand. Very tall, slightly stooped, with a high brow and a partly bald pate but with abundant hair at the back of his head (Maurice Barrès referred at one point to his *tête de pianiste*), he was always an impressive and distinguished figure at the podium of the Assemblée.

Ribot was marked by a complete and widely recognized integrity of character—a quality that contrasted sharply with much that was to be seen in his political environment of the time. Though courteous and conciliatory in official contacts, he was never the popularity-seeker, was consistently reserved in personal relations, and seldom, if ever, sought the favor of others for reasons of political expediency. He no doubt had that measure of self-esteem—or even of ambition, if one will—without which no one rises (or perhaps even should rise) to eminence under a democratic system; but this was not the ruthless ambition of the power-hungry parvenu. Largely devoid of enemies but equally devoid of intimate political collaborators, he remained throughout his career more the jurist and the parliamentarian than the partisan political leader.

Not that he was entirely an "independent" in politics. His undeviating attachment to the principle of republican-democratic rule kept him from association with the parties of the Right, whereas his innate conservatism held him similarly aloof from those of the radical Left. He found his most suitable (if not always comfortable) place, therefore, on the moderate flank of the liberal "Centre-Gauche," vaguely described at that time as the camp of the "Opportunistes." Here he seems to have enjoyed universal respect, even on the part of his most deeply committed political opponents; but he tended to be called on for high executive office primarily at times of unusual external stress or danger, only to find himself rejected again, sometimes quite unjustly, in the intervening doldrums of political squabbling and maneuvering.

As in the case of so many prominent French gentlemen of that period, Ribot kept his private life very private indeed. His wife was an American-born woman, daughter of a Chicago banker. Her parents' marriage had been broken up after a painful and sensational divorce proceeding in one of the Chicago suburbs; and the daughter was taken to Paris by her father at a young age and reared in a fashionable *internat pour jeunes filles* at Fontainebleau. At the time she married Ribot she was a woman of striking beauty. By then she had broken all ties with the United States (which she was never again to visit) and was entirely assimilated into French society.

Ribot's appointment as foreign minister in 1890 marked his real entry into national prominence. In the years to come, he was destined to serve five times as prime minister, in addition to occupying several other cabinet positions and to serving once again as foreign minister in the difficult wartime year of 1917. As he took over his new post in 1890 he was, of course, relatively new to the problems of diplomacy. He already had an extensive acquaintance with England and America, largely the product of his long-standing interest in English law. Of Germany, on the other hand, he appears to have known very little, and of Russia (where he had never been) almost nothing at all. Russia must, one can only assume, have appeared on his horizon, as on that of so many other Frenchmen, only as a major military power, a close relationship with which might serve to liberate France from the humiliating position of diplomatic and military isolation in which she had found herself since 1871.

Other things being equal, Ribot would probably have preferred to see this liberation achieved by a greatly strengthened relationship with Great Britain. But France's relations with that power were then being increasingly marred by colonial rivalries, not to mention temperamental differences. Ribot himself was destined to find his efforts to improve relations in that quarter heavily frustrated during his first months at the Quai d'Orsay, particularly in the case of the Egyptian question, where the perceived interests of the two countries were coming increasingly into conflict. These frustrations could not help but heighten his interest in the possibility of a closer relationship with Russia.

It had been, as of 1890, years since the Quai d'Orsay had been in the hands of anyone who combined an interest in Franco-Russian relations with so high a degree of energy and ability as did Ribot. Emile Flourens, a personally insignificant man who had served as French foreign minister in 1887 and 1888, had indeed been passionately devoted to the dream of a Russian alliance and had done what he could to promote this objective; but, being inexperienced and erratic, he had pressed the cause so clumsily as to harm it more than to help it. His successors in the 1888–1890 period (René Goblet and Eugène Spuller) were both colorless men who had little interest in the possibility of a Russian alliance and were, in any case, either disinclined or too timid to pursue it. With Ribot's advent to the foreign ministry, all that changed.

Given the extensive powers of the French presidency in the field of foreign policy, the personality of the incumbent of the presidential office of that day, Sadi Carnot, must also be mentioned. In contrast to his predecessor, the skeptical and disillusioned Jules Grévy, whom he had replaced in 1887, Carnot took a keen interest in the possibility of an alliance with Russia and did all in his power to further the project. His role in this effort was seldom a publicly active one; indeed, it could scarcely be that, for the negotiation and conclusion of the Alliance were kept strictly secret, and this was a requirement Carnot was careful to observe. But his influence behind the scenes was not unimportant. His initial approval of the formation of the Freycinet cabinet, with Ribot as foreign minister, was influenced by a belief on his part that these men might be able to make greater progress towards such an alliance than had been made by their predecessors. And in the coming period, as we shall see, Carnot, aware of the Tsar's strong aversion to the introduction of new personalities into the delicate process of communication between the governments, would use his influence to assure that the two men—Freycinet and Ribot—were kept in office as long as possible, even when circumstances would otherwise probably have led to their removal.

In the years ahead, Carnot would naturally take no active part in the negotiations with the Russians. That was the task of the ministers. But he would be consulted at the crucial stages of decision, and his reaction would invariably be supportive of the effort.

All three men—Freycinet, Ribot, and Carnot—shared to the full the general feeling of the educated French public of that day that the successful development of France's armed forces, to a point where they were now (at least statistically and on paper) not inferior to those that faced them on the German side of the line, had given France a new prestige and had placed her in a position where she could well afford to pursue a more self-confident and far-reaching foreign policy than had been possible in the 1870s and 1880s. They were aware that the French public was strongly in favor of an alliance with Russia. They were all keenly conscious of the political credit that would accrue to anyone who could claim to have been the architect of the achievement of this dream. This gave them, to be sure, an aim in common; but it also gave them an incentive to rivalry, for it was obviously possible that one of them might receive more credit than the other. Particularly was this true of Freycinet and Ribot. Their political relations had not always been of the best in earlier years. And Freycinet was scarcely the man to sacrifice to the impulses of collegial camaraderie any conceivable political advantage. This rivalry would have its effect, as the period of their collaboration ran its course, not on the end they were pursuing but on the paths and methods by which they respectively pursued it.

It was against this background that the French pressures for a closer tie with Russia were exerted with renewed vigor after the advent to power of the Freycinet-Ribot combination in the spring of 1890. It is idle to ask whether the effort was inspired by defensive or offensive considerations. The two concepts were not easily separable. The French statesmen of that day were certainly not envisaging any early attack on Germany even in the event that the alliance with Russia could be achieved. They did, however, wish to place themselves in a military position from which they could view with confidence the outcome of any serious conflict with Germany, from whatever cause it might arise; and this was something that required an alliance with Russia.

Throughout these years the revision of the humiliating Treaty of Frankfurt, by which Germany had sealed her victory over France in 1871, remained at all times the supreme and undeviating objective of French statesmanship. There may well have been some who thought that if the Russian alliance could be achieved, and French policy advanced to the new level of self-assurance and authority this would imply, then it might also be possible to find some peaceful path to the treaty's revision. It is, however, the sad duty of the historian to report that most influential people in France, as elsewhere, accepted another European war as ultimately inevitable. They did not know how it would begin; that would depend on circumstances impossible to foresee at the moment. But since this war *was*, in their view, inevitable, one had to plan for it and to prepare for it. And only the fewest of them perceived that precisely this planning and preparing, now going on all over Europe, would have the effect of making that war inevitable, whether or not it would really have been that in other circumstances. In the welter of interaction among such things as suspicion, intention, apprehension, prediction, misunderstanding, and resignation, questions of offensive or defensive motivation lost their clarity and much of their meaning. The forces that were carrying Europe towards war ran deeper, and were more complex, than any simple offensive or defensive intentions.

. . .

In the first months of their combined authority, there was not much that Freycinet and Ribot could do to promote the Russian alliance. Ribot, in particular, was heavily pressed by the numerous ulterior duties of his office. And the experienced (if somewhat colorless) French ambassador in Petersburg, Antoine de Laboulaye, warned against trying to go too far and too fast in this direction. The Tsar, he argued, was not prepared for it. Coming to public attention, any Franco-Russian agreement of this nature could only have the effect of strengthening the Triple Alliance of Germany, Austria, and Italy, due to come up shortly for renewal. And this, he thought, would be doubly unfortunate, because there were serious prospects that if the respective parties were not frightened by a sensational Franco-Russian rapprochement, the Triple Alliance might not be renewed at all. Finally, Laboulaye pointed to the thorny question of the need for parliamentary ratification of any Franco-Russian agreement. The French constitution, in his understanding, failed to allow for the conclusion of such treaties by the executive power alone, without consultation and consent of the legislative body. This appeared to preclude the element of secrecy on which, he was confident, the Russians would insist. Unless the latter could be reassured on this score, they were not likely, he thought, to agree to any written alliance at all.

Circumstances, then, were not favorable to the taking of any very active steps in the first few weeks of the existence of the new French cabinet. There was, however, one small step that *could* be taken to make a favorable impression on Russian official opinion; and this the French government promptly took.

For years past, a constant bone of contention between the French and Russian governments had been the tolerance shown by the French authorities for exiled Russian revolutionaries who had chosen Paris as their place of residence and who continued to conduct from there their efforts to undermine and overthrow, particularly by acts of terrorism, the tsarist government in Russia. Occasionally, when these people went too far and violated French law in the course of their political activities, the French authorities had taken action against one or another of them; but seldom had that action been severe. On more than one occasion men and women whom the Russian government would have liked to see extradited to Russia as common criminals had been granted by the French the status and privileges of political refugees and permitted, much to the annoyance of the Tsar, either to pursue their activities with impunity or to leave France unscathed. Now, in May 1890, the French police, acting under orders from the new minister of the interior, Constans, suddenly moved in on an entire coterie of such people, caught them *in flagrante delicto* in the concocting of explosives presumably destined for the assassination of the Tsar, arrested several of them, and hauled them before the courts of law.

Although this action appears to have been in response to a specific request from the Russian government (better informed, no doubt, than the French themselves as to what these people were up to) and was thus not entirely a French initiative, the Russian reaction was instantaneous and enthusiastic. Upon the Tsar, in particular, its effect was highly favorable—and lasting. The Russian minister of the interior, acting on orders of the Tsar, at once paid a formal visit to the French ambassador in Petersburg to express appreciation. Similar steps were taken in Paris. The Russian ambassador there, Baron Arthur Mohrenheim, never a man to neglect an opportunity to take credit upon himself, was prompt to claim that it was only upon his insistent urging that the final action had been taken by the French authorities; and he appears in this way to have succeeded to some small extent in further ingratiating himself with the Tsar. But this did not detract from the latter's sense of appreciation for what the French had done.*

It might be well to note that as of the early 1890s this was not the only way in which the French leaders felt they had placed the Russian government in their debt. In 1888 and 1889 the French cabinet had agreed to assist the Russian government, at the latter's request, in developing a new infantry weapon designed for the use of smokeless powder— an innovation that had important military advantages, defensive and offensive. Not only had the French consented to make available to the Russians, for inspection and study, a specimen of the new Lebel rifle they were then developing, but they had agreed in principle to permit the governmental munitions plant at Chatellerault to manufacture for the Russians the first half million of a Russian version of the new gun. This step had required cabinet-level decision; and in taking this decision, the French had made it clear to the Russians that they regarded the action as a first step towards more extensive collaboration in the military field. And in all of this Freycinet, as minister of war, had been prominently involved.

Beyond this, the French statesmen of 1890 had prominently in mind the fact that within the preceding year and a half French bankers had

---

*It is revealing of the Tsar's inner-emotional state that one finds no record of any similar gratitude on his part towards the Germans, despite the fact that they had never permitted such people to carry on in Germany in the first place.

made four major loans to Russia, enabling her to convert to easier and more manageable terms a large portion of her external indebtedness. While it was true that the motivation for these operations on the part of the bankers had been primarily financial and commercial rather than political, the transactions had enjoyed the benevolent encouragement, in some instances even the active support, of the French authorities; and in the case of at least one of the bankers (the Danish-Parisian Emile Hoskier), political sympathies had played a part both in the French initiative and in the Russian response.

In the light of all these gestures, the French statesmen felt that they had gone out of their way on more than one occasion, voluntarily and unilaterally, to oblige the Russian government, and had thus built up a certain political credit on which they should, at some point, be permitted to draw. This feeling deserves notice; for it was destined to play a part in the impatience that the French would show, in later phases of the relationship, with the frequent tergiversations and prevarications of Russian policy. As noted above, Ribot and Freycinet had little opportunity in those first weeks of the new Freycinet ministry to attempt to draw on this credit; but it was very much in their minds, and they never doubted that the time would come when they would be able to use it to good effect in connection with wider and more important negotiations.

. . .

In Russia the reaction to the events of the spring of 1890 was more complicated. Bismarck's departure had removed from the active scene, to be sure, a formidable rival figure whose successes had aroused in Russia that peculiar form of resentment that only envy can arouse. For the chauvinist-nationalist elements of Russian opinion Bismarck had long served as the ostensible source of all evil and the target of much indignant rhetoric. Yet it was grudgingly admitted, sometimes even in these self-same circles, that Bismarck was a man with whom you at least knew where you stood and what to expect; whereas the young Kaiser William II, who appeared to have taken over many of his powers—a histrionic, vainglorious, and highly erratic man—inspired no such confidence. On the contrary, he only aroused new anxieties, previously unfelt.

As for the lapse of the Reinsurance Treaty: only a handful of people in Russia—five or ten at the most—had been aware of its existence. Only these could, therefore, have been aware of its termination. For them the main effect of the treaty's lapse was simply to deprive them of the formal assurance, which the treaty had hitherto provided, that in the event of a war with England they would not find Germany, too, arrayed against them. In the eyes of the Tsar the disappearance of this assurance was no great loss. As the first of the tsars to have serious concern for any section of Russian opinion (in his case, it was nationalistic opinion, particularly in higher court and family circles), Alexander III had lived in constant anxiety lest the existence of the secret treaty with Germany become known and expose him to criticism from the nationalist side. The lapse of the treaty relieved him of this anxiety; and he was quite willing to pay for this relief with the sacrifice of whatever additional security the treaty might have provided.

The same was true of the few military leaders (there were possibly only two—Vannovski and Obruchev) who were in the know. They saw little reason to fear a German attack on Russia, even in the case of a Russian war with England. They were themselves sure, and they thought the Germans must be equally aware, that in the event Germany should attempt to join the British in an attack on Russia, the French would at once strike for the recovery of Alsace-Lorraine and the Germans would then be faced with the two-front war they were obviously concerned to avoid. Feeling themselves thus protected by the realities of the situation, the Russian military leaders saw little need for the retention of the formal assurance of German neutrality.

The only person in high governmental circles to whom the retirement of Bismarck and the lapse of the treaty relationship with Germany gave real concern was Giers. Well aware of the dangers that any major military involvement at all, even one nominally successful in the military sense, would hold for Russia in view of her parlous internal state, Giers had of course valued the tie to Germany for the restraints it imposed on the Germans; but he had valued it even more for the restraints it imposed upon the Tsar, and through him upon the hotheads within the Russian establishment itself. For this reason he saw in the state of isolation in which Russia now found herself dangers not visible to most of the others.

Giers had little confidence in the use many Russians might try to make of the "free hand" that, as they conceived it, Bismarck's retirement now allowed them. Remembering the Crimean as well as the Russian-Turkish wars, he had no sympathy for Russian imperialist aims in the Balkans or at the Straits. The Balkans were a region in which he had spent a large part of his life—a region whose problems he probably understood as well as anyone in the diplomatic world; and he saw little to be gained for Russia by any dabbling in its obscure and complex affairs. He had equally little enthusiasm for the exploits of various Russian generals in central Asia. He deplored the accesses of chauvinistic fervor with which these exploits were greeted in the popular Russian press. He regretted particularly the added and unnecessary strain they were placing on Anglo-Russian relations. He was reluctant to believe that a Russia prepared to mind her own business and to follow a policy of restraint would have much to fear either from England or from Austria. He had held these views throughout the Bismarckian period, recognizing very well that Bismarck had no designs on Russia and was concerned primarily only to keep Russia aloof from Western European quarrels and Germany aloof from Balkan ones. In this last he and Bismarck had in fact seen eye to eye. But how all of this would be now—with Bismarck gone, with German policy apparently in the hands of the inexperienced and mercurial young Kaiser, with Russia's own policy now cast loose from the contractual anchor to Germany that had held it steady for some nine years, and with the Tsar's essentially vacillating judgment now at the mercy (or so it must have seemed to Giers) of every military adventurer and chauvinistic hothead who could gain access to him: all this was a question that filled Giers with dismay and foreboding.

Giers had nothing against France. He wished that country well. He even saw value in a closer Franco-Russian relationship that could serve as a restraining influence upon what now appeared to him as a relatively unreliable and incalculable Germany. But he was aware of a fundamental incompatibility in French and Russian aims. He knew that France, in the last analysis, would be as little inclined to fight for the achievement of Russian aims in the Balkans as Russia would be to fight for the recovery of Alsace and Lorraine by France. And he feared that a full-fledged military alliance with France, in addition to being based on this fundamental divergence of aims, would split Europe into rival military camps and would open the way for all those wild and adventuristic tendencies in Russian policy—those demands for military actions in the Balkans and elsewhere—that for nearly a decade he had successfully opposed, but only barely successfully, and not without cost to his position, his influence, and his health.

For the excitements of the years 1885 to 1888, when Giers had been forced to defend his policies and his position against powerful and sometimes unscrupulous attacks from within the Russian journalistic and governmental establishments, had not only taken their toll of his energies:

they had also inflicted a certain erosion on his relations with the Tsar. Too often, as we have already noted, he had found himself obliged to strain those relations by keeping Alexander from moving in chauvinistic directions, urged upon him by other people, in which he was temperamentally inclined to go. In these obscure contests between servant and master, Giers had been able to make good use of the formidable figure of Bismarck: of the dangers of opposing him, of the advantages of keeping him formally on your side. Now this argument, to the Tsar's secret satisfaction, could no longer be invoked; and Alexander, in these circumstances, felt a greater freedom to undercut his foreign minister, to listen more often and more freely to contrary advice, to encourage the pursuit through other channels of policies of which he knew that Giers would not approve—and this without informing him, keeping him in the dark.

Alexander had no disposition to get rid of Giers entirely. The latter's experience was too valuable; his disappearance would have lent itself to undesirable interpretations; there was no one who seemed fitted to replace him. But despite the fact that in matters of foreign policy his was still the wisest and soundest head Russia possessed (that of Lamsdorf perhaps excepted), from 1890 on we shall see in the person of the Russian foreign minister a tired and enfeebled figure, partially disowned, no longer always fully informed, fighting a losing battle against both the inroads of age upon his own physical frame, and tendencies in Russian official opinion in which he was able to discern nothing but trouble, confusion, and ultimate tragedy.

Chapter 3

THE NARVA MANEUVERS

For a full five months after the initial German refusal, in March 1890, to renew the Reinsurance Treaty, Giers was unwilling to abandon the hope that Berlin could be induced to change its mind. On several occasions he talked long and earnestly with the German ambassador, General Lothar von Schweinitz (a wise and highly experienced man), about the matter. He admitted to Schweinitz (March 31) that the Tsar had no interest in seeing the treaty renewed. "His Majesty," Giers said, "never had much interest in the treaty, but I do have it, and I have good reasons for having it."[1] And in a later talk between the two men (May 14), Giers explained what at least one of these reasons was. "I don't want to praise myself," Giers said, "but you know that I constitute the last resort, on which the present Russian policy depends. Tomorrow this chair in which I am sitting may be occupied by another man; and for this eventuality I would like to leave behind me something in the way of a binding commitment."[2]

Schweinitz scarcely needed to be told Giers' reasons for wishing to have some sort of a written commitment from the Germans. He knew those reasons well and shared the views on which they were based. In his dispatch summing up the discussion with Giers of March 31 he described the way that the European situation of that moment looked in Giers' eyes: the three Central powers (Germany, Austria, and Italy) joined by publicly known treaties; England being drawn steadily towards a closer relationship with Germany; French upper-class enthusiasm for a war of revenge against Germany being somewhat moderated only by the unmistakable desire of the French people for peace (with the implication that a France of this disposition would be more acceptable as an ally in Russian eyes); Austria-Hungary, freed from the strict but benevolent control of Prince Bismarck, at liberty to pursue her own imperialistic aims in the Balkans; and on the other side—Russia, now quite alone, devoid of any agreement with Germany or anyone else, vulnerable to any and all temptations.

Schweinitz, finding himself under the necessity of guarding his fences in Berlin, took care not to associate himself directly with this view

37

of the European situation; but there is no doubt that he shared it. He even elaborated on it by pointing out that Germany's Central European allies (it was of course Italy that he had in mind) had certain ties with England —ties that Germany herself had promoted. And he went on to observe that in these circumstances "no one should be surprised if he [Giers] looks elsewhere [than to Germany] for an attachment."

He drove this last point home, and even more bluntly, in reporting the talk of May 14. Giers, he said, "must have sound reasons . . . for returning once more to this request for a written agreement of some sort which would have the effect of depriving the Russian government of the possibility of coming together with France in a coalition for the purpose of realizing certain common aims."[3]

In the light of these passages in Schweinitz's reports, it is impossible to say that the German government was not fairly warned that failure to ratify the treaty could well be the start of a process leading to a Franco-Russian alliance.

Schweinitz's dispatch of April 3, describing the talk with Giers of the 31st of March, evoked in the higher echelons of the German foreign office a whole flock of startled and outraged memoranda from persons who opposed renewal of the agreement. The reasons adduced were numerous —too numerous to be exhaustively recounted here. The most important of them have already been mentioned in Chapter 1; but there were a number of others, many of them ingenious and well argued.

What strikes the historian of another age (from the advantage, of course, of hindsight) is the little attention that was given, in all these German documents, to the central point at which Schweinitz had hinted: that in the absence of some piece of paper in the nature of the expiring treaty, Russia would be bound to seek an alliance with France. Only in two instances does the German chancellor, Caprivi, appear to have addressed this point in the repeated instructions he gave to Schweinitz, directing him to continue to oppose renewal of the treaty. Referring to Schweinitz's argument that a treaty along these lines would at least assure Russian neutrality over the first weeks following the outbreak of a Franco-German war, Caprivi wrote that this would be of little value; the Germans would have to keep a considerable portion of their army on the Russian border anyway. Beyond that, he argued, an alliance with France would be useless to Russia because what the Russians were really interested in was to attack Turkey in order to obtain control of the Straits, and for this purpose an alliance with France would hold no advantages.

One marvels at the lack of realism in these statements. The soundness of the first of them, denying in effect the value of keeping Russia inactive during the first weeks of a European war, is belied by the great and central importance the French were shortly to place, in the negotiations for the alliance, on the principle of "immediate and simultaneous mobilization." This appeared to them as the very essence, the vital principle, of any Franco-Russian alliance—the feature without which such an arrangement would have no value at all in their eyes. If a German-Russian agreement had done no more than to prevent immediate Russian mobilization in the event of a conflict between France and Germany, it would have vitiated in French eyes the entire value of any political-military agreement between France and Russia.

Caprivi's second observation—that Russia would not be interested in an alliance with France because this would not facilitate a Russian conquest of the Straits—is even more astonishing. That some sort of Russian control at the Straits, giving Russia the power to prevent the passage through those waterways of foreign warships, was a long-standing objective of Russian policy is indisputable. But to believe that Alexander III was animated, as of 1890, by a determination or intention to launch an early attack on Turkey for the realization of this aim, and that the question of an alliance with France would be looked at by him primarily from the standpoint of the extent to which such an alliance would or would not promote this objective —to believe these things was to entertain a seriously erroneous view of Russian policy, not to mention of the character of the Tsar. The problem of the Straits was no longer a fundamental factor in Russia's relations with either Germany or France. Giers, in fact, repeatedly offered to omit all mention of this question in any renewed Reinsurance Treaty if this would make things easier for the Germans—although the old agreement had indeed included a clause by virtue of which the Germans had assured the Russians of a free hand in this connection.

Be that as it may, the Germans held steadily to their refusal to renew the treaty or to consider anything that might take its place. And here the matter stood when, at the beginning of June 1890, Giers left for his usual summer vacation in Finland. With that, the exchanges on this subject necessarily came to an end.

.   .   .

In 1889 the Tsar had visited Berlin in order to return (most reluctantly) the visit the young German Kaiser had paid to him the previous year. In Berlin, the two emperors appear to have come to a vague under-standing (surely the result of the Kaiser's initiative) that William II would come to Russia the following summer for attendance at the annual grand maneuvers. These were to take place from August the 18th to the 22nd at or near Narva, on the shores of the Gulf of Finland, near the historical Russian-Estonian border.

The Tsar, one may be sure, would have been only too happy to forget this earlier discussion and to let the idea of such a visit fade into oblivion; but the Kaiser, being inordinately fond of such occasions, was not at all so disposed. There was nothing to be done, therefore, but to go through with it.

Narva, a small town near the place where the river of that name falls into the sea, was not a community that lent itself to anything so grand as an imperial summit meeting. It housed only two large structures. One was that of the well-known Crenholm textile mills, the greatest mills of their kind anywhere in the world, a huge complex of gloomy dark stone buildings perched upon the river bank. The other was the villa of the wealthy Secretary of the State Council of the Empire, A. A. Polovtsov, son-in-law of the owner of the mills (the banker, Baron Steiglitz). In preparation for the maneuvers and the imperial summit meetings, the villa and two wings of the mills were converted into premises for the imperial parties, palm trees and other tropical rarities being imported in large numbers from the Crimea to enliven their grounds and walls.

Narva having no proper port facilities, it was arranged that the Kaiser, traveling on the battle cruiser *Hohenzollern* with the escort of a second naval vessel, should make his arrival at the port of Revel (the present Tallinn) on the same south coast of the Gulf of Finland, some 125 miles west of Narva. This he did on the 17th of August, posing grandly on the bridge of his flagship, attired in the resplendent Russian general's uniform the Tsar had once given him. He and his party were met at the dock by two brothers of the Tsar, the grand dukes Vladimir and Aleksei (the latter then minister of the navy), who took the German guests by rail (the entire railway having been taken over by the army for the duration of the maneuvers) to Narva, where the Tsar received them. Four days were then passed, at or around Narva, exchanging entertainments and attending the maneuvers, after which the two emperors and their suites moved farther along the coast to Peterhof. There, there was a final gala dinner, after which, on the 23rd, the Kaiser took his departure from the nearby naval base at Cronstadt.

Thus the honors were done, in accordance with the customs of the day. And when the visit was over, everyone assured everyone else that so far as relations between the two monarchs were concerned, things had gone off excellently. Some of the Germans even congratulated themselves on the fact that the Tsar had appeared to become increasingly cheerful and relaxed as the visit ran its course. This they tended to attribute to the Kaiser's charm and warmth of character. (The latter, for all his faults, was indeed not devoid of these qualities when he wished to display them.) But those who took this view had not looked deeply into the murky depths of Alexander's emotional constitution. A more plausible hypothesis would have been that the evident improvement in his spirits, as the visit progressed, was induced by the pleasing awareness that it was closer, with each passing day, to its termination. Indeed, some of the foreign correspondents covering the visit came away with the impression that the Tsar's reception of his German cousin, and indeed the entire atmosphere of the visit, had been distinctly cool and perfunctory.

. . .

Officially, this visit was supposed to be a personal one between the two family-related monarchs; but the presence of the German chancellor, General Caprivi, made it clear that some mention of political matters was not to be avoided. The Tsar, having in mind no doubt his differences with Giers over the question of the renewal of the Reinsurance Treaty, had at first instructed the latter not to come to Narva; it would be sufficient, he had said, for Giers to meet the German party only during their short stay at Peterhof. But Caprivi's presence made this impracticable. Caprivi was German foreign minister as well as chancellor. He had to have an opposite number. So Giers was summoned to Narva after all, if only to be present for the arrival of the German party. There, as later in Peterhof and Petersburg, in addition to paying a perfunctory and very brief courtesy call on the Kaiser, he did manage to talk a bit with Caprivi about the problems of Russo-German relations; but he was barred, by the Tsar's orders, from bringing up the subject of the renewal of the treaty.

The Tsar, meanwhile, was having his own occasional political exchanges with the Kaiser. When the visit was over, he at once summoned Giers and gave him the benefit of those exchanges as well.

The upshot of these various talks was satisfactory as far as it went. The Germans agreed about the formal illegality of the regime of Prince Ferdinand in Bulgaria (something very dear to the heart of the Tsar) and promised, at least by implication, not to support him. They also assured the Russians that their policy towards the problems of the Turkish Straits would be based strictly on the existing treaties of 1856 and 1871. (The delicate question of the interpretation of these treaties, on which the Russians and the British disagreed, seems to have been, by mutual consent, tactfully avoided.) Most important of all, the Germans reiterated on all occasions that while they were not disposed to sign any new agreement (this, they insisted, would not be understood, if it became known, either by their Central European allies or by the German public), their policy towards Russia had undergone no change. In general, the visit may be said to have gone off better than the earlier one of 1888; but the Austrian chargé d'affaires in Petersburg, Count Lexa Aehrenthal, was speaking from sound experience when he warned his government that it would have no appreciable effect on the suspicion of Germany that prevailed in influential Russian circles.[4]

Giers, looking back on the visit after the Kaiser's departure and seeing in the outwardly friendly atmosphere by which it had been marked a last faint possibility of getting some sort of a signed document out of the Germans, resorted in his desperation to a small ruse. He drew up a digest of the principal points on which, in the light of his own talks with Caprivi and those of the Tsar with the Kaiser, the two sides had appeared to be in agreement. This document he then sent, as a species of aide-mémoire, to the Russian chargé d'affaires at Berlin, Count Michael Muraviev, with instructions to show it to Caprivi and to solicit the latter's confirmation of its accuracy.* Since the Germans had, after all, maintained throughout the Narva discussions that their failure to renew the treaty did not mean that there had been any change in their policy towards Russia, and since that policy had, so long as the treaty was in effect, included a promise to remain neutral in the face of any actual attack on Russia by another power, it was no doubt Giers' thought that if he could confront the Tsar with some sort of a formal confirmation that this was indeed (if only by implication) still German policy, he would have in hand something on the basis of which he could argue that the conclusion of a military alliance with France, as distinct from a moderate political rapprochement with that country, was unnecessary.

It seems highly probable (the Germans, in any event, were later wholly convinced that this was the case) that Giers also asked Muraviev

*The text of this document seems to be nowhere available in published form.

to try, when showing this aide-mémoire to Caprivi, to induce the latter to put in writing in some way, if only by signing the document, his acknowledgment that its contents correctly represented German views and German policy. Muraviev, however, was instructed not to reveal that the suggestion had come from Giers himself.

On the 8th of September Muraviev had the required interview with Caprivi. He showed him Giers' document and suggested he should sign it or otherwise indicate in writing his acknowledgment that it was a correct summary of the discussions. Caprivi's reaction may be surmised from two documents of the time. One was a memorandum drawn up by Caprivi on the heels of the interview and dispatched to Schweinitz at Petersburg. In the accompanying instruction to Schweinitz, Caprivi summed up (very briefly and sketchily) the main points of Giers' paper, and then added:

> Count Muraviev added the request, as coming from him personally, that I should confirm in writing that he had read this paper aloud to me and that I was familiar with its content. Although I could have done this with good conscience, I declined to put anything in writing, pointing out that M. von Giers would content himself with an oral statement on my part.[5]

This laconic statement by Caprivi hardly gives the true tenor of the exchange. There is also Muraviev's report of the conversation; and this was much more explicit: "Why, this seems to me entirely useless." Caprivi is quoted here as saying:

> I am completely resolved not to put anything in writing. You have been instructed to read to me a dispatch which, I agree, reproduces very faithfully the political views exchanged between M. de Giers and me. You have done so. But to address anything of the sort to you in writing? No. I have not the political strength of Bismarck, but I am loyal, and you can rely upon our loyalty, which will never fail you.[6]

When Muraviev countered this statement by saying that the suggestion was his own, Caprivi responded by saying, rather archly:

> I know it well. M. de Giers could never have charged you to ask it of me, since I have often told him that I would absolutely refuse to give him anything in writing relating to our exchange of views on political questions. . . .

Muraviev also reported that Caprivi, in terminating the interview, took occasion to emphasize to him once again what the Kaiser had attempted, during the course of their conversations at Narva, to impress upon the Tsar: that Germany had serious internal problems to which, in the coming period, she would have to address herself; and that it was in the overcoming of these problems, not in external adventures, that the Kaiser wished to seek and establish the glory of his reign.

Such expressions of peaceful intent were all right in their way, and they were probably quite sincere on the part of the Kaiser, who, while he liked to boast about Germany's military strength, did not actually wish to see it employed in a highly destructive war between great powers. But (as Caprivi should have known, for Schweinitz had repeatedly emphasized the point in his dispatches) these expressions failed completely to satisfy Giers' need for something more specific, in writing—something that would have committed not only Caprivi's successors but, by implication, those of the Tsar and Giers as well, to the continuation of the recent relationship.

With this rather desperate, pathetic, and wholly unsuccessful effort, Giers had exhausted all the possibilities open to him for avoiding a military alliance with France—an alliance in which he could see nothing but the splitting of the European community into warring camps and the likelihood of an eventual major war. The absence of any assurance of German neutrality in the event of a British or Austrian attack on Russia meant that the latter country now found itself in a state of total military-political isolation, devoid even of near-allies, and vulnerable to an Austro-German attack, even to one—worse still—with which the British might associate themselves. He, Giers, may well have doubted the likelihood of any such developments; but in such matters the military imagination, as he well knew, was always feverishly active. The military would be bound to argue —and in this the Tsar would support them—that such a situation of vulnerability was intolerable. There was nothing for it, they would argue, but to attempt to find some sort of escape from this isolation, and what could this be other than an arrangement with France?

Giers hoped, wearily and without much confidence or enthusiasm, that the new relationship with France might be confined to certain purely defensive arrangements that would not preclude, at some more distant date, the revival of a similar relationship with Germany; for he believed, as did Bismarck, that secret defensive obligations could be assumed with relation to more than one other power, even when these latter were not in good relations with each other, this not being equivalent to the deceit or betrayal of either of them. But this was a very slender hope; and in entertaining it at all, Giers was ignoring—perhaps he felt compelled, in his desperation, to ignore—the momentum of military competition that, as we have seen, soon obliterates the distinction between offensive and defensive motives and leads all parties, however motivated, relentlessly to the eventual resort to armed force.

.   .   .

The pathetic quality of this effort on Giers' part to save the last remnants of the Russian tie to Germany is highlighted, from the perspective of the historian, by another set of exchanges that was taking place in and around Petersburg at just the same time—exchanges of which Giers was himself in all probability ignorant.

At some point in midsummer 1890 (around the 20th of July), with the Kaiser's visit now less than a month off, Giers had asked the French ambassador, Laboulaye, to transmit a personal invitation from the Tsar to General Boisdeffre to attend both the annual public maneuvers at Krasnoye Selo and the real maneuvers, near Narva, that were to follow them. This invitation was probably inspired in the minds of Obruchev and the minister of war by the fact that the Kaiser had already announced his intention of bringing with him to Narva not only Caprivi, who was himself a high military figure, but also two other senior military officers. The presence of Boisdeffre at the maneuvers was desired as a counterweight to that of the German generals, lest the public be misled into thinking that some sort of Russo-German military discussions were contemplated. While Laboulaye later claimed that the idea of the invitation to Boisdeffre had originated with him and that it was to his suggestion that the Tsar had reacted, there is little reason to doubt that the thought had been put into Laboulaye's head by the assistant French military attaché, Colonel Louis Moulin, acting at the instigation of Obruchev.

The suggestion, in any case, had its effect. The invitation came as a surprise to the French government—or as much of it as was on duty in Paris in those days of the midsummer vacations. Freycinet, however, at once perceived the importance of the gesture (perhaps even overrated it) and proceeded with energy to follow it up. Boisdeffre was promptly recalled from his own vacation in the Midi and dispatched to Petersburg, where he arrived on the 8th of August, just in time to attend the tattoo taking place on the opening day of the maneuvers at Tsarskoye Selo.

In the ensuing days Boisdeffre was treated with marked attention and courtesy by the Russian imperial couple. This was immediately noted by various officials and courtiers in the Tsar's entourage. They were quick to sense in it a change in the political atmosphere and to reflect this impression in their behavior. One result of this was that the German ambassador, Schweinitz, was treated with such unusual coldness and reserve that he canceled his plans to spend another twenty-four hours at Tsarskoye and immediately returned to Petersburg, no less well aware than were the others (but more unhappily so) of the implications of Boisdeffre's presence and treatment.

Over the ensuing two weeks Boisdeffre had daily opportunities for conferring with Obruchev, with Vannovski, and finally, on the day of the Kaiser's departure, with the Tsar. He recorded the results of these conversations in a long report, dated the 27th, portions of which appear in the *Documents diplomatiques français.*[7] This report leaves something to be desired, because Boisdeffre deliberately failed to make clear from which of these three conversation partners various specific statements cited in the report were forthcoming. But this, where it is not specifically clear, can be generally surmised; and the report, recounting as it did the first serious and authorized exchanges between French and Russian officials concerning the requirements and possibilities for a military alliance, is of high importance.

It is plain from the wording of this document that Freycinet, in dispatching Boisdeffre on this mission, had instructed him "to attempt to ascertain at long last just what the Russians would do if war were to be declared on us, and within what limits we would be able to count on their assistance."

Boisdeffre began his talks by maintaining to the Russians, somewhat illogically, that while the strength of the French forces was now such as to permit France to "view calmly all eventualities," outside assistance was nevertheless necessary. Such assistance, he further affirmed, was just as necessary, and just as desirable, from the standpoint of the giver (he obviously meant Russia) as from that of the receiver. The outcome of the Franco-Prussian War of 1870–1871, he maintained, had already signified a considerable deterioration of Russia's security. That security could be even more importantly weakened if France should suffer defeat in a second war of this nature.

To this the Russians replied (we are following, throughout, Boisdeffre's account) by emphasizing that the first thing they had made clear to the Kaiser during the course of the latter's visit was that Russia could not permit injury to be brought to France—that France's continued existence and strength were indispensable to the European balance of power. The Russians then went on to raise the question whether the same thing would be true the other way around, particularly in the light of the mercurial quality of French governmental arrangements. Could they, in other words, be sure that France would always stand by Russia?

Boisdeffre replied to this by affirming, more vigorously, the willingness of the French to go to war if there were no honorable alternative. And he drove home his point by expressing at the start France's willingness to accept the principle of a simultaneous mobilization on the part of the two powers. He did not need to point out, he said, that this would preclude all possibility of the Germans' launching the totality of their power against Russia alone; for it was clear that faced with such a mobilization on France's part, the Germans would be obliged to keep a very large portion of the forces on their western border, and probably (since the French would scarcely be willing to pass up so favorable an opportunity for a war of revenge) to use them there as well. And he even went on to say that while he was not authorized to propose this formally on the part of his government, he felt sure that the latter would be prepared to sign a formal military convention in which this principle of simultaneous mobilization would be embodied.

To this his interlocutor (probably in this case Vannovski) replied by asking whether it would not be better just to leave this as an oral understanding, without writing anything or signing anything. "A convention, once written and signed, would not be kept secret," the interlocutor said. "I think it would be better for both of us to restrict this to a tacit understanding."

Without dwelling further on this exchange, Boisdeffre went on, in his report, to describe the Russian view (here, he was clearly quoting Obruchev) of the situation that could be expected to arise in the case of any major conflict that engaged the forces of the Triple Alliance. This was by no means encouraging from the French standpoint. The Germans, Obruchev thought, could be expected to launch an initial offensive either against Russia or against France and to go onto the defensive, for the time being, against the other party. Should it be Russia against whom this initial offensive was launched, the thrust would probably be made from the north (i.e., from East Prussia) against Bialystok, the objective being to divide the Russian armies. The Russians proposed to counter this strategy by retreating and adopting a scorched earth policy, seeking only to hold a large triangle south of Warsaw. From this triangle as an area of deployment, they would at once launch an attack on Austria. If, on the other hand, the Germans should launch their initial attack against France, the Russians proposed to launch an immediate attack of their own, but again—against Austria, not Germany. And their advice to the French for this contingency was: go first onto the defensive; give up Nancy; fall back on your strong forts (the reference was presumably to the new fortifications at Verdun, Toul, Epinal, and Belfort); and let the Germans blunt their teeth in the effort to assail these redoubts. Then, the Germans having thus weakened themselves and the Russians having in the meantime presumably defeated the Austrians, both of them, French and Russians together, would see what could be done about defeating the now weakened and isolated Germans.*

Boisdeffre of course objected strenuously to this view of the situation. But Obruchev held his ground, insisting particularly on the necessity of a prior destruction of Austrian military strength before concentrating on the Germans.

There is no indication, in Boisdeffre's report, that these particular discussions produced any reconciliation of the obvious conflict of views. This was, after all, only a preliminary exchange of opinions.

What Obruchev had said was clearly not, for the most part, what Freycinet and Ribot desired to hear. But Boisdeffre, in summing up the exchange, was at pains to show that what was reflected in the Russian statements was not entirely or even mainly discouraging. He was convinced, he wrote, that Alexander III would not repeat the mistake made by his father in 1870–1871; the mistake, that is, of standing idly by and permitting France to be crushed while Russia looked on. "I believe," he wrote,

> that if today war were to break out without there having been any provocation on our side, Russia would mobilize. I believe this all the more because the Tsar would be doing this not at all for us (for whom his affection is decidedly limited) but solely in the interests of Russia herself. Besides, the

*The reader will note how strikingly this response reflected a long-standing and deeply rooted tendency in Russian strategic thought: namely, the concept of luring the enemy deep into one's own territory, to a point where he weakens himself by the lengthening of his lines of communication and by the resulting problems of supply as well as by the necessity of attempting to find and to crush an elusive enemy fighting on his own ground and enjoying the central position; and then, when this weakening of the enemy has occurred, of going over to the counterattack. The value of this concept, particularly for a vast country such as Russia, which could always trade territory for time, had been discovered in the efforts at defense against the Asiatic hordes in the Middle Ages. The concept had been invoked again, with a measure of success that was never to leave the Russian consciousness, in the struggle against Napoleon. It was destined to be invoked once more on a grand scale in the defense against Hitler.

Russians are not entirely sure, in the bottom of their hearts, that they would not be the first to become engaged in such a war, and they would not be in the least unhappy to see us engaged too. The Tsar is of a very honest, very firm, and very pacific temperament. He does not, perhaps, have many ideas; but he has, by the same token, a firm idea of what he wants; and in general he sees things quite correctly.

This being the case, I believe that we could today count on his help, and that is the important thing. It is perhaps regrettable that he would take the offensive against Austria and not against Germany; but what is important is that Russia would go to war in the face of an attack on us; and this, I believe, is what she would do.

In addition to these observations on the main question he had been instructed to clarify, Boisdeffre mentioned two or three other points of incidental interest flowing from his visit.

For one thing, he had urged the Russians, he wrote, to proceed vigorously with the development and fortification of Libau (Libava in Russian, Liepāya in Latvian), an ice-free port on the seacoast of what is today Latvia, instead of basing their Baltic fleet on Cronstadt, at the head of the Gulf of Finland, ice bound for several months of the year, where the fleet could readily be bottled up by the German navy in case of war. The money for this had already been appropriated, as he understood it; and he had urged the Russians to get on promptly and vigorously with the work of construction. (This—the question of how far to go in creating a major naval base at Libau—was a question destined to come up shortly in a more acute form in connection with the necessity of making a choice between Libau and Murmansk as the main base for the Russian navy on the Atlantic-Baltic side of the Russian empire.)

Before termination of the maneuvers, Boisdeffre was received in audience by both the Russian and the German emperors—in the latter case, at the Kaiser's specific request. Nothing was said, in Boisdeffre's report, of the audience with the Tsar. Baron Boris Nolde, however, who seems to have seen more documents than he actually cited in his book,[8] wrote that the Tsar was much impressed by what Boisdeffre had to say about France's military progress and about her great financial strength. These were points that would have commanded respect on almost anybody's part in that Victorian age, when money and military strength were supreme values; and Nolde's statement that the Tsar was impressed by them is borne out by various statements attributed to Alexander by those who talked with him in the ensuing months.

It is evident that the question of the French form of government was also discussed by the Tsar both in his talk with Boisdeffre and in his conversations with the German Kaiser; but the upshot of these exchanges is cloudy. Rumors at once circulated in German and Austrian circles that Boisdeffre had tried to persuade Alexander of the desirability of a monarchist restoration and that the Tsar had expressed a preference for a return of the Orléans dynasty. The reality appears to have been quite different. If anything, Boisdeffre appears to have impressed the Tsar with his accounts of the true state of affairs in France; and there is little doubt, in the light of some of Alexander's later statements, that the latter came out of the interview both persuaded that the royalists actually had no political future and greatly reassured about the quality of a republican France as a possible partner in an alliance.

As for his interview with the Kaiser, Boisdeffre said in his report that the German monarch had been extremely courteous and pacifically minded. But beyond that, Boisdeffre's account is quite unsatisfactory, particularly because he appears to have confused, even within a single sentence, the Kaiser's remarks to himself with observations allegedly made by the Kaiser and by Caprivi to the Russians. He quotes both of those men as having "contrary to precedent" demanded nothing in the way of a free hand to move against France; and his reference to the fact that such demands were *not* made on this occasion, as being something unusual and unprecedented, is revealing for the sort of misunderstanding—the sort of exaggeration and distortion of German policy—that had by this time become ingrained in French official thinking. At no time, then or in recent years, had the Germans demanded of the Russians a free hand for another attack on France. Indeed, the language of the Reinsurance Treaty, concluded in 1887, had specifically left the Russians quite free to take whatever action they might wish to take in the face of such a contingency.

. . .

It is not easy to assess the exact significance of these Franco-Russian exchanges of the summer of 1890. They represented the first serious move in the direction of an alliance. It is noteworthy that this move took place under the very noses of the Germans, during the course of an imperial German visit in and around the Russian capital. These were of course only preliminary soundings; but they brought all the principal parties perceptibly closer to the goal of a formal alliance: Giers, because the German refusal to renew the treaty or anything like it persuaded him for the first time of the inevitability of a much closer relationship to France; the Tsar, because this last encounter with his German guest had left him, if anything, even less inclined than before to preserve a close political and military relationship with Germany, and because Boisdeffre had been effective in reassuring him about the merits of France as a potential partner; Obruchev, because the French offer of a military convention binding the parties to simultaneous mobilization held important advantages for Russia; Freycinet and Ribot, because the professed Russian readiness to mobilize if the French did, even though they were not yet ready to put this in writing, practically assured Russian participation from the start in any future Franco-German war. In these circumstances, Boisdeffre had good reason to be satisfied, as he declared himself to be, with his effort.

The only mystery here is the obtuseness of the Germans, who, besides being unaware that all this was occurring in the Russian capital during their own presence there, unwittingly encouraged it. In the case of the Kaiser this can perhaps be explained by his firm conviction that important political results could be obtained by successful personal encounters among crowned heads, and by his belief that he was capable of making a sufficiently favorable impression upon his imperial-Russian cousin to make unthinkable any such duplicity on the Russian side. In the case of the various military and political figures in the Kaiser's entourage, however, the lack of concern is harder to explain. One can only suppose that they regarded an eventual Franco-Russian military collaboration as a foregone conclusion, already taken full account of in their military plans. It seems in any case never to have occurred to them that, by retaining the previous contractual relationship to Russia, they could at least have had a chance of preventing such a development of Franco-Russian relations.

Chapter 4

THE "ENTENTE CORDIALE"

Some of those who have glanced, in retrospect, at the history of the Franco-Russian Alliance may have wondered at the fact that this arrangement (as we shall shortly have occasion to see) took the form not of one document but of two; that the respective negotiations out of which these two documents proceeded were separated by an entire year; and that their respective contents were partially overlapping, to the extent that each contained the crucially important provision for immediate and simultaneous mobilization in case either power should become involved in a war with Germany.

It will be easier to understand how this curious result was achieved if it be borne in mind that there were two forms such an agreement could conceivably take. One would have been a full-fledged political alliance, identifying the common political interests and purposes of the two parties, defining the conditions under which each would expect the other's support, and committing the governments as a whole, either directly or by action of their foreign ministers, to the fulfillment of the terms of the treaty. The other would have been a purely military-technical agreement, describing in detail the exact military support each of the parties might expect from the other in time of war, but committing only the two general staffs or the respective ministers of war, or both. These alternatives were of course not mutually exclusive. There was in fact a wholly reasonable question as to whether one could properly have the military agreement without the political one; for unless the general political purposes of the alliance were to be clearly defined and agreed upon, either side could easily find itself fighting someday for purposes it had never approved and never intended to fight for.

Depending on which of these alternatives was chosen, or at least which was to be given precedence in the process of negotiation, there were two channels through which negotiations might proceed. For negotiation of a full-fledged political alliance the proper channel was of course the

52

political-diplomatic one: that is, communication between the respective foreign offices or, possibly, even the heads of state. Negotiations for a purely military convention might proceed, however, directly between the two military establishments.

It was mentioned above (chap. 2, p. 29) that Freycinet and Ribot, although colleagues in the same cabinet (Freycinet as premier and minister of war, Ribot as minister for foreign affairs), were in a sense long-standing political rivals. Note was further taken of their common recognition that the bringing to completion of an alliance with Russia would be regarded by the French public as a signal triumph of French statesmanship. This meant, of course, that great political credit could be expected to accrue to anyone who could plausibly claim to have played the leading role in this achievement.

All this being the case, it must have been clear to Freycinet that he, in his position as premier and minister of war, would be well situated to control negotiations for a military convention and to receive major credit for their successful accomplishment, whereas in the case of a political pact it would normally be the minister for foreign affairs who would be most prominently involved. As for Ribot: it was only natural that he should be aware of the dangers of any arrangements concluded at the military level that were not covered by clear political understandings. It will not have failed to occur to him, in particular, that should the military arrangements be pursued in advance of the political ones, he would be in danger of losing control of the entire process of negotiations and would be vulnerable to serious reproach for having failed to meet his responsibility, as foreign minister, for seeing that the political interests of France were adequately identified and protected in the new and more intimate Franco-Russian relationship these military arrangements would imply. He could, in these circumstances, only be sensitive to anything that appeared as an effort on Freycinet's part to deal with the Russians through military channels without his (Ribot's) knowledge or without consulting him.

All this must be borne in mind if the further course of the Franco-Russian relationship is to be fully comprehensible.

. . .

Ribot had had no part in preparing the instructions by which Boisdeffre was guided in his exchanges with the Russians in the summer of 1890. It is even questionable whether Boisdeffre's written report on those talks[1] even came into his hands at the time; for when Boisdeffre, on returning from Russia, called on him and gave him an oral account of the exchanges, Ribot was startled to learn that Boisdeffre, although not so authorized, had taken upon himself the responsibility of offering to conclude a written agreement providing for immediate and simultaneous mobilization. "Comment, général?" Ribot is reported to have exclaimed. "Mais c'est très grave ce que vous avez fait! Comment avez-vous osé prendre une telle initiative?"*[2]

Ribot will have been relieved, of course, to learn that the Russians had shown themselves unwilling to conclude any such written agreement at that time. But the incident must have made him more sensitive to the dangers of any serious military-level communication with the Russians over which he had no control. In any case, he appears to have perceived, in those first months following the Narva-Petersburg discussions, no reason for forcing the pace in further exchanges with the Russian government. He evidently preferred for the moment to wait and see whether the Russians would not themselves take a further initiative, as they had done in inviting Boisdeffre's mission the preceding summer and as he thought it likely they would do again.

Giers, his health failing badly, remained in the country for some weeks after Boisdeffre's visit. It was not until the month of September had passed that Laboulaye had an opportunity (October 9, 1890) to see him once again and to discuss with him the state of Franco-Russian relations. What Giers said on that occasion, all of which Laboulaye promptly reported to Paris, must have confirmed Ribot in his view that he had not heard the last from the Russians with respect to the prospects for a closer Franco-Russian relationship. For Giers had first observed (while admonishing Laboulaye not to mistake this for an "avance") that he could see nothing, not even anything in the French form of government, that could constitute a serious source of dissension between the two governments—a statement that surely reflected the favorable impression made upon the Tsar by the recent explanations of both Laboulaye and Boisdeffre concerning the form of government in France. And Giers had gone on, then, to say that although nothing had been signed between the two governments at the time of the Narva maneuvers, "It was as though something had been."

---

*In English: "What, General? But this is a very serious thing you have done. How could you have dared to take such an initiative?"

Finally, Giers had made a significant observation with respect to a minor press incident that had just taken place in Paris. A rumor had been circulating there to the effect that the Russian chargé d'affaires in that city, Ernest Kotzebue, had approached the Quai d'Orsay with proposals for an alliance. The rumors were clearly false. Kotzebue had publicly denied them. But he had done so in such a way as to leave open the question as to whether such an alliance might not have been a real possibility in the first place. This had caused some comment; and Giers had asked himself whether he ought not to place an item in the official *Journal de Saint-Pétersbourg* strengthening Kotzebue's denial. But he had refrained from doing so, he explained to Laboulaye, because he feared that this might be taken as a repudiation on his part of the very idea of such an alliance.

Laboulaye was not slow to get the hint and to call it to Ribot's attention. It could serve, he observed in his message to Paris, as a fitting reply to those who claimed that a republican France could never have as an ally the autocratic "Tsar of all the Russias."[3]

. . .

The European press of the first weeks of 1891 was preoccupied with two developments, both of which, while not of much importance in themselves, suggested a possible weakening of the Triple Alliance and thus tended, at least momentarily, to throw a certain doubt over the necessity for a Franco-Russian alliance as a response to it.

The first of these developments was the fall, on January 31, of the strongly anti-French Italian premier, Francesco Crispi, and the attempt of his successor, the Marquis di Rudini, to improve relations with France. This effort was inspired primarily by Italy's financial distress of the moment and her need for the support of the Paris bankers. But the French statesmen not unnaturally saw in this development a possibility of buying Italy off from her adherence to the Triple Alliance. For some time they devoted themselves eagerly in talks with the Italians to the exploration of this prospect. But they demanded, as a part of the deal, that the terms of the Triple Alliance should be revealed to them. This demand, requiring in effect an Italian breach of faith with the other members of the Triplice, was too much. Rudini's parliamentary position gave him no authority to go this far. Nor would the Italian king have accepted it.

Nothing came, therefore, of Rudini's brief effort at a rapprochement with France. On the contrary, it only gave rise to increased bitterness on both sides. But while it lasted—roughly from mid-February to mid-April 1891—it was naturally seen by some in France as a potential alternative to a closer relationship with Russia.

The second development was the unhappy visit to Paris, in late February 1891, of the dowager empress of Germany, Queen Victoria's daughter "Vicki," widow of the recently and tragically deceased Kaiser Frederick III. It was a visit undertaken for the most worthy of motives: to encourage participation by French artists in an exhibition of modern art scheduled soon to take place in Berlin; but it was one that, in its execution, reflected credit on none of the parties involved. The very idea of including French artists in this exhibit was probably not a good one in the first place. Beyond that, everyone made mistakes. The German government neglected to give proper notification to the French government of the lady's coming. She herself destroyed what was supposed to have been her incognito by insisting on visiting the studios of several French artists, to the acute embarrassment of some of the proprietors. Coming to public attention, these visits aroused the fury of the French chauvinists, notably the poet Paul Déroulède and the violently *revanchiste* military artist Edouard Detaille; and their angry protests led to hostile public demonstrations. The royal visitor played into the hands of these enemies by prolonging her stay beyond its appointed time, and then by having the tactlessness to visit Versailles, where, only two decades earlier, the establishment of the German empire had been proclaimed over the prostrate bodies of the defeated and humiliated French. The French government, attempting to cope with the attendant protocol problems, vacillated awkwardly between a desire to ward off unnecessary unpleasantness and a reluctance to offend aroused nationalistic opinion. In the end the unfortunate ex-empress had to be virtually smuggled out of Paris to avoid hostile demonstrations. What had begun as a goodwill mission ended as the occasion for angry wrangling among all concerned.

When Giers went to Gatchina on the 3rd of March for his weekly report to the Tsar, the two men had before them a whole series of reports about the ex-empress's visit and the various European reactions thereto; and they decided to take advantage of the occasion not only to make their own position clear in the face of this episode, but also to remind the French of the seriousness with which they continued to view the recent strengthening of the relations between the two countries. Giers was instructed to draw up, for distribution to the Russian diplomatic missions in Europe, a circular instruction setting forth the official Russian view of the Paris episode; and it was agreed that this instruction should be accompanied, in Mohrenheim's case, with a private letter detailing the implications of this event for Franco-Russian relations. In addition to this, the Tsar gave his final approval in principle to the bestowal upon the French President, Sadi Carnot, of Russia's highest decoration, the Great Ribbon of Saint Andrew. This last was to be, ostensibly, in appreciation for the hospitality about to be bestowed upon the Russian heir apparent, Prince Nicholas, who was at that time performing a highly publicized journey around the coasts of Asia and was about to set foot for the first time on French soil (as it was then regarded): the territory now known as Vietnam. Mohrenheim was to be instructed to inform the French government of the Tsar's intention to bestow this decoration upon the President, explaining that the actual ceremony of presentation would take place at a later date.

All this was done as agreed; and in the special letter to Mohrenheim, Giers expressed satisfaction over the failure of what had seemed (namely, the dowager empress's Paris visit) to be a German effort to lure France away from her rapprochement with Russia. He then went on to say:

> The *entente cordiale* that has happily been established between Russia and France represents a factor essential at this moment not only from the standpoint of the mutual interests of the two parties but also, insofar as it assures the most favorable balance of forces, for the creation of a certain counterweight to the influence of the Triplice. At a time when the Triple Alliance . . . is ruining itself in military preparations, the agreement between Russia and France, promoting as it does the gradual and natural development of their power and prosperity, genuinely guarantees the preservation of peace.*[4]

One can only be puzzled, at first glance, over the reason for these decisions of the 3rd of March. Nothing in the official reports or in the press publicity attending the Paris visit of the dowager empress gave the two Russian statesmen the slightest reason to suppose that the enthusiasm of the French government for the rapprochement with Russia had been in any way weakened by this episode—quite the contrary. Besides which, the pretext for the bestowal upon Carnot of Russia's highest decoration was a flimsy one; and the Russians must have known that high political

*The original of this letter was presumably written in French. The only copy available is a Russian version appearing in the published Russian translation of Lamsdorf's diary. There is, of course, a possibility that this Russian text *was* the original and that Lamsdorf either inserted it into the diary in its original form or translated it into French—the normal language of the diary.

significance would be attached to the gesture.* We shall have to return to this question at a later point in this narrative.

If Giers and the Tsar did not intend these two steps to be taken as a major diplomatic initiative, they failed to reckon with the freewheeling and not always predictable propensities of their ambassador in Paris, Baron Arthur Mohrenheim. An intensely ambitious and not overly scrupulous man, a glib, compulsive talker and shameless intriguer, Mohrenheim had by no means been Giers' choice for the position he then held at Paris. He owed this position to the influence of the Empress Dagmar, with whom he had succeeded in ingratiating himself when serving in Copenhagen in earlier years. He was intensely envious of Giers (of whose dislike for himself he was not unaware), had dreams of replacing him as foreign minister, and seldom lost an opportunity for undermining his reputation in the eyes of the French. All this being the case, he was naturally anxious to insert himself as prominently as possible into the process of Franco-Russian relations and to establish himself in both French and Russian eyes as the real architect of the Alliance.

Upon receiving Giers' letter, Mohrenheim, although without any formal authority or instruction to do so, at once approached Ribot with the request for a special and immediate interview—a request that in itself conveyed the suggestion that he had something of major importance to impart. He then showed to Ribot (though again, quite without authorization to do so) the text of Giers' letter to himself, pointed out that the phrase "entente cordiale" was new in Russian usage, suggested that its use on this occasion represented a departure of major significance in Russian policy, and coupled this with the communication of the Tsar's intention to confer the decoration on Carnot.†

Ribot, startled by this approach and at a loss to know what to make of it, dismissed Mohrenheim with the normal expression of gratification

---

*Two months later, in May 1891, another order (the Alexander Nevski Order) was bestowed on Freycinet and Ribot, to the high satisfaction of the latter, but to the embarrassment of the former, who had made it a rule not to accept foreign decorations but found it impossible to decline this one.

†In reporting to Petersburg on his visit to Ribot, Mohrenheim was less than candid about what he had done, concealing the fact that he had actually shown Giers' letter to the foreign minister. Giers, however, learned of this—through the interception by his Black Chamber of Ribot's telegram to Laboulaye about the visit. Giers was too experienced, of course, to reveal to Mohrenheim what he knew, or how he knew it; but he no doubt derived a certain malicious pleasure in expressing to Mohrenheim, in a subsequent letter, his gratification that Mohrenheim had held the earlier one in strict confidence, since it had, he wrote, not been intended for French eyes (Lamsdorf diary, March 5/17, 1891).

This, incidentally, was not the first time, nor would it be the last, that Mohrenheim would take, in his relations with the French, initiatives for which he had no proper authorization—always with a view to promoting his own involvement in the preparations for an alliance.

over the decoration and with the assurance that the French government "appreciated the full importance of Giers' communication." He then went off to inform Carnot and Freycinet of what had happened.[5]

These latter were also puzzled. Particularly so because the approach came at a moment when their suspicions had been aroused by Russian behavior in another matter, one that concerned an existing Franco-Russian collaboration—clandestine collaboration at that—in the military field. Mention was made above (p. 32) of the fact that in the late 1880s the French government had given important aid to the Russian Ministry of War in the latter's effort to develop a new infantry weapon designed for the use of smokeless powder. In early December 1890 a contract had been signed for the manufacture for Russia (or partial manufacture; some parts, it would appear, were to be made in Russia) of 500,000 of the new guns by the French governmental arms plant at Chatellerault. The arrangement had been confirmed by a French governmental decree of the 26th of December. Since that time, the Chatellerault concern had been holding itself in readiness to begin the work. But the Russians had dragged their feet, had failed to come across with the design for the new gun, and, characteristically, had been less than communicative about their reasons for the delay. The great plant thus remained largely idle over the winter, at the cost of considerable inconvenience and financial loss. Meanwhile, the French were getting reports that delegations of Russian officers were traveling around Europe, visiting other arms manufacturers, including the Enfield plant in England. And about all this, too, the Russians had said nothing to the French.

It was now the turn of the French to become suspicious. And the retiring French military attaché at Petersburg, Colonel Briois, did nothing to allay these suspicions. "I consider," he wrote to Freycinet on the 24th of January,

> that we cannot be too wary of the bad faith of the Russians in business matters. It is not impossible that despite the assurances given to General de Boisdeffre by . . . Vannovski and repeated to me by Colonel van der Oven, the Russian government, having in mind the possibility of manufacturing the guns in Russia, is trying to wriggle out of its undertaking to us, and that all these procrastinations and beautiful words have no other purpose than to wangle out of us the things they lack, such as powder, machines, tools, know-how, etc.[6]

Impressed by such warnings, Freycinet himself began to have serious misgivings. It was he, after all, who had taken personal responsibility for the Chatellerault deal from the start. Was it possible, he now had to ask himself, that the Russians had been just playing games with them all along, and that Mohrenheim's friendly approach was only a smoke screen, designed to keep them quiet while Petersburg explored other possibilities?

Ribot, too, was aware of the Chatellerault situation and was equally puzzled. It occurred to both men, therefore, that it was high time they took matters into their own hands and attempted to find out what was really going on in the Russian mind. But, significantly, each set out to do this in his own way. It will be instructive to see what these ways were.

To understand the direction Freycinet's efforts took, a further word of background is necessary. There is considerable evidence that at just this time he was in contact with, and to some extent under the influence of, the former French foreign minister (1887–1888), Emile Flourens (son of the well-known physiologist of that name). Still a parliamentary deputy but otherwise now an outsider to governmental matters, Flourens remained an enthusiastic adherent of the project of an alliance with Russia. Not only this, but he had become firmly persuaded (probably by Mohrenheim) that to make any progress in that direction it was necessary to bypass Giers and to establish direct communication with the Tsar. This, he further reasoned, could most easily be done when the Tsar was spending his annual vacation in Denmark as guest of his wife's parents, the King and Queen of that country; for on these jaunts, which usually occurred in late summer and lasted for several weeks, Giers never accompanied the imperial couple. When himself serving as foreign minister in 1887, Flourens had exploited this possibility by sending to the Tsar at Copenhagen, through secret emissaries, a number of documents calculated to persuade that monarch that Bismarck was deceiving him and treacherously undermining his purposes in the sensitive question of policy towards Bulgaria. These documents, as it turned out, were forgeries; and Bismarck, to whom the Tsar showed them (without revealing their source), at once published them and named them as such.[7] Flourens's part in getting them into the Tsar's hands remained unknown to the public and even to the diplomatic world of that day; but it is evident that he looked back on the episode with pride and with undiminished faith in the usefulness of getting at the Tsar during the latter's Danish vacations.

Flourens's highest ambition, in the years of the early 1890s, appears to have been to continue to play a role in Franco-Russian relations and particularly to ingratiate himself with Alexander III. One must suppose that the motivation for these efforts was the hope of obtaining either a second appointment as foreign minister or the post of ambassador in Petersburg and thus appearing as the true architect of the Alliance.*

Flourens was close to Mohrenheim. In the days of Flourens's foreign ministry, the two men had collaborated extensively; and it cannot be doubted that Mohrenheim's influence was exerted, then as afterwards, to strengthen the other in the view that Giers should be avoided wherever possible and bypassed in the effort to realize the alliance. While the two men had of course dealt directly with each other in official matters in the days of Flourens's incumbency at the Quai d'Orsay, they had also kept in touch, unofficially and more intimately, through the services of a curious intermediary, Jules Hansen by name, normally a journalist by profession but at that time functioning simultaneously as an honorary official of the French foreign office (with the title of Counselor of Embassy) and as a paid assistant to the chief of the intelligence section of the Russian embassy in Paris, P. I. Rachkovski. The Russians certainly knew of his official French status. Whether the French knew of his Russian connection is not apparent. It was Hansen who had served as one of the emissaries who brought the false documents to the Tsar in 1887. Now, in 1891, he appears again as secret emissary (a calling to which he was passionately attached), but this time not for the French foreign minister of the day, Ribot, with whom he evidently had no relations of confidence, but between Freycinet and Mohrenheim, to the latter of whom he was greatly devoted.†

A number of indications suggest that beginning in the late winter of 1891 and continuing for more than a year thereafter, Freycinet directed his efforts primarily to the conclusion of a military convention, and this through channels other than the French and Russian foreign offices. In this effort he seems to have made use of Hansen, just as Flourens had used him in earlier years, as a confidential emissary. The first instance of that

---

*Flourens, as we shall see shortly, made journeys to Petersburg in the first months of both 1891 and 1892 and succeeded in seeing the Tsar on both occasions, much to the annoyance of the respective French ambassadors in that city. In 1894 he produced a highly hagiographic and largely valueless book about Alexander III, with the evident purpose of elevating himself in the eyes of that ruler. Alexander's death in November of that year obviously robbed the book of whatever effect it might otherwise have had in this direction; and with that disappointing turn of events, Flourens's interest in Franco-Russian relations appears to have subsided. (The book in question was entitled *Alexandre III* [Paris: E. Dentu, 1894].)

†Hansen was the author of two small books dealing with the Franco-Russian relations of the period: *L'Alliance franco-russe* (Paris: Ernest Flammarion, 1897) and *Ambassade à Paris du Baron de Mohrenheim* (Paris: Ernest Flammarion, 1907). Journalistic in style and superficial in content, these books add a little, though not much, to the history of the preparation of the Alliance.

employment came just after Mohrenheim's dramatic visit to Ribot in March 1891, and apparently by way of reaction to that event. It took the form of a request by Freycinet to Hansen to get in touch with the military attaché of the Russian embassy, General (Baron) Fredericks, and to ask the latter to inquire, through Freycinet's opposite number, the Russian war minister Vannovski, (a) where the matter of the Chatellerault deal stood, (b) whether the Russians did not consider that there was need for a military convention; and if so, (c) whether this was not something that could be discussed directly between the two ministers of war (i.e., without the involvement of the respective foreign offices).

It must be noted that the normal channel for an inquiry of this nature would have been through the French military attaché in Petersburg. Had this channel been used, however, the French ambassador there would also have had to be informed, and the matter would thus have come to the attention of the two foreign offices. This avoidance of the involvement of the diplomats is the only apparent reason for Freycinet's selection of the other channel.

The innuendo behind the sequence of Freycinet's two questions was, of course: "Yes, we will be glad to pursue the question of a military convention—and this, directly between the two war ministers; but first you must tell us what you are up to in the matter of the Chatellerault deal; otherwise we shall have to revise our ideas about further military collaboration."

.   .   .

Hansen and Fredericks did their parts as requested. Fredericks obviously consulted his principals in Petersburg (in this instance, surely, Vannovski); and on March the 24th he transmitted the Russian reply to Hansen. With respect to the Chatellerault affair, there were soothing words: the French need not worry; the Tsar had approved the transaction; it was taking a bit longer than had been anticipated to decide on the design of the rifle, but this was not serious—all would be well. And as for the rest: there was no reason why the two war ministers should not discuss the question of a military convention, if the Tsar approved. But was this, it was then asked, really what the French wanted? Such a convention could, of course, be useful, even if no formal political alliance existed. But was not the existing unwritten "entente" just as good? A written instrument might cause one or the other of the parties to be restricted in its freedom of action long after all justification for this had ceased to exist. It might even provoke the very war against which it was intended to guard.*

It is significant that this reply reflects very accurately what are known to have been Vannovski's personal views. While unwilling to exclude the possibility of a military convention (for he knew that the Tsar had not fully made up his mind about this), and while anxious to have the benefits of an informal understanding with the French for simultaneous mobilization and common action in the event of a German attack, Vannovski had, and would long continue to have, doubts about the wisdom of concluding a written convention. The reply indicates, however, that he was at that time not averse to establishing direct communication on these matters with his French opposite number, excluding the two foreign offices and the diplomatic channel generally.

.   .   .

So much for Freycinet's reaction to the Russian *démarche* of the 9th of March, 1891. Let us turn to that of Ribot.

How much Ribot knew about Freycinet's feelers through Hansen is not clear. The wholly misleading document that reposes in the files of the Quai d'Orsay may have come to that ministry at a later date; and the distortion of its content suggests that it was not intended that Ribot should know the whole story, in any case. He may, however, have had his suspicions. He must have realized that relations with Russia had now moved into a more active and serious phase, possibly involving the formalization of a closer relationship, and that this involved his responsibilities in the most intimate way. Plainly, he would be remiss in his duties if he permitted such a process to go forward without his involvement, and particularly so if there were a possibility that this might occur exclusively through military channels.

The first effect of Mohrenheim's *démarche* must have been to make Ribot painfully aware of the insufficiency of his own sources of informa-

---

*The substance of this Russian reply will be found in *DDF*, vol. 8, no. 319, pp. 439–441, March 25, 1891; but the form in which it is there enclosed was a most curious one: namely, that of a verbatim record of a supposed casual conversation between Hansen and Fredericks. That this was a deliberate mystification is evident from the fact that the full written text of the Russian reply, as an independent document quite devoid of mention of any questions by Hansen, is to be found in the Boisdeffre mss. Presumably, the intended victim of this mystification was Ribot, from whom it was evidently not thought prudent to conceal the Russian reply, but who was not to know that it was the response to a query by Freycinet himself. He was to be allowed to suppose that this was only a casual reply by Fredericks to a casual query by Hansen. It is out of the question that Fredericks would have ventured to come forward with these views to such a man as Hansen otherwise than in response to specific instructions from a very high level in Petersburg.

tion. He had had no forewarning of this development from the French embassy at Petersburg. Where, he will have asked himself, had been his ambassador there, Laboulaye, while this Russian move was being prepared? Why had the Quai d'Orsay received no reports of what was cooking, and no guidance from Laboulaye in the interpretation of it? Was it not the latter's business to know about these things, to inform Paris about them, and to give his interpretation?

Laboulaye was a competent and experienced career officer. He had been stationed in Petersburg as a junior officer in earlier years, and had now been there four years as ambassador. He was not one to press himself forward professionally or otherwise; and he was skeptical, for serious reasons, of the possibility and desirability of a formal alliance with Russia. But the record suggests that he had been doing his job in Petersburg just about as effectively as anyone could have done it, considering the unusual handicaps under which the work of a foreign envoy in that country had always to be performed. These last included the ingrained Russian passion for governmental secrecy, the tendency to regard every foreign representative as a spy, the remoteness of the sovereign from all informal contact with the diplomatic corps, and the timidity of the various ministers when it came to discussions with foreign diplomatic representatives.

Ribot, however, will have had little understanding for these handicaps. It is not certain that he would have been able to picture them clearly, even had Laboulaye endeavored to describe them.* This being the case, the thought will have occurred to him that if he wished to take into his own hands the reins of France's policy towards Russia, the first step must be to find for the Petersburg post an ambassador who would be of more use to him both as a source of information about what was happening at the Russian end and as a line of communication with the Russian government.

For several weeks, as it happened, Laboulaye had been requesting for personal reasons (his wife had recently died and he had new family responsibilities) a long leave of absence. Ribot had resisted this, being reluctant on general principles to permit him to leave his post at so important a time. On the 5th of March, Laboulaye had written once more, insisting this time on the necessity of a leave. The letter must have reached Ribot at just the time of Mohrenheim's *démarche*. Three days

---

*On one occasion, Ribot wrote to Laboulaye suggesting that the latter (evidently with a view to the improvement of his contacts with the Russian government) should invite the Tsar to dinner. This suggestion would have been greeted with derisive laughter on the part of anyone familiar with the ways things were, and were not, done at the Russian court at that time.

after that event Ribot replied to Laboulaye's letter, saying, rather brutally though in delicate terms, that since Laboulaye was no longer able to reconcile his official duties with his personal obligations, his resignation from the diplomatic service would be accepted.[8]

This decision raised a delicate question. Alexander III, as noted above (chap. 1), did not like new faces, even in the diplomatic corps. Some years earlier, he had been deeply offended when Laboulaye's predecessor, General Félix Appert, had been abruptly yanked from his ambassadorial position, and this, incidentally, by none other than the same Freycinet who was now premier. The action had been taken without prior notice to him or to Giers. His anger over this procedure had nearly led to a total break in diplomatic relations between the two countries. It had been months before he could be induced to give his consent to the appointment of a new ambassador to take Appert's place. Now, in 1891, it took all Giers' tact and experience to prepare the suspicious and sensitive monarch for the news of Laboulaye's sudden removal and to get his consent on principle to the acceptance of a new appointee.

Not only this, but there appears to have been some difficulty at the Paris end with regard to the choice of a successor. Just who the leading candidates were is unclear. Possibly Flourens was one of them. However that may be, Ribot could find, for the moment, no one who was to his taste and was acceptable to those others who had a say in the matter. The result was that he was obliged to revise his decision about Laboulaye's recall, to the point of agreeing that the latter should have his three months' vacation before abandoning the ambassadorial position, after which time (this would be in midsummer) he could return to Petersburg, present his letters of recall, and take his final departure.

Even this decision raised a further complication. In the preceding summer, at the time of the Narva maneuvers and Boisdeffre's visit, the French had inquired in Petersburg about the possibility of sending a French naval squadron on a formal visit to Cronstadt, the island naval base for the Petersburg area. The Russians had indicated their consent in principle, but it had proved too late to arrange the visit for that summer and the matter had been permitted to lie over. Now, under the impact of Mohrenheim's approach, Ribot took the matter up again, and it was arranged that the visit should take place in late July 1891, just before the annual military maneuvers and the ensuing departure of the Tsar for his annual vacation in Denmark. Since, however, it would be awkward to have a new ambassador arriving just at the time of the fleet visit, it was decided that Laboulaye, upon returning to Russia after his leave of absence, should remain there over the days of the visit and only then, after the ships had departed, should present his letters of recall and take his departure. On this understanding, matters rested over the spring.

. . .

However, before Laboulaye could leave Petersburg (circa April 6), a further development took place, one even more intriguing for the historian than the decisions of the 3rd of March. During one of Laboulaye's last visits to Giers (and probably the last one, at the beginning of April), Giers appears to have hinted to the ambassador that perhaps the time had come to make more precise (presumably in written form) the unwritten "entente" that already existed between them. It is of course possible that this approach was so delicately phrased that Laboulaye, preoccupied with his own personal troubles and forthcoming departure, failed to appreciate its significance. But even this is uncertain. There is no specific reference to the episode in the French documents.* In the account that Ribot drew up many years later (1913) of the origins of the Alliance, published in 1937 in the *Revue d'Histoire de la Guerre Mondiale*, [9] he merely observed, speaking of this period, that "the entente of which M. Giers had spoken was indeed in need of being made more precise." And he went on to explain why the French had not pushed the matter at that time. "We had," he wrote,

> no reason to pause along the path that led to an alliance; but we in Paris did not wish to force the pace. We did not find it desirable to show ourselves too eager. We thought it would be wiser on our part to give the Russians time to allow their decisions to mature and to overcome the hesitations caused by the differences in the political institutions of the two countries, and by the fear that the French government, subject as it is to ministerial vicissitudes, would not know how to preserve that secrecy that the emperor Alexander III considered as the primary condition for a formal agreement.†

It is of course possible that Ribot's memory may, at the distance of so many years, have betrayed him, and that he confused one period with

---

*The evidence that there *was* such an approach by Giers will be seen in a later chapter. The Austrian embassy in Paris picked up a rumor to the effect that Laboulaye, on the occasion of this last visit to Giers before leaving for France, had clumsily *proposed* an alliance and had been rebuffed by Giers. This seems unlikely; but the rumor would seem to support the thesis that the subject was discussed in some way on the occasion in question.

†The quoted passage (translated, of course, from the French) does not appear, curiously enough, in the original text of Ribot's account, as contained in the Ribot mss. at the Quai d'Orsay, but it does appear in the version of the document published (for the first time) in 1937 in the *Revue d'Histoire de la Guerre Mondiale*.

another. But barring this contingency, the historian can only conclude that the French were reacting, in that spring of 1891, to what they took to be a suggestion from Giers, conveyed orally to Laboulaye in early April, that the existing unwritten entente cordiale should be made more precise by being formalized in some sort of a written document. Possibly this suggestion, never recorded in writing, was merely recounted orally by Laboulaye to Ribot upon their first and only encounter following the former's return from Petersburg. But again, since this encounter was rumored to have been a very stormy and unpleasant one, owing presumably to Ribot's recent action in dismissing Laboulaye from the diplomatic service, it may also be that Laboulaye, in the heat of the moment, neglected entirely to mention it.

· · ·

Before leaving these events of the late winter and early spring of 1891, it may be well to glance back briefly at the three Russian initiatives of that period—the bestowal of the decoration on Carnot, the communication to Mohrenheim of early March, and Giers' suggestion to Laboulaye of early April—and to reflect on their possible significance.

The first thing that strikes the eye is that the initiative for all three steps appears to have come from the Tsar.

In the case of the decoration for Carnot, Lamsdorf's diary makes it clear that the Tsar plainly regarded this as *his* decision but was vacillating in the last days of February and the first days of March as to whether to proceed with it. This was a matter affecting primarily the Tsar, as head of state; and the initiative is unlikely to have come from Giers.

As for the *démarche* of early March by Mohrenheim: here, the Tsar's behavior was most peculiar. When Giers came to him, on the 17th of March, with the evidence that Mohrenheim had taken unauthorized and improper action in the matter, the Tsar's reaction, far from suggesting any discontent with Mohrenheim, was one of a weak and embarrassed effort to defend the latter's conduct. Lamsdorf's diary entries on this subject even leave the reader with the impression that the Tsar already knew what Mohrenheim had done and that his embarrassment was occasioned by the revelation that Giers, contrary to his expectations, had inadvertently learned of it.

And finally, the initiative for Giers' approach to Laboulaye in early April is most unlikely to have come from the foreign minister himself. He was pleased enough with the existing state of affairs: a situation marked by the fact that there was no written engagement but "it was as though there were one." He would clearly have preferred that Russia retain the maximum of freedom of action for unpredictable future contingencies. And in any case, he was decidedly not the man to take any initiative of this sort except on the Tsar's authority and in conformance with the latter's wishes.

What, then, had moved Alexander to take these steps, and to take them precisely at the time in question? Neither Lamsdorf's diary (the most sensitive and reliable reflection of the communications between the Tsar and his foreign minister) nor the pages of the Russian newspapers Alexander was in the habit of reading indicate anything coming to the latter's attention over the winter to stimulate him to such initiatives.

The conclusion is inescapable that just as the French had been waiting to see whether some further initiative would not be forthcoming from the Russian side, so the Tsar had been waiting to see whether the French would not come forward with the next step, and was hoping that they would—hoping so, not only because he preferred, on principle, to let initiatives come from others rather than to take them himself, but also because he really wanted, in his heart, to get on with the conclusion of the alliance. His three steps of the period in question were the expression of this impatience; and that it was *his* impatience, and not that of Giers, seems to be amply clear.

But if this was the case, then one is obliged to look to the events of the year 1890—the French crackdown on the Russian revolutionaries in Paris; the German refusal to renew the Reinsurance Treaty and the resulting danger of Russian isolation; the poor impression made by the young Kaiser on his visit to Narva; and above all, Boisdeffre's reassuring words about the French governmental system—as the decisive factors shaping the Tsar's readiness, on principle, to pursue the project of a genuine alliance with France. To be sure, many impediments remained to be overcome, many hesitations to be experienced and cleared away, before this goal could be attained; and these will be recounted in the following chapters. But the desire for the alliance was there from the summer of 1890. It was Alexander's desire, not that of his foreign minister. And such was the stubborn persistence of this crowned head, once the mind was made up, that while the various impediments and hesitations would be the occasion for long delays and setbacks, even appearing at times to be insurmountable, Alexander's disposition to proceed along this path, albeit in his own way and in his own time, would never waver until the goal had been achieved.

Chapter 5

PRIVATE STIRRINGS

The French foreign office and Ministry of War were not the only places in Paris where serious interest was being taken in 1891 in Franco-Russian relations generally and the possibility of an alliance in particular. There were in the early 1890s, as there had been ever since 1875, several private circles greatly interested in promoting these possibilities, circles that sometimes even formed themselves into what would today be called "lobbies" with a view to putting pressure on the government to get ahead with the task.

In the late 1870s and early 1880s such activity had been centered primarily in journalistic circles—this, incidentally, not without a certain amount of judicious financial encouragement from the Russian embassy in Paris, which tried to promote pro-Russian tendencies as a means of combatting the influence of the bitterly anti-tsarist Russian exiles living in that city. The most consistent and impassioned champion of the cause of a Russian alliance among the journalists was the intensely chauvinistic publisher and editor of the literary-political journal *La Nouvelle Revue* (an organ she had herself created)—Juliette Adam. This formidable woman, for whom hatred of Germany was a life's dedication, was, like her counterpart in London, the well-known Olga Novikova (friend of Gladstone and lobbyist for the Russian-Slavic cause), a great enthusiast for the Slavs in general, for the Russian Pan-Slav cause in particular, and especially for a French alliance with Russia. For many years, she pursued her advocacy of such an alliance undeviatingly, with all the force of her impulsive personality, all the power of her untiring pen, and all the influence of the bourgeois-literary salon that she regularly conducted.

In the late 1880s Mme. Adam and her sympathizers, who had been among the first to sponsor this cause, found themselves joined—in part to their gratification, in part to their embarrassment—by two powerful allies: one, in the person and following of the charismatic but indecisive minister of war, General Georges Boulanger; the other, the chauvinist-poet, Paul Déroulède. Both of these men exerted themselves vigorously for a time (primarily in the late 1880s) to promote the cause of the alliance; but political failure followed by exile and death, in Boulanger's case, and a wild impracticality on Déroulède's part, soon put an end to, or frustrated, their efforts. More persistent, if not much more effective, in the advocacy of the alliance was Flourens (see chap. 4 above). He remained consumed with the desire to reinsert himself in some way into the picture of Franco-Russian relations; and we shall encounter him at several points on the pages to follow.

In 1888 Juliette Adam had attempted to give organized form to her pro-Russian lobby by the creation of an organization labeled, somewhat misleadingly "L'Association Artistique et Littéraire Franco-Russe." The enterprise found favor, however, neither with the French government nor with the Russian one. Both governments feared, although for different reasons, that private pressures of this nature could unbalance the delicate orientation of their policies and impede rather than promote the strengthening of Franco-Russian relations. In the face of the French government's opposition the association had to be abandoned; but two years later, in 1890, it was recreated under another name: La Société des Amis de la Russie. High-ranking and influential supporters were now recruited: among them, the former foreign minister Flourens; the former French ambassador to Russia, General Félix Appert, together with his wife; and the widow of another former ambassador to that country, General Antoine Chanzy. Both of those ambassadors had enjoyed marked and unusual favor at the Russian court. But even this, as it turned out, was not enough. Once again, the two governments withheld their favor. And it was Mme. Adam's old friend Freycinet, now premier, who was obliged to insist on the closing down of the new society. This was no doubt a bitter disappointment to the society's founder; but it did not diminish her enthusiasm for the cause. She continued to pursue it wherever she could, despite the fact that her relations with Mohrenheim and the rest of the Russian embassy were of the worst, they and she being rivals rather than collaborators in the effort to bring the alliance about.

· · ·

Those who have read the earlier volume in this series may recall that Alexander III had ruled out any Russian participation in the great Paris Exposition of 1889—the centennial commemoration of the French Revolution. Alexander III could not see himself joining in the commemoration of a revolution that had achieved its culmination in the beheading of a king. The absence of Russian participation in this exposition had naturally been greatly regretted by the private French enthusiasts for a closer

Franco-Russian relationship, as well as by some of the Russian ones.

At some time in late 1889 the idea arose of filling this regrettable hiatus by staging a French exposition—a smaller edition of the Paris one —in Russia. A man by the name of Watbled, formerly honorary French consul in Moscow, took the lead in the effort to give reality to this dream. He appealed to Spuller, the French foreign minister of that day, for governmental support. The appeal was refused. Not only Spuller but the premier, Pierre Emmanuel Tirard, was firmly against it. Watbled, however, was not to be discouraged. In January 1890 he went to Russia, saw the finance minister, Ivan Aleksandrovich Vyshnegradski, and succeeded somehow or other in getting his support. Then he went on to Moscow and procured a similar endorsement of the idea by the governor general at that place, Prince V. A. Dolgorukov, a man of strongly pro-French inclinations, who was close to certain of the more prominent and sophisticated of the businessmen in that community (particularly the financier and railway magnate, Polyakov). The matter was then further pursued in Petersburg; and on May the 2nd, 1890, the Tsar personally gave authorization to Watbled to proceed with his plans, and for this purpose placed at his disposal (through 1891) the grounds and buildings at Moscow formerly used for the all-Russian Exposition of Arts and Industries of 1882. (The land in question was the well-known Khodynskoye Polye, destined to be, some seven years later, the scene of the tragic disaster that occurred on the day of the coronation of Nicholas II, when many hundreds of persons were trampled to death as a result of blunders in the handling of the arrangements.) These grounds and buildings had been laid out in the grand manner to which the Russians were accustomed; and they fully sufficed for a great international exposition.

Mystery still surrounds this success of Watbled's promotional effort. While he had gone to Russia armed with a letter, apparently from the French minister of commerce, identifying him as a *"consul de France en mission officieuse, pour étudier les meilleurs moyens de developper les relations commerciales entre la Russie et la France,"*[1] and while he claimed later to have had the personal support of the French ambassador at Petersburg, Laboulaye, there is no evidence that the French foreign office, particularly under Spuller, favored the undertaking; and it was unlike Vyshnegradski and the Tsar to go so far as they did in authorizing and patronizing a French undertaking that did not have strong French diplomatic support. (There is, incidentally, no evidence that the Russian foreign office, for its part, favored or supported the project at any time or was even consulted on the question of its authorization.)

Returning to France, armed with this impressive Russian support, Watbled was fortunate enough to find that Spuller and Tirard had now just fallen from office and been replaced by Ribot and Freycinet. Freycinet, in particular, while insisting that the enterprise must remain a private one, was sympathetic to the idea, conceiving that the exposition would contribute to the strengthening of relations between the two countries. Watbled was able, after all, to point not just to the political aspects of the enterprise but also to the need to do something to strengthen Franco-Russian commercial ties. Despite the massive financial assistance that France had already given to Russia, trade between the two countries had remained of minor significance compared to Russia's trade with Germany and England. Taking both imports and exports together, France had accounted, in 1889, for only 5.1 percent of Russia's trade, as compared with 31 percent for England and 26.3 percent for Germany.*

With all this in his favor, Watbled was now permitted to proceed with his plans. He enlisted the enthusiastic support of Juliette Adam and Flourens and set up under the guidance of the French minister of commerce (who had evidently been authorized to supervise the operation) a semiofficial commission, composed largely of prominent figures who had been extensively involved in the 1889 Paris exposition, to carry the project to completion. Financial support, to the initial amount of 1,500,000 francs, was obtained from a Paris banker by the name of Jouanno against the prospective revenues from the sale of tickets.† And thus the project was launched. The final attitude of the French government was set forth in a letter of July the 3rd, 1890, to Watbled from the Ministry of Commerce (Roche), in which it was cautiously stated that the Ministry of Commerce,

> as far as it is concerned, would view with pleasure the success of an enterprise designed to open new export possibilities for our industry and to promote the development of commercial relations between France and

*These figures, published in the *Nouvelle Revue* (vol. 69, April 1891, pp. 449–460), were probably provided by Watbled himself; but they coincide with the official ones. While England was by far the largest importer from Russia by reason of her extensive purchases of food and raw materials there, it was Germany that, with her shipments of machinery and equipment, occupied the leading position as exporter to that country.

†Confusion continues to surround this question of the ticket monopoly. *The New York Times* Berlin correspondent alleged one year later (May 24, 1891) that two prominent members of the Moscow Jewish community, Polyakov and Grunwald, had loaned the French committee large sums against the security of 1,200,000 tickets, and that the Tsar was incensed over this involvement with Jewish financiers and declined to visit the exhibit until the arrangement was canceled. While this was obviously gossip, there was evidently some germ of truth behind it.

Russia, but [an enterprise] that remains, and can only remain, essentially a private one, and one that must not be permitted, consequently, to engage in any way or in any degree the responsibility of the [French] government.[2]

There is some evidence that this undertaking, in addition to the cautious support that it received from the minister of commerce, also enjoyed some special attention from military circles. The exposition, as finally mounted, contained an entire *"pavillon militaire,"* which included, in addition to products of several French arms manufacturers, the entire French army camp, complete with wax figures attired in the real and proper uniforms, that the French Ministry of War had contributed to the 1889 Paris Exposition. It could only have been the same ministry, headed by Freycinet, that made this elaborate exhibit available for showing in Moscow.*

Despite this support from the two governments, overt in the case of the Russians and veiled in the case of the French, the very idea of the exposition was seriously misconceived. Moscow, with its pious, xenophobic, and strongly anti-Semitic old-Russian merchant community, was hardly the spot, in the first place, for a great international exhibit of this nature. The protectionist instincts of these merchants were bound to be aroused by the public display in the old Russian capital of the wares of some 1,500 foreign competitors. But beyond this, the timing could not have been worse. Only two months before the scheduled opening of the exposition, sinister changes appear to have been taking place in the disposition and policies of the Tsar—changes that quite altered the atmosphere for any undertaking of this nature. Somehow or other, the antiforeign and anti-Semitic pressures from the Moscow clergy got through (the intermediary was surely the Oberprokuror of the Holy Synod, Pobedonostsev) to Alexander III and induced that monarch to put in hand a series of curious and highly reactionary measures relating specifically to Moscow. The liberal governor general, Prince Dolgorukov, known especially for his moderation towards the Jews, was abruptly removed from his post. In his place was appointed the reactionary and viciously anti-Semitic brother of the Tsar, the grand duke Sergei Aleksandrovich. And these dispositions were followed by an imperial ukaz (March 27, 1891) requiring the expulsion from

*One notes, too, that French military authors played a prominent part as contributors to the volume entitled *La France à Moscou—Exposition de 1891,* published in Paris while the exposition was in progress. Other indications as well point to a deliberately concealed, but not insignificant, involvement of certain French military circles (probably not the General Staff) in the promulgation of the exposition.

Moscow, and removal to the Jewish "pale" in the western districts of the empire, of all Jewish artisans and traders established in that city.*

What these measures reflected in the way of a change in the general dispositions of Alexander III, and whether this change was one that had implications for his foreign policy as well, is an interesting question.

The timing of the dismissal of Dolgorukov and his replacement by the grand duke Serge (as he was usually known to foreigners), who had long coveted the position, seems to have been determined by the conversion to Russian Orthodoxy of Serge's German-born wife, the grand duchess Elizabeth (sister of the future empress, Alexandra). Elizabeth had long resisted this act; but her resistance was worn down by long and heavy pressure, particularly from Pobedonostsev. The ceremony of conversion was finally carried out at the palace in the presence of the Tsar and Tsarina, on April 24, 1891. This having been accomplished, Pobedonostsev, who detested the tolerant and humane Dolgorukov, happily assented to the latter's removal and his replacement by the grand duke; and at approximately the same time the anti-Semitic measures were put in hand, with the confidence that, with the grand duke now on the scene, they would be enforced with the desired harshness (as indeed they were). The whole affair was regarded as a spectacular victory for Pobedonostsev.

The Moscow press was permitted to interpret these measures as a certain turning-of-the-back by the monarch on the oversophisticated, cosmopolitan, and deplorably un-Russian capital of Petersburg, allegedly corrupted by foreign (especially German and Jewish) influences and contacts and by a largely de-Russianized bureaucracy; and, accordingly, as a gesture of self-identification on Alexander's part with the old virtuous Moscow, traditional seat of the Russian throne, center of the true religious orthodoxy and Russian patriotism, and bulwark of resistance to the insidious influences of a heretical outside world. There was, undoubtedly, something to this. One senses in these measures a new and intensified manifestation of Alexander's long-standing dislike for the German influences that pervaded the Petersburg-Baltic region, of his aversion to the sophisticated, cosmopolitan cultural tastes of the Petersburg intelligentsia

---

*The Vienna *Neue Freie Presse*, May 22, 1891, reported, in a long article about the background of these measures, that whereas it had been agreed that 25,000 Jews would be permitted to live in Moscow, the actual number had grown to five times that figure. In one section of the city they had replaced so many Russians that the Orthodox Church revenues had declined heavily, angering the local clergy, whose complaints to Moscow touched off the deportations. Dolgorukov, brokenhearted over his disgrace, at once left Russia and died within a matter of months.

The number of Jews actually affected by this ukaz would appear to have been in the neighborhood of 6,000.

and nobility, and of his implacable hatred for the revolutionary tendencies that had led to the assassination of his father on the Petersburg streets. In Moscow, there was indeed a less questioning acceptance of the autocracy, a greater approval of Alexander's reactionary policies, and more sympathy for the dark suspicions with which he viewed the German and Austrian-Catholic worlds that lay to the west.

Whether these things were in Alexander's mind when he authorized the mounting of the French exposition in Moscow is hard to tell. The very embodiment of this old-Muscovite spirit had been, up to his death in 1887, the great Moscow editor and publicist Mikhail Nikoforovich Katkov. Katkov had been, in his final years, the leading advocate in Russia of the break with Germany and the strengthened relationship with France. And France, curiously, despite the Jacobin origins of the existing Republic, evidently lay outside the area of Alexander's strongest aversions. It seems, in any case, never to have occurred to this tsar that the sort of xenophobia and anti-Semitism he was encouraging in Moscow was not favorable to any international exhibit, even a French one. Or perhaps he never thought of it at all. The two decisions, after all, were taken at different times.

. . .

The Moscow exposition was not the only point at which, in that spring of 1891, Russian commercial and financial policies fitted poorly with the political requirements of foreign policy. Another such point could be found in the field of international finance.

From the period of the Crimean War (1854–1856) down to the mid-1880s, the Russian treasury, its resources drained by the Crimean War, the Polish uprising of 1863, and the war with Turkey in the late 1870s, had been obliged to turn to the outside world for loans. Initially, it had been the old family banking houses of London and Antwerp, later those of Berlin, that had supplied these needs. Rarely and only in minor degree had the Paris market been tapped. But by the mid-1880s the conditions for Russian borrowing in London, Antwerp, and Berlin were, for various reasons, no longer favorable; and it was into the resulting gap that the French then moved.

Large-scale Russian borrowing in Paris began in the autumn of 1888, when a wide international syndicate, in which French bankers put up most of the money, made available to the Russian treasury the sum of 500 million francs (125 million rubles), to be used in large part for the conversion of one of the earlier German loans to a longer maturity period and a lower rate of interest.* The negotiation of this loan was the work of two French bankers: Charles Sautter, head of the well-known Banque de Paris et Pays Bas (colloquially shortened to "Paribas"), and a Danish-French banker, Emile Hoskier, whose operations were also based in Paris. The former put up most of the money; the latter contributed much of the initiative and enthusiasm.

Hoskier's interest in promoting this and other loans to Russia was not exclusively financial. He was the brother of the wife of the former French ambassador at Petersburg, General Appert, referred to above. Mme. Appert, a Danish-born woman, was well connected at both the Danish and the Russian courts. She and her husband had enjoyed the marked favor (rare among diplomats at that time) of the Russian imperial couple. In addition to which, Hoskier's wife was Russian-born. He therefore had, beyond his interest in lending money on advantageous terms to the Russian treasury, strong pro-Russian inclinations of a personal and political nature. He was particularly close to Mohrenheim, who had once served in Copenhagen. Indeed, there is evidence (in the memoirs of Giers' son Nicholas) that Mohrenheim regularly received a cut from the interest paid on each of Hoskier's loans to the Russian treasury.

The first major French loan, of 1888, was followed in 1889 by two further ones—both arranged, this time, by the powerful competitor of the Sautter-Hoskier syndicate, the Paris Rothschilds. This time, the amounts involved were much larger—nearly two billion francs (500 million rubles) in all. And the following year, 1890, witnessed the extension of one more loan from the Hoskier-Paribas combination, and of another two from the Rothschilds. Thus by the beginning of 1891 the Russians had received six major loans from French sources, to a total of something over three billion francs.†

Up to 1890, these had been conversion loans, involving the conversion of 5 percent issues into 4 percent ones. However, since the bonds issued in France had sold well under par, the actual interest received by the French investor was higher, amounting to something like 4.3 percent on the Russian paper, as compared to the 3.3 percent to be derived (on an average)

---

*On their earlier borrowings from foreign sources the Russians had normally been obliged to pay 5 percent interest. The conversion loans from France of 1888 and the immediately following years were designed to reduce the figure to 4½ or 4 percent, at the cost, of course, of the acceptance of longer periods of amortization.

†In addition to this: in view of the rising prices for Russian paper in Paris, quantities of Russian securities previously held in London, Amsterdam, and elsewhere had now floated to Paris, so that by the summer of 1891 the French holdings of such paper were understood to be approximately four billion francs.

The Tsar Alexander III

Princess Valdemar of Denmark (Princess Marie)
at the time of her marriage

N. K. Giers, Russian foreign minister

Count Vladimir Lamsdorf,
confidential aide to Foreign Minister N. K. Giers

from internal French bond issues. By the beginning of 1891, however, the prices for the Russian bonds were beginning to rise with the growth in the confidence of the French investor. The result was that their effective yield was declining to something approaching the 4 percent par, and their relative attractiveness as investments was beginning to decline accordingly.

It was in the face of this situation that negotiations were again undertaken with the Rothschilds at the end of March 1891 for a more ambitious project: the conversion, this time, not of a 5 percent issue into a 4 percent one, but of a 4½ percent issue into one bearing only 3 percent interest. The sum envisaged was large: 1,800,000,000 francs (450 million rubles); and great hopes were placed in Petersburg on the successful conclusion of the deal.

But suddenly and quite unexpectedly, in the month of May, disaster occurred. The Rothschilds backed out of the whole affair, causing a sensation on the Paris exchange, sending the prices for Russian bonds spinning all over Europe, and forcing the Russian treasury to enter the market itself and to buy up some two hundred million rubles' worth of its own bonds in order to avoid a complete collapse of Russian credit. What had caused this reverse?

The general assumption, then and later, was that this was an angry response by the Rothschilds to the anti-Semitic measures that had been ordered by the Tsar to be carried out in Moscow. Unquestionably, this had its effect on the Rothschild decision. One may even suppose that it was the principal causal element.* But it was not the only one. Professor René Girault, leading historian of the Franco-Russian financial relationship in the years in question, believes that other considerations also played an important part.[3] The various loans were not, Girault pointed out, the only irons the Paris Rothschilds had in the Russian fire. They controlled the Société de la Caspienne–Mer Noire, one of the three major enterprises (the other two were Russian owned) then exploiting Baku oil, and the only one engaged in exporting the oil for refining outside Russia. Beyond that, they had been encouraged to hope that they would be permitted to take a prominent and profitable part in financing the sale of French railway equipment for the construction of the recently authorized

---

*It was understood in Petersburg diplomatic circles that the Russian finance minister, Vyshnegradski, had personally assured Alphonse Rothschild, head of the Paris house of that name, in the previous November, that no further anti-Semitic measures would be taken in the coming period. This is entirely plausible. Vyshnegradski, like Giers, was firmly opposed to these measures; and he must have felt as brutally disavowed as did Giers by the Tsar's behavior, generally, in the spring of 1891. Should such assurances really have been given, the bitterness of the Rothschilds would have been all the more understandable.

Trans-Siberian Railway and for the railway then in process of construction from the Caspian Sea into central Asia. In both of these projects, as it happened, they had met with disappointment during the first months of 1891. In mid-March, the Russian finance minister (Vyshnegradski) had seen himself obliged to pay a special visit to the French chargé d'affaires in Petersburg to break the sad news that the Russian government had decided, in response to protectionist pressures from the Russian competitors of the Rothschilds, to levy a tax on crude oil exported from Russia —a measure of which the Rothschilds would be the sole victims. And on the 4th of May there was issued in Petersburg an imperial ukaz directing that equipment for the Trans-Siberian line should all be of Russian manufacture. To this should be added the report, circulating at that time in well-informed Paris diplomatic circles, that both Ribot and the French minister of finance, Rouvier, considering the Paris market to be overloaded with Russian paper, had told Alphonse Rothschild, head of the Paris house, that the French government had no interest in seeing another French loan made to Russia at that time.[4]

Surely it is somewhere among these developments, all just preceding the Rothschild decision to back out of the projected loan transaction, that the motivation for that decision must be sought. Whatever the motivation, however, it is clear that the Rothschild decision did not improve the atmosphere for the Moscow exposition, which was at that time just on the point of being opened.

. . .

The preparation and opening of the French exhibit in Moscow was a long succession of difficulties, frustrations, and absurdities. The undertaking was not quite the total fiasco the British ambassador joyfully described it as being, in his dispatches; but it appeared to be the victim of what would be known in America in another century as "Murphy's Law": that if anything *could* go wrong, it would. Dolgorukov's removal had deprived the undertaking of its only enthusiastic local patron. The grand duke Sergei Aleksandrovich showed no interest in it, timing his triumphant arrival in Moscow just *after* its opening, and paying it only one perfunctory visit. The Moscow press was partly hostile. Preparations suffered endless delays. The exhibits were only partially in place when the opening occurred. This led to bitter recriminations between the French organizers and their Russian hosts. On the unhappy opening day (May 11) the weather was cold; it poured rain; the lights went out repeatedly; the food supplies ran out; the great balloon (also imported from the Paris

Exposition) refused to rise. Attendance, then and later, was disappointingly small. The Paris bank of M. Jouanno, who had put up the money for the show in return for a monopoly on the ticket sales and who was on hand for the opening as a member of the organizing committee, suddenly went bankrupt while he was there, in consequence of which he appears to have hastily sold his ticket monopoly to a local Jewish fur merchant, one Grunwald, and disappeared not only from Moscow but indeed from the European world in general, including his Paris creditors.

The managing director of the exposition, M. Auguste-Lucien Dautresme, who had held a similarly high position at the Paris exposition and had apparently been selected by Freycinet to take charge of this one, had now had enough. After a bitter conflict with his French associates on the organizing committee, he left abruptly in a huff before the exposition was fairly under way.

Altogether, the enterprise was one long series of setbacks and disappointments. It never drew the public attention its organizers had hoped for. But it continued, nevertheless, and ran its course through most of the year 1891.

In mid-May, just after the exposition's opening, Flourens, also a member of the organizing committee, appeared in Petersburg. Somehow or other, without the official knowledge of Giers and apparently without the support of the French embassy, he succeeded in obtaining an audience with the Tsar and evidently persuaded the latter to pay a personal visit to the exposition.*

All this was most remarkable. Normally, the Tsar would not have received a private French citizen without the approval of Giers and without sponsorship on the part of the French embassy. And it was just four days after Flourens's visit, one notes, that the Tsar publicly announced his decision to decorate Freycinet with the Grand Cordon of Saint Alexander. Why, one asks, just at this time? And on whose recommendation? Hardly that of Giers.

It seems clear from all these evidences that throughout those early months of 1891 some ulterior influence was being brought to bear on Alexander III. It is impossible to say with certainty what this influence

---

*Giers and Lamsdorf learned of Flourens's audience with the Tsar only through the decoding by the foreign office's Black Chamber of the messages between the Paris foreign office and the French embassy at Petersburg. Giers cannot have failed to recognize, from these circumstances, that he was being bypassed somewhere along the line by other influences—and this in matters that were very much his proper concern.

was; but the process of exclusion (not a difficult one to pursue, for the circle of those who dealt personally with the Tsar was so small) points strongly to the French circle of Freycinet-Hansen-Flourens as its inspiration, and to Mohrenheim, probably acting through the intelligence chief at his embassy, Rachkovski, and through Rachkovski's superior, the minister of the interior, as the channel through which much of it was exerted. It is also possible that urgings from this quarter found support with the Empress Dagmar, always well inclined towards Mohrenheim and quite differently inclined towards Giers.*

The Tsar's visit to Moscow seems also to have been attended by complications. Difficulties developed between Grunwald and the committee over the ticket sales. For some days, it would appear Alexander, annoyed anyway over this involvement of Moscow Jews in the exhibit, held up his own departure pending a settlement of the dispute.[5] But the matter was somehow composed; and on the 28th Alexander, together with Dagmar and his daughter Olga, set off for the old Russian capital.

It was the Tsar's first visit to Moscow in over two years; and it was given the official character of a state visit to that city, ostensibly celebrating the entrance upon his new gubernatorial duties of the grand duke Serge, who had made his ceremonial arrival a few days before. Giers was not asked to go along. Aside from the members of his family and personal attendants, Alexander took with him, significantly, only the ministers of war and the interior. On the 30th he paid his visit to the exposition, arriving in great style with Dagmar and Olga behind a troika of magnificent black horses and spending more than three hours, in intense heat, inspecting the various exhibits. The members of the French organizing committee, including Flourens, were all there to receive him, and there was great excitement all around. The Tsar, however, did not entertain specifically for the French visitors. At the first of the formal dinners the French committeemen were not invited at all. They were included only the following evening, as incidental guests, at a dinner given primarily for the senior officers of the Moscow military garrisons.

The French chargé d'affaires at Petersburg, Vauvineux, learned only at the last minute, and then by chance, of the Tsar's intention to visit the exposition. He hastily wired the foreign office in Paris asking what he should do. He was told to go to Moscow and to join in greeting the Tsar

---

*It may also be noted that Hoskier, too, was in Petersburg in mid-May, trying to pick up the pieces from the wreckage of the Rothschild deal. His influence, never friendly to the Russian foreign office, may also have been brought to bear on the Tsar at that time.

upon his arrival at the exhibit, something for which he required no invitation from the Russian side. This he did; but he left again immediately afterward and took no part in the remaining festivities.

. . .

All this, and particularly the demonstrative exclusion of the Russian foreign minister from the entire affair, did not escape the attention of the more sophisticated Petersburg observers. The faithful Lamsdorf, well aware that the Tsar was being affected by influences quite other than that of his foreign minister, and seeing in this a significant diminution of his chief's prestige and authority, took a dark view of the entire trend. He confessed, in his diary, to experiencing

> heavy thoughts over the fact that our minister was not invited. . . . The situation of M. Giers is indeed fairly pathetic. Obolenski thinks that the trouble is his exaggerated modesty and retiring disposition—this constantly vacillating and self-deprecatory manner in which he conducts himself at court. Nobody knows, of course, how he really speaks with the Tsar and how many real services he has performed for the country. When he was first appointed, he said that his motto would be "not to have the reputation of being, but really to be." It is a fine thought; but unfortunately, by disregarding the outward appearances, he has reached a point where no one any longer gives him any credit. One highly influential lady once said of him: "Say what you will, the figure of Giers is an insult to the country." Our foreign ministry, never very popular, finds itself, under the present reign, in a state of prolonged disfavor. There is nothing but general, pitiless ill will on every side.[6]

The Tsar returned from Moscow on the 2nd of June. Giers went out to Gatchina the following day to render his usual weekly report. He took the occasion to request permission to retire for some time to his dacha on the banks of the Saimaa Canal in Finland, some four hours' journey, at the least, by rail and steamer from Petersburg. The reason given was the state of his health, and this argument was plausible enough. But surely, the conclusions he had been obliged to draw from the Tsar's recent behavior also had something to do with it. The request, in any case, was granted; and Giers left the next day—with a feeling, one senses, of both despair and relief: despair over the extent to which somebody had succeeded in discrediting him in the Tsar's eyes and over the evidence that things were getting seriously out of hand; relief over the fact that now, sick at heart as well as in body, he would be able to escape, at least for a time, from his unhappy official position.

Chapter 6

THE DISCUSSIONS RESUMED

When Nikolai Karlovich Giers, then completing his eighth year as Russian foreign minister, left for his Finnish dacha after his meeting with the Tsar on the 4th of June, 1891, he no doubt hoped, and thought it likely, that he would never return to his duties at the Singers' Bridge. But Fate was not to be thus kind to him. The Tsar, while not averse to taking an occasional flier of his own under some invisible ulterior influence, was too well aware of his need for Giers' experience and judgment to try to dispense entirely with his advice and help where serious matters were involved. And that serious matters *were* then involved, or appeared to be involved, was something that was becoming evident just in those same first days of June and in the weeks that followed. To understand what these serious matters were one must go back a bit in time.

The secret arrangement known as the Triple Alliance, or the Triplice, among the governments of Germany, Austria-Hungary, and Italy, had been originally concluded in 1882, for a five-year term. It had consisted, initially, not of a single document but of a bundle of bilateral agreements among the respective parties. It had been renewed, in 1887, for another five-year term. Formally, then, its second term should not have expired until 1892. The Italians, however, were not satisfied with it in its existing form, and they began to plead in early 1891 for its immediate renewal, in a modified form, for a third term. The other two parties agreed to this procedure. In March 1891 negotiations to this end were put in hand. And the effort received new impetus when, in mid-April, the Italian premier, Rudini, was finally obliged to recognize the failure of his efforts (mentioned in the preceding chapter) to patch things up with the French and was obliged to look around for alternatives. On May the 6th, agreement was reached among the three powers on a new and slightly modified version of the original treaty; and on the 17th this was ratified by all three parties. News of the renewal of the treaty (the existence, if not the text, of which was already widely known) was not officially released until the end of June. But Giers had learned of it even at the time of its ratification; and rumors about it began to circulate widely in late May.

In itself, this development did not change a great deal in the international situation with which the French and Russians were faced. Only perhaps for the French, who were already seriously concerned about the treaty in view of their relations with Italy, did the mere fact of its renewal lead to heightened anxiety.

But as of early June a new level of significance was given to the matter by the emergence of an abundant crop of rumors to the effect that Britain had adhered, or was about to adhere, to the pact. This, obviously, was a suggestion that gave serious concern to both France and Russia: to France, because it raised the specter of the acquisition of joint naval control in the Mediterranean by the English and the Italians, to the jeopardy of France's recently established position in Tunisia and perhaps of the security of the French Mediterranean fleet; to the Russians, because a British-Italian-Austrian combination would strengthen the British naval position in the entire Mediterranean basin, including the Aegean Sea and the approaches to Constantinople.

Seldom does one find, in the history of diplomacy, serious anxieties, influential in affecting the course of history, for which there was less real substance or justification than these Franco-Russian fears of an adherence by Britain to the Triple Alliance. At no time was there any serious possibility that Britain could be brought into such an arrangement. Constitutional traditions, the mood of Parliament, and the deepest instincts of English statesmanship all spoke against it, as the French and Russian statesmen should have known.

Such slender substance as actually existed behind these rumors amounted only to this. In 1887, when the Triplice had consisted simply of a bundle of separate agreements among various members of the group, the Italians were anxious that these agreements should be supplemented by another one—this time between the British and themselves, on Mediterranean problems. They took up the matter in London. Their effort was supported by the Germans. But what came out of it was only an exchange of notes in which, in effect, each party stated its own position. Among other things, the British government, in its note, expressed agreement with the Italian government on the desirability of preserving the status quo on the littorals of the Black and Aegean seas (which meant, primarily, opposition to any effort by the Russians to establish control of the Straits), and declared its disposition in principle to cooperate with the Italian government in this and other Mediterranean problems. It insisted, however, on retaining full liberty to decide, in any given instance, what form that cooperation might assume.*

This, as will readily be seen, was something less than a serious commitment to any particular course of action at any future time. It actually changed nothing from the standpoint of the Russians, since it did no more than to affirm what was already a known firm objective of British policy, exchange of notes or none.

Now, in 1891, in connection with the renewal of the Triplice, the Italians told their two allies that these assurances of 1887, while all right so far as they went, did not satisfy them: they wanted to obtain from the British new and (as they hoped) more far-reaching ones, relating this time to the western Mediterranean—assurances that would give them reason to expect British political support in case of further encroachments by the French (who had already taken Tunis) in North Africa, and British naval support in case it should come to an actual war with France. These were rather extravagant aims. (The Italians were never exactly modest, in those days, in the demands they placed either on their allies or on others.) But it was thought in Rome that the prospect of assured Italian help in keeping the vulnerable yet strategically important Italian coasts out of French hands in time of war would be of such importance to the English that it was not entirely unrealistic to hope for such a commitment on Britain's part. And since the Italians did not, for various reasons, consider their ambassador in London a suitable vehicle for this sort of effort, they asked the Germans to assist them diplomatically and to undertake the necessary soundings in London.

Holstein and his friends were not loath to assume this task. They saw in it a way of easing Britain into the Triplice, of making a quadrilateral alliance out of a triple one, and thus in effect of achieving the alliance of England with Germany that had long been their dream. Beyond which, they had persuaded themselves that unless Britain could be brought to associate herself in some way with the Triplice, the Italians, for whom the strained relationship with France held serious disadvantages, might decide to leave that alliance entirely. They therefore charged the able German ambassador in London, Count Paul von Hatzfeldt, with the task of taking the initial soundings.

Nothing, of course, came of this. As noted above, there never was

---

*This position was reaffirmed in a British note to the Austrian government in December 1887. (See G. P. Gooch, *History of Modern Europe* [New York: Holt and Co., 1923], pp. 150–151.)

the remotest possibility that Britain could be eased into the acceptance of such a commitment. Hatzfeldt, sensing this, could approach his task only in the most tentative manner; and Lord Salisbury, the British foreign secretary, had no difficulty evading the approaches and stringing the matter along until the Germans were obliged to recognize the futility of the effort and to desist from its continuation.

But something of all this leaked, as it was bound to do. Among other things, there were interpellations in the House of Commons about Britain's relationship to the Central European powers. In response to one of these interpellations, the foreign office spokesman was obliged to confess, on the 4th of June, that in 1887 there had indeed been "an exchange of views" with the Italians on the subject of the preservation of the status quo in the Mediterranean—nothing more.

This was not much; but rumors had already been circulating about a possible association of England with the Triplice, and this confession on the part of the foreign office was enough to give new sustenance to them. In the general atmosphere of hyperimaginative speculation that then prevailed, further wild inferences were drawn from the otherwise not greatly sensational news of an impending British naval visit to the Austro-Hungarian port of Fiume (the present Rijeka) on the Adriatic coast and of plans for a similar visit by a German squadron to England, to take place in midsummer.

In the face of this rather slender body of evidence, rumors of British adherence to the Triplice now flew thick and fast through the journalistic and diplomatic centers of the Continent. They reached Russia, as they did every other place; and they appear to have commanded extensive credence in the congenitally suspicious Russian mind—even at the foreign office. This was not really so surprising; for the rumors found support in the dispatches of three of the most strategically placed and influential Russian ambassadors.

Mohrenheim, in the first days of June, reported finding Ribot depressed over France's isolation in the face of the renewal of the Triplice, which treaty, Ribot had said, had been "widened by the effective adherence of England, whose relations with Germany and Italy appear to be becoming closer and closer."[*1]

*It is interesting to note that this view, attributed to Ribot, was in flat contradiction to the opinion of the French ambassador in London, Waddington, who stoutly denied the existence of anything that could properly be called an "alliance" between England and Italy. (See DDF, vol. 8, no. 369, pp. 493–494. Dispatch, Waddington to Ribot, June 4, 1891.)

On June the 9th Nelidov, the ambassador at Constantinople (always a great breeding house for diplomatic rumor), was referring to the Triplice in one of his reports as an arrangement "to which England has in some way adhered."[2] In another dispatch, a month later, there was a more cautious, but still confirmatory, reference to England's adherence "if not by treaty then at any rate in fact."[3]

One notes, too, in dispatches from the ambassador in Vienna, Lobanov-Rostovski (like Lamsdorf, a future foreign minister), a statement to the effect that ". . . the adherence of England to this so-called League of Peace, in whatever form it may have occurred, is beyond question."[4]

In the face of such reports it is not surprising that credence in the rumors of Britain's adherence to the Triplice was widespread (if not universal*) in Petersburg in the summer of 1891.† Even Lamsdorf, in early July, was noting sadly in his diary that "the Triplice is loudly announcing its existence. England, apparently, has joined it."[5] And the imperial family appears to have been much affected. The French chargé d'affaires, Vauvineux, reported in early July on a talk he had had with one of the grand dukes (probably the Tsar's brother, Vladimir) in which the latter professed the belief that England was now "participating" in the Triplice. Vauvineux added that this view was shared by other members of the imperial family, and he predicted, significantly, that this impression would have its effect at the time of the impending French fleet visit.[6] And the Tsar himself, when receiving Laboulaye some weeks later, observed that he thought the British were now "coming to regret the part they had taken in the Triple Alliance."[7]

Giers, as usual, was somewhat more cautious; but he would shortly be referring, as we shall see presently, to a fourth power's having joined the Triplice *"pour certaines éventualités"* and to *"l'accession plus ou moins directe de l'Angleterre."*

There can be no doubt, then, that Russian statesmanship was seriously affected in the late spring of 1891 by the impression that Britain had in some way associated herself with the Triplice. And the seriousness of this impression must not be underestimated. Since the lapse of the

---

*The new chief of the Asiatic section of the Russian foreign office, Count D. A. Kapnist, gave to the French chargé d'affaires a quite accurate assessment of the real relationship of Britain to this pact.

†A dispatch of July 30 from the Austrian chargé d'affaires at Petersburg, Aehrenthal, suggests that even he, no doubt poorly informed by his government (which must have known better), believed the reports of England's adherence to be true.

Reinsurance Treaty with Germany, Russia had already been effectively isolated among the great powers. But up to this point the British orientation had remained an open question. If, now, Britain was to be in some way associated with Germany and Austria, this was a significant development, which could not be ignored.

. . .

It will be recalled that after the 4th of June Giers was living at his dacha in Finland, several hours' journey from Petersburg in the best of circumstances; but it had been arranged that he should return once every fortnight for his regular report to the Tsar. This he did on June 16, perhaps again on the 30th. But on the first of July the Tsar himself left with his family for his customary summer yachting cruise in the Finnish archipelago, and was no longer available for another two to three weeks.

One is compelled to conclude that at one of these meetings in June it must have been agreed that when Laboulaye returned to present his letters of recall and take his final departure (he was expected in the middle of July), Giers should find some way to receive him and to renew the soundings that he had tried once, in April, to take, with respect to the possibility of a further step in the direction of an alliance. There is no direct documentary evidence of such a decision; indeed, considering the way such things were then handled, there is no reason to suppose that any such documentary evidence ever existed. But we may deduce that something of this sort must have been discussed and agreed upon between the two men—may deduce it from the fact that when Laboulaye returned, Giers, as we shall see, did indeed approach him with such suggestions; and this is something he would never have done (of this we may be sure) without the Tsar's express authorization. These audiences of Giers with the Tsar in June were the only occasions on which such authorization could have been given. After the end of June, with the Tsar away on his yacht, Giers had no further opportunity to consult him before Laboulaye's return; Giers showed, actually, some nervousness over this fact, complaining to certain of the foreign diplomats about the Tsar's inaccessibility.[8] All of which would suggest that the instructions Giers had received in June about approaching Laboulaye were not too clear or specific and that he would have welcomed a chance to clarify them.

Nevertheless, the conclusion that he had received some such authorization during his June meetings with Alexander is inescapable; and it conduces to curiosity about the motivation for this renewed interest in approaching the French, and particularly about the sense of urgency that dictated that the approach be made to Laboulaye (who was only going to be in Petersburg for a brief time before leaving the French diplomatic service forever) rather than waiting for the arrival of a successor (as yet unnamed). The successor might, after all, be supposed to enjoy a higher degree of Ribot's confidence, and would be in a position to follow up on any initiative that might be taken.

We have already seen the evidences of a disposition on the Tsar's part, even at a much earlier date, to prod gently and delicately in the direction of a further step in the establishment of a close political and military intimacy with France. Up to this time, however, he had shown patience and had made only one cautious move, authorizing Giers to sound out Laboulaye in April, before the latter's return to Paris. Now, however, a new sense of urgency seems to have come into his inclinations in this direction. Not only was there the encouragement given to Giers to undertake a new approach to Laboulaye; but there is evidence, as we shall see in a later chapter, that in the first days of June Alexander also (probably unbeknownst to Giers) authorized Obruchev, then about to leave for his summer vacation in France, to undertake similar soundings with Boisdeffre or Miribel (the chief of the French General Staff) concerning the possibilities for a military convention.

What had occasioned this new sense of urgency, so unusual in a man normally so phlegmatic and unhurried as Alexander III? It could, one must suppose, only have been the effect of the recent reports about a possible adherence of Britain to the Triplice.

In the case of Giers, the question of motivation is more complicated. We do not know whether the idea of approaching Laboulaye in this way was one with which he agreed, or partially agreed, or, if he accepted it as an order, whether he did so pretending to agree or only after voicing objections and being overruled. He too had been affected, though not so strongly as the Tsar, by the rumors about Britain and the Triplice. He was well aware of the dangers of a total isolation of Russia that these rumors implied. The evidence suggests that he was not averse to restrained demonstrations of a closer Franco-Russian relationship—such demonstrations as the impending visit of the French fleet to Cronstadt might be expected to provide. Gestures of this nature could usefully serve, in his view, as a warning to the Germans that Russia was not dependent on them —that she had alternatives to their friendship. But he had never wanted, and never would want (his future conduct would make this clear) to see the Tsar bind his own hands and those of his successors by written pacts that could limit Russia's freedom of action in remote future contingencies, now impossible to envisage. On the other hand, he dared not go too far, or be too emphatic, in opposing a step to which the Tsar was emotionally committed; for this involved the risk that the latter, offended, might pursue the same goal exclusively through military channels, and then Giers would lose all control over the negotiating process.

. . .

On July the 9th the French chargé d'affaires in Petersburg, M. de Vauvineux, reported to his foreign office that the Petersburg *Novoye Vremya*, generally regarded as a mouthpiece for the Russian foreign office, had carried a statement (apparently in an editorial) that ". . . the hour is approaching when the simple logic of facts will render inevitable the transformation of the mutual sympathies between France and Russia into a formal alliance."9

Whence, one wonders, this highly accurate observation? Had someone leaked? All the major actors in the drama were at that moment away from Petersburg. The main ones were not in the habit of leaking things to the press, anyway. One suspects the grand-ducal entourage of the Tsar. It was only in the most intimate family circle that Alexander would have discussed the sort of decision he and Giers had taken.

In any case, on July the 12th, three days after Vauvineux reported this newspaper item to Paris, Laboulaye, returning from his long leave of absence, arrived in Petersburg. When, two days later, he paid his routine official call at the foreign office, Vlangali, the acting foreign minister, invited him, on Giers' behalf, to visit Giers immediately for a day or two at the latter's Finnish dacha.10 This was most unusual. Giers and Laboulaye were not close. Giers was not normally a very social person. He seldom received in the country.

Laboulaye may have thought that Giers, being too ill to come to Petersburg, wanted an opportunity to take leave of him before his final departure from Russia. In any case, he accepted the invitation and made the necessary daylong journey. On the 16th of July, in the leisurely atmosphere of the peaceful Finnish countryside, the two men talked at length. They first discussed a relatively minor incident that had brought their two governments into conflict over their respective positions as protectors of Christian religious rights in Jerusalem. Laboulaye then asked Giers how he felt about the renewal of the Triplice. Giers replied (according to Laboulaye's later report) that there was a new fact of which one had now to take account, namely the "more or less direct" accession of England to that pact. One had to recognize, after all, that a fourth power had just joined, "for certain eventualities," the other three. This was what was most serious.

In these circumstances, Giers went on to say, he had come to the point where he was obliged to ask himself "whether we should not take one more step along the path of the entente." He and Laboulaye had spoken of this, he seemed to recall, on one occasion, before Laboulaye went on leave. He had subsequently mentioned the suggestion to the Tsar. The latter had "not said 'no.' " In revealing this, he added, he was speaking in strictest confidence. He had not even whispered a word of it to Mohrenheim.

"Your Excellency is no doubt thinking," Laboulaye replied, "about the conclusion of a military convention that would place the two general staffs henceforth in an established relationship to each other. In case we should be taken by a surprise attack, it would indeed be well that our efforts should be shaped in such a way as to avoid loss of our forces."

"Why not," replied Giers (ignoring Laboulaye's suggestion), "an agreement between the two governments?"

Laboulaye seems wholly to have failed to grasp the significance of this approach. He ended the discussion by simply asking Giers to reflect further on the matter and to let him know if he had any further thoughts about it that he wished to communicate. And in the brief telegraphic report that he submitted to his government immediately after his return to Petersburg (July 18), he said only that the renewal of the Triplice and the "indirect accession of England" to that pact had brought *the two of them* to ask themselves "whether another step on the path towards the entente was not desirable."[11] He said nothing, in that telegram, to suggest that it was Giers alone who had made the suggestion; nor did he point out that Giers could only have been speaking under instructions.* He did, to be sure, even before receiving Paris's reaction to this telegram, set forth in two confidential personal letters to Ribot (drafted on the 19th and 20th of July[12]) a more detailed account of his talk with Giers, making it plain for the first time that the suggestion of a further step had come from Giers

---

*There is, of course, the possibility that Giers, always on guard against telegraphic intercepts and Black Chamber decodings (of which he made liberal use himself), asked Laboulaye not to mention his (Giers') initiative in any telegraphic message, restricting himself rather to the use, for this purpose, of private letters sent by diplomatic pouch.

and was not just something that had occurred casually to the two of them on the spot. But it seems not even to have occurred to him that Giers' suggestion was anything to which the French would wish to react. He mentioned the matter only in the second of the two letters (the first being devoted to the Jerusalem affair), and then treated it on the assumption that the French would simply wait to see whether Giers would bring the subject up again at some future time. For the moment, he said, he rather doubted that Giers would. He had found the foreign minister aged and fatigued, claiming to be unable to come to Petersburg in the near future. However, he added philosophically, this was perhaps not so important in a country where the cabinet ministers were only *"des commis."*

This detailed report from Laboulaye was not received in Paris until the 30th of the month. Before we turn, however, to the reactions of the French governmental leaders to the Russian initiative, it becomes necessary to note certain other things that were occurring at just this time. For the final days of July 1891 witnessed a great precipitation of events in the relations between France and Russia—events of which the secret communications between the two governments about a written accord were, while of outstanding importance, only a part.

. . .

Neither Giers nor Laboulaye is likely to have known, when the two talked together at Giers' country cottage on the banks of the Saimaa Canal, that another discussion of equal importance was taking place that same day at another country house some two thousand miles away—at the château of Mme. Obruchev in the Dordogne—between Obruchev and Boisdeffre. The background of that encounter, too, is not without interest.

Some weeks earlier, in June 1891, the Obruchevs, man and wife, accompanied by Vannovski, had been taking the cure at Vichy. During their stay there General de Boisdeffre had appeared (not wholly surprisingly) and showed himself interested in renewing the discussions he and Obruchev had conducted in Petersburg the preceding summer. Obruchev had demurred. Such discussion, conducted in Vichy, would be too apt, he thought, to come to public attention and to arouse comment. Boisdeffre had then suggested that Obruchev, who was planning anyway to proceed by way of Paris to the Dordogne upon completion of his cure, should stop off at Paris and have discussions there with the chief of the French General Staff, General Miribel. Again Obruchev had objected. He approved on principle the renewal of the discussions (something, incidentally, that he would not have done without high-level authorization), but Paris, he thought, was not the place. He was, he explained, *"en froid"* with Mohrenheim. It would be hard for him, in these circumstances, to preserve his incognito. The proper place was his wife's château at Jaurès. He hoped that Miribel (his opposite number) could be persuaded to join him there.

Boisdeffre reported all this to Miribel, who found the suggestion bizarre. *"Quels drôles de gens que ces russes!"* was his reaction. Here was Obruchev declining to spend an afternoon with him in Paris, where the meeting could easily be kept secret, but wanting him to come down to the country, where his presence would be almost sure to become known. Besides, he said, if he went there in person and talked with Obruchev, he would have to report both the fact and the results of the visit to Freycinet, who would not only offer picayune objections to anything they might have agreed upon but would no doubt reveal the entire matter to Mohrenheim. No—Boisdeffre, as a longtime friend of the Obruchevs, should go in his place.

This statement by Miribel is revealing for the light it sheds on another aspect, not mentioned above, of the rivalry between the two governmental channels of communication and negotiation about the Alliance. In the face of this rivalry, the two general staffs, it would seem, found themselves on the side of the respective foreign offices, not of Freycinet and Mohrenheim. Obruchev could not endure Mohrenheim. Miribel's feelings towards Freycinet, and probably those of Boisdeffre as well, were plainly less than cordial.* All three of these senior staff officers appear, on the other hand, to have had entirely acceptable relations with their respective foreign ministers and, in the French case, with the French ambassador in Petersburg.

A second interesting aspect of this exchange was Obruchev's unhesitating readiness to resume with Boisdeffre the discussions of the

---

*Freycinet's relationship to the Boisdeffre-Obruchev talks of 1891 is unclear. Miribel apparently changed his mind and took Freycinet into his confidence about the talks; for both the instructions with which Boisdeffre departed for Jaurès and the fact that his subsequent report was addressed to Freycinet as well as to Miribel indicate that Freycinet was kept informed. Mohrenheim, however, threw much confusion into this question by reporting later to Petersburg that Freycinet had been greatly discontented with these talks, had denied that Boisdeffre had been authorized to conduct them, and had said that he found them appropriate. The record shows these statements to have been so flatly incorrect that one suspects a deliberate effort on Mohrenheim's part to mislead his own government with a view to discrediting Obruchev.

preceding summer. Since he and Vannovski were together at Vichy, he must have been acting with Vannovski's knowledge and approval. But Vannovski, too, who took a very cautious attitude towards the entire idea of a military convention, would not have given this approval without authorization from the Tsar. Both men, however, had left Russia in early June. The Tsar's approval must therefore have been obtained before that time. This only strengthens the evidence, apparent from Alexander's behavior in March and April, that his desire to press on with talks with the French at both diplomatic and military levels was something that had matured well before the summer of 1891 and even before the rise of the various anxieties concerning Britain's relationship to the Triplice.

Obruchev, in any case, soon went on from Vichy to his wife's château at Jaurès. Here Boisdeffre joined him for a short visit in mid-July. On the 15th and 16th of that month, just as Laboulaye was paying his visit to Giers in the Finnish countryside, the two generals sat down, as they had done the previous year, for a serious discussion of the prospects for a military alliance.

Boisdeffre at once went on to the attack.[13] To this point, he said, the French had had only words, and words which, after all, did not commit the Tsar. The various Russian generals who had come to Paris had seemed to be fearful of compromising themselves by too close relations with their French colleagues. Why could not the Tsar say out loud the things that Obruchev and others were saying to the French in confidence? In short, he concluded,

> when I tell people in France that you would act alongside us and would mobilize simultaneously with us, they ask: Why, then, does all this have to remain vague? Why do we not sign an official convention that would put an end to the uncertainties, the equivocations, and the insecurity—a convention that would simply state that if France or Russia should be attacked by Germany, they were prepared to conduct a general and simultaneous mobilization, and this at the earliest possible moment?

The French government, he was able to state, would be prepared to follow Russia along this path if the Tsar was similarly inclined.

Obruchev, in reply to this sally, took refuge in the well-known Russian position that the integrity of France was essential to the European equilibrium. Giers had even said this, officially, to Caprivi the year before, at Narva. What more did the French want?

Boisdeffre rejoined that he did not doubt Obruchev's words; nevertheless, this was still not an official commitment.

"But," said Obruchev, significantly, "has M. de Giers not made a communication along these lines to your ambassador?"*

"Not that I know of" was the frank and honest reply. (Boisdeffre obviously could not know of what was being said to Laboulaye that very same day at another country house two thousand miles away.)

Obruchev, at this point, was overtaken by the congenital suspiciousness that has marked Russian statesmen of all ages. How, he asked, could we be sure that *you* would march if *we* were attacked? Suppose the Germans were to offer to give back Alsace if you would remain passive?

Boisdeffre pointed out that this suspicion only proved the need for a formal convention.

"I know," replied Obruchev. "But we have to know where we stand. Of course I shall talk with the Tsar; but he has to be sure what it is that you want and what you are prepared to do." A mere convention stipulating that both parties would mobilize in the event of a German attack would be, he said, quite insufficient. One had to take into account the interests of the two countries in other parts of the world, and the sort of wars in which they might become involved. Either party might be drawn into war by questions of national honor: the French by an incident on the German frontier, the Russians by some incident in the "East."† In this latter case, it would not be the Germans who would be initially attacking Russia; Germany would be hiding behind Austria and Turkey; and then, when Russia had been sufficiently weakened, Germany, if she had not actually joined in the struggle, would enter a peace conference where, with her two million bayonets, she would lay down the law just as easily as if she had fought a victorious war.

"Well, then," Obruchev concluded, "if we faced a war in the East, or against Austria alone, for example, would you be with us?" For Russia, a war with any one of the powers of the Triplice would be, he pointed out, the same as a war with all of them, whether the others joined immediately and directly or whether they merely threw in their weight at the peace conference.

To these reflections, so obviously inspired by memories of the 1877–

*Obruchev's posing of this question throws an interesting light on the timing of the Tsar's decision to pursue these feelers. Obviously, Obruchev was aware that Giers was preparing to approach Laboulaye along these lines. But Obruchev had been gone from Petersburg, and was quite out of touch, since early June. The Tsar's decision to authorize this step on Giers' part must therefore have been taken before that time and was probably communicated to Giers at their meeting on June 4.

†By "East" Obruchev evidently meant the Balkans—then a common usage of the term.

1878 war with Turkey and the ensuing Congress of Berlin, Boisdeffre responded by asking whether conversely, if France were to become involved in a war with Italy alone, Russia would feel herself obliged to join.

"Certainly," Obruchev replied. This, he went on, was the only proper basis for an alliance. One had to mobilize at once and to start the war on the day of mobilization. The Russians would do this; and they would follow it up by sending out their cavalry at once to destroy the enemy's railways.

Very well, Boisdeffre replied, but what the Russians were demanding amounted, then, to a general alliance against everybody. In this case it was a matter that had to be treated at the diplomatic level—as a political treaty.

To this, Obruchev agreed; and he went on to outline the objectives Russia would be pursuing in any war that might occur. One was the conquest and incorporation of the province of Galicia, then under Austrian rule. The other was the acquisition of "the key to the Straits." By this, he explained, he did not mean the actual possession of Constantinople. What was wanted was merely an arrangement that would give Russia assurance that the English would not be able to enter the Black Sea. And what, he then asked, would be the equivalent aims of the French?

Boisdeffre's answer was instantaneous: the recovery of Alsace and Lorraine.

Obruchev was suspicious. "Would you not also," he asked, "wish to extend your borders to the Rhine and to break up Germany? (One senses here the effects of Giers' warnings against Russia's associating herself with any such far-reaching aims.)

Boisdeffre, in response to this sally, was evasive. One would first have to know what success one had had on the field of battle. "Let us begin by beating them; after that it will be easy."

Obruchev saw no point in pursuing this further. But he pointed out that even if the two governments could agree on this question of war aims, the two general staffs would still have to be consulted, and a special agreement between them would still be useful.

Boisdeffre agreed; and he went on to outline the two points on which the French would have to insist in any such military agreement. The first was general and immediate mobilization. The second was the deployment of the respective armed forces in the manner most conducive to the earliest possible defeat of the enemy (meaning, of course, Germany). This last purpose, he observed, would not be served merely by the Russians hurling themselves initially against Austria, any more than it would be served by the French hurling themselves against Italy.

But Obruchev was not to be shaken. Austria? Germany?—it was all, in Russian eyes, one and the same enemy. Let us attack that enemy, he said, where the resistance is weakest; and if that happens to be a point defended by Austrians, what of it?

On this note, the discussion ended. Boisdeffre, in reporting its tenor to Freycinet, observed that the Russians had at least, in contrast to the year before, come to the point of accepting the need for a military convention. If the French could accept the idea of a general, rather than a specific, alliance, and if the two parties could agree on the question of the respective war aims, he anticipated no difficulty in negotiating such a convention. With this, he left it to the French government to make the necessary decision.

It seems clear from this account that the Russian military leaders, still haunted by memories of their unhappy experiences in the Crimean and Turkish wars, viewed an alliance with France primarily as a means of keeping the Germans off their backs while they settled their scores with the Austrians and the British, whereas in the eyes of the French it appeared quite simply as a means of inflicting upon the Germans a defeat from which these latter would never recover. Plainly, the Russians were prepared to mobilize and to enter into a state of war with Germany if that latter country should attack France; but their views as to how they would then conduct hostilities, as well as their concept of the aims they would be pursuing in any conflict with the parties to the Triplice, still differed very significantly from those of the French General Staff. Indeed, the two approaches stood in sharp conflict with each other.

. . .

So much for what might be called the preliminary exchanges, diplomatic and military, of July 1891. Let us now turn to the great precipitation of events that marked the latter part of that month.

Chapter 7

CRONSTADT

On the morning of Thursday the 23rd of July, 1891, just a week after these exchanges in Finland and in the Dordogne, a Russian cruiser squadron, drawn up in line, was lying at anchor in the roadstead off the island naval base of Cronstadt, some twenty-five miles out to sea from Petersburg. It was awaiting the arrival of a squadron of French vessels, composed of three armored cruisers and five smaller ships, under command of Admiral Gervais, arriving to pay a formal visit to the Cronstadt base, and—in effect—to the Russian capital.

The approach of the French squadron was signaled to the Russian ships, and to the armada of small private welcoming vessels assembled around them, by the release of a balloon from a promontory some sixteen miles westward along the coast. A Russian ship was at once dispatched to act as escort. An hour or two later, the French ships were slowly and precariously pushing their way, amid a great booming of artillery salutes and endless cries of *"Vive la France!"* through the throng of waiting vessels at Cronstadt. Among the latter was one greatly festooned ship bearing the entire French colony of Petersburg. From the deck of another the famous Slavyanski choir was singing the "Marseillaise"—to Russian words composed for the occasion.

Thus was inaugurated a fortnight of public festivities, demonstrations, and general political and social frenzy such as the city of Petersburg, and indeed Russia generally, had never seen the likes of, and would never see again. One dinner, luncheon, ball, and reception for the hard-pressed French officers followed another, some on shore, some on the ships. For ten full days there was not a moment's respite.

The city of Cronstadt inaugurated the festivities with a sit-down dinner of four hundred and eight places. On the 29th the French officers were taken up the Neva River for a visit to the capital itself. Debarking among huge and wildly enthusiastic crowds, they were first driven, behind galloping troikas, on a tour of the islands of the delta and of the city itself; after which there was a tremendous reception at the city hall, on which occasion each of the French ships was presented with a magnificent silver punch bowl and each of the officers (to the number of 120) with an *objet d'art russe;* whereas 2,200 cigarette boxes, with views of Petersburg, were supplied for presentation to the ratings aboard the ships.

A special evening of entertainment for the French officers was tendered, on behalf of what was known as "high society," by "Missi" Durnovo, wife of the interior minister and daughter of the Mistress of the Court, Princess Kochubei, at her villa on the banks of the Neva. Here the jaded officers were entertained until two in the morning with fireworks, music, dancing, and everything else that this immensely wealthy lady could offer. Towards the end of the visit there was even an excursion to Moscow, where similar extravagances of hospitality were undergone.

The high point of these festivities was a gala dinner tendered by the Tsar at his summer palace at Peterhof for a hundred sixty guests, including all the senior French officers and a great many of the highest Russian dignitaries. Here the Tsar electrified Europe by standing bareheaded while the orchestra played the "Marseillaise"—the marching song, that is, of those who, a hundred years before, had beheaded a king.

This episode made a profound impression everywhere in Europe—an impression more dramatic, in truth, than the circumstances warranted.* Actually, it was only after troubled consultations with Giers that the monarch had consented to make the gesture. He would much have preferred to omit it. But the two men saw no acceptable alternative. The "Marseillaise" had been played, and similarly honored by the heads of state, when the French squadron visited Copenhagen and Stockholm on its way to Russia. A refusal by the Tsar to accept its playing in Russia would, therefore, have been all the more conspicuous and offensive. "After all," Alexander grumbled to Giers, as he reluctantly agreed to take the step, "I can't invent another hymn for them." And although he did go so far as to stand bareheaded for the opening strains of the piece, he stopped the rendition halfway along its course by motioning to the orchestra and saying: *"Assez, assez."*[1] But the press and public of Russia and Western Europe were in no mood at that time to take a measured view of events. The episode became firmly planted in the historiography of the period as a significant political demonstration on the part of the Tsar.

Nothing like this reception of the French squadron, be it reiterated, had ever before taken place in Petersburg. Ever since the tragic day of the abortive Decembrist uprising, some sixty-six years before, the authorities

---

*The Austrian chargé d'affaires in Petersburg saw in the Tsar's gesture an omen as fateful for the tsarist regime as was, for the French monarchy, the appearance of Benjamin Franklin in Paris in 1776.

had frowned on any and all sorts of street crowds and demonstrations. There were not lacking, even on this occasion, those in high Petersburg society and in the diplomatic corps who saw in the existing permissiveness a dangerous precedent, in the light of which crowds might some day appear in those same streets for purposes less agreeable to the government. The Austrian ambassador, Wolkenstein, declined to believe that the street demonstrations (what he termed "this saturnalia") were not deliberately organized by some delicate hand behind the scenes; and he came, by process of elimination, to the conclusion that it could only have been the Russian General Staff, and Obruchev personally, who had inspired it.[2]

Laboulaye himself, like many others, was amazed. He had tried to warn his government, in advance of the visit, that it should not expect too much in the way of a reception. The Russians, he had pointed out, were not normally allowed to demonstrate; besides, the only people who could be expected to develop much enthusiasm would be the bourgeoisie, of which Petersburg, he thought, had few.

He was wrong on both counts. Petersburg had more bourgeoisie than he thought. And even the lower classes turned out in great numbers, with every sign of high enjoyment. One may well wonder whether it was not the holiday mood, the fine summer weather, and the opportunity to stroll the streets in company with many other people, rather than any great enthusiasm for the French, that brought them out. The fact is, they came, they strolled, they stood, they peered and cheered—to the point, in fact, where all of Europe was impressed with the accounts of the spectacle.

Although unaware of what was occurring behind the scenes, the European chanceries and newspaper offices attributed to the Cronstadt visit a significance remarkably similar to what would have been assigned to it by someone in possession of all the facts: they saw it, that is, as the symbol of a real alliance between the two countries—an alliance of such firmness that no written document, as they thought, was required. And nothing, actually, could have suited the Tsar better than the currency of this impression; for it conveyed the image of a significant intimacy of understanding between the two countries, without requiring him (essentially a timid and hesitant man in these respects) to set his signature publicly to any specific document. For many years to come, persons in Western Europe, unaware of the written exchanges between the two governments, would speak of the Cronstadt visit as though it and it alone had been the foundation of the Alliance.

This impression served, of course, as both French and Russians intended it should, as a useful reminder to the Germans and the other members of the Triplice that they could not expect, in another European crisis, to settle their scores separately with either the French or the Russians. Yet any tendency that might have existed in Germany and elsewhere to view the visit as an immediate military threat was attenuated by the fact that the French squadron, having completed its visit to Cronstadt, proceeded immediately thereafter to the south coast of England to pay a similar visit to the Queen of England. This gesture brought raised eyebrows and some discontent to a number of the more sanguine French and Russian figures; but it also suited excellently the purposes of the Tsar and Giers; for there was nothing they less wanted than to stir up serious trouble with the Germans at this point and thus to become dragged into a war for which they were as yet by no means prepared.

· · ·

Not all the Germans underestimated the significance of the Cronstadt visit, or failed to sense what was occurring behind the scenes while it was in progress.

Six days after the departure of the last of the French ships from Cronstadt there took place the annual maneuvers, so called, at Krasnoye Selo:—"so called" because they were more in the nature of carefully rehearsed military-theatrical displays, mounted for the benefit of the foreign military attachés and other distinguished visitors, than of serious military exercises. In attendance—for he had no other choice—was the German ambassador, General Lothar von Schweinitz, an honorable and cultivated man who had served some sixteen years at Petersburg in that capacity—whose professional life had been devoted, in fact, to the cultivation, from one position or another, of the intimacy among the three imperial courts of Germany, Austria-Hungary, and Russia. Although naturally not informed of all that was taking place behind the scenes during the Cronstadt visit, he was too sensitive and thoughtful a person not to sense the full gravity of the change in the political atmosphere, and too much of a realist not to recognize in it the destruction of what had always appeared to him as the central purpose of his life's work.

It may not be superfluous, therefore, to note, as an example of the cruel moments that the necessities of diplomacy can sometimes impose on those individuals who devote their lives to the service of it, the letter that Schweinitz, sitting in a guest room at Tsarkoye Selo near the parade ground on the opening day of the maneuvers, wrote to his wife, whose birthday it was, then staying with their numerous children at their country home in Germany:[3]

My dearly beloved wife:
   May God bless you and give you all the happiness we human beings are capable of receiving in this world. It is now nine in the morning, and I am thinking of how it all looks at this moment at the Schwedenpfad: the children all in excitement with their flowers and their little poems, the tall Wilhelm giving the commands, the little Friedrich gaping in wonder but still taking his part.
   Here, the regiments are marching past, behind the blaring bands, on their way to the parade ground. The weather is fine. It is the sixteenth time that I have attended this military display; but I do it today with wholly different feelings than in the past; because even if I have been taught nothing new by the pro-French madness of these last weeks, I nevertheless now have the painful conviction that the dynastic policy—the solidarity of the monarchs against the Revolution—has been definitely laid to rest. In the thirty years that have passed since I was Military Attaché in Vienna . . . I have collaborated in the three-emperors policy; and today I shall ride in the parade, with the decorations of the Black Adler, of Saint Stephan, and of Saint Andrew* on my breast, as a living anachronism. My political activity of thirty years thus ends in the breakdown of all the principles for which I have striven. It does not occur to me to regret what I have done, or to regard it as a mistake; but it is sad to end it all with a fiasco.
   From these reflections I turn my thoughts once more to the table full of flowers in the drawing room; I see you and the dear faces of the children clearly before me, and I pray to God to bless and keep you all.

It was, then, in the midst of all the hysteria of the Cronstadt visit that the negotiations flowing from Giers' delicate suggestion of the 16th of July to Laboulaye ran their course.

---

*These were, respectively, the highest decorations of the three imperial courts that a man in his position could be given.

At just what point Ribot was made to realize that the Russians were now prepared for serious discussions is not clear; but all the evidence suggests that this realization came to him both as a surprise and as a great blessing and relief. As late as the 22nd of July the Austrian chargé d'affaires in Paris, ignorant of all these happenings, was reporting to his government that Ribot's fortunes had fallen grievously; that he was now the weakest member of the cabinet; that the last shred of his prestige had disappeared with his failure to achieve the alliance with Russia; and that while he would probably last until the passage of the 1892 budget, there would then be a cabinet crisis and he would be the first to be jettisoned. One can imagine with what eagerness Ribot, in the face of the currency of such impressions in Paris, must have welcomed any shred of evidence that the Russians were now prepared to do serious business.

It will be recalled that Laboulaye, in his initial telegram of the 18th of July reporting his interview with Giers in the country, merely mentioned that it had occurred to Giers and to himself that one might consider a further step along the road of the entente. He said nothing to indicate that the suggestion had come, initially, from Giers; nor did he say anything to indicate that he himself attached any great importance to the exchange.

Ribot appears, however, to have sensed very accurately what lay behind this report. For he at once went into action. He first dispatched a telegram to Laboulaye, demanding further information about what it was that had led him and Giers to talk about a further step in the consolidation of the "entente," and what it was that Giers had in mind in speaking of this possibility. He added that should Giers return to this subject, Laboulaye was not to discourage any overtures he might be inclined to make.*

After sending this message, Ribot at once got in touch with Freycinet and with President Carnot. And on the 23rd of July, the very day of the arrival of the French squadron at Cronstadt, the two ministers sat down to work out the initial draft of what was destined to become

---

*This telegram, like most of the messages addressed by the Quai d'Orsay to the French embassy at Petersburg, was intercepted and decoded by the Russians. Giers, who gained from it the impression that the French did not propose to pursue the matter unless he took some further step, was disturbed, and sent the intercepted message to the Tsar with this interpretation. The Tsar, on this occasion, was wiser. "Let us just wait," he wrote on the margin of the message. "The French government would really find it hard to say anything more explicit on the basis only of a single telegram from Laboulaye; the matter is too important for them." (Lamsdorf diary, July 11/23, 1891)

the political portion of the Franco-Russian Alliance.*[4]

It was a revealing document. Stressing at the outset the importance of a stable balance of power in Europe, the two statesmen described that balance as "seriously compromised" by the conditions under which the Triple Alliance had recently been renewed. They further noted that the renewal of the engagements constituting that alliance—engagements that had been "assiduously held secret"—had coincided with exchanges of views between England and one of the parties to it (Italy, of course, was meant)—exchanges that would appear to assure to that grouping "the more or less direct support of Great Britain." In these circumstances a due devotion to the cause of peace made it obligatory for France and Russia, they concluded, to recognize the need for

1. an agreement to concert their efforts in all questions that could threaten the peace of Europe; and
2. an agreement to the effect that both of them would mobilize immediately, simultaneously, and without need for further communication, in case any member of the Triple Alliance mobilized.

Ribot immediately wired the substance of this document to Laboulaye and dispatched the full text of it to Petersburg with a special courier (Laboulaye's own brother). Later that same day (July 24), he and Freycinet conferred with the President, Sadi Carnot, following which discussion they wired again, giving Laboulaye even more detailed instructions. And some days later (July 29), after receipt of Laboulaye's complete written account of his visit to Giers, Ribot wired once more, not only expanding on the earlier instructions but expressing the hope that even in the limited time before Laboulaye's scheduled final departure from Russia (then believed to be little more than a week off) he would be able to agree with Giers on the language of a formal written accord.

Laboulaye, finally made aware in this way of the importance being attached in Paris to his recent discussion with Giers, found himself in a difficult position. The fleet visit, with its multitudinous demands on his

---

*The speculations among the foreign diplomatic representatives in Petersburg as to what was going on at that point sometimes appear, in retrospect, in an ironic light. On July 21, the Austrian chargé d'affaires reported, in a letter to his foreign office, the statement of a high Russian foreign office official to the effect that: "There is no written treaty between France and Russia; not a single written word has been exchanged between Petersburg and Paris." This was literally true. Aehrenthal obviously could not know that while he was writing those lines, the first project of a written agreement was being drawn up in Paris.

time, was now at its height. He had been spending some six hours a day just in steamer and rail journeys between Petersburg and Cronstadt and Peterhof, not to mention the time spent at the various functions and ceremonies themselves. At the moment when this particular message reached him he had just returned (thoroughly exhausted, one must suppose) from the great reception for the French officers at the Duma. He, now a widower (see chap. 4), was himself preparing to give a formal dinner for the officers at his residence the following evening. In addition to which he was preparing to break up his household, in anticipation of his own departure. Only some ten days actually remained before the scheduled presentation of his letters of recall and the Tsar's departure for Denmark after the summer maneuvers. Giers, ill and still in the country, was not expected in Petersburg for another four days. How, in these circumstances, could Laboulaye expect to conduct secret negotiations of the highest importance? He had, it seemed to him, neither the time, the leisure, nor the facilities for such a task. He wired all this, despairingly, to Ribot, and begged for mercy; but the latter was unbending. He must, Ribot insisted, do his best.

Giers returned to town on the 2nd. Laboulaye could arrange to see him only for a few minutes, during which time he tried, hastily, to outline to him the French proposals. The following day the two men met once more, in Peterhof, where the Tsar's final dinner was being given for the French. Giers, so ill that he had to cancel his presence at the table, mingled briefly with the guests beforehand; and there, standing among the splashing fountains on one of the great terraces that surveyed the flight of cascades leading down to the sea, he and Laboulaye exchanged a few more hasty, whispered words. The Tsar, Giers said, was being consulted; his reaction would soon be available. It was not until two days later, however, the 5th of August, that Laboulaye was finally able to call upon the exhausted minister at the latter's apartment in the foreign office. Pale and uncomfortable, Giers rose from a sick bed to receive him; and now for the first time they came to grips with the vital question.[5]

The Tsar, Giers said, had been consulted. He had accepted on principle the idea of a written exchange. He had in fact described such an exchange as the natural "sanction" of all that had been taking place in those recent days. But an agreement of the two powers to concert their efforts in all questions that threatened "the peace of Europe" was not, Giers said, enough. Europe was not the only place from which the peace could be threatened. They would have to widen the scope of the proposed document in such a way as to take account of the possibility of wars arising from events in other parts of the world, such as Egypt, or even China. (He would not, Giers added pointedly, speak of Turkey, which was itself a European power.*) It would, therefore, not be enough to limit the agreement to defense against an action initiated by one of the members of the Triple Alliance. There now existed, after all, some sort of a quadruple alliance in place of the earlier Triple one; and it might well be England who would be the first to spark the conflagration. In any case, Giers said, he would undertake to produce the draft of an agreement and to show it to Laboulaye as soon as he had obtained the Tsar's approval of it.

The following day (August 6) the two men met once more. Giers had ready his draft of the agreement. It was much like the French one, but the commitment to immediate mobilization was watered down to give it a less binding quality and to leave greater flexibility for future decisions. They went over it together and agreed on an edited version, which Laboulaye promptly wired to Paris. Giers at that time conceived of the document as a letter he would expect to address to Laboulaye over his own signature, whereupon Laboulaye could then acknowledge it, saying whatever the French thought it suitable to say in reply.

Ribot and Freycinet were pleased with Giers' document. They had only minor, though not insignificant, suggestions for changes of language. A reference to the two "cabinets" should be replaced, they thought, by the term "governments"—a reasonable enough suggestion, since the term "cabinet" had a different meaning in Russia than in France and most of the Russian ministers had not even been consulted. And the French, equally sensibly, urged that a somewhat tortured phrase in the second paragraph of the Laboulaye-Giers draft, by which the two parties undertook "to study the means of agreeing in advance" on the measures each would take in certain situations, should be shortened to read that they would simply "agree" on these measures.

Giers, having taken the responsibility for consenting to the first two of these changes, demurred on the second but consented to leave the decision to the Tsar and went to see the latter on the 7th. The monarch's reaction was wholly unexpected and brought Giers up short. He accepted the language of the revised draft, as far as that was concerned; but he then went on to voice startling procedural objections. First, he thought the

*The hint was clear. Even under an agreement relating to matters affecting only the peace of Europe, Russia would expect French support if complications arose with England over the regime of the Straits.

time too short for completion of the whole matter in Petersburg before the respective departures of himself and Laboulaye. But secondly, he thought that Mohrenheim should be brought back to Petersburg and commissioned to transmit the text of the Russian note to Ribot in Paris.

This was a severe blow to Giers. He had thought it important to keep Mohrenheim out of the whole affair. But there was no way of arguing with the Tsar at that point. He had no choice but to accept this dictum and to communicate it to Laboulaye, who promptly relayed it to his government.

On August the 10th Laboulaye went out to Peterhof to present his letters of recall to the Tsar. The latter explained to him, partially at least, the decision to which he had come. "One must not be hasty," the monarch said. "The terms of such an agreement are not something that one defines over the telegraph wire. To act in that way would be dangerous. M. de Mohrenheim, who ought to be consulted, will come to Petersburg; and I expect that by October or November we shall see more clearly into the situation." And he went on to observe that England, which could not afford a conflict with France, was already—or so he thought—coming to regret the part it had taken in the Triple Alliance. This, in his view, was the interpretation to be given to the forthcoming French fleet visit to England.

One is somewhat puzzled over this reaction on the Tsar's part. Insofar as it concerned Mohrenheim—it was not pleasing to Giers, and could not have flowed from his advice. At no time had Giers wanted Mohrenheim to have anything to do with the affair. He distrusted the latter's vanity as well as his garrulousness. He had specifically warned the French not to mention the matter to him. The Tsar's decision to bring Mohrenheim back and to entrust him with the transmission of the Russian note can have come to Giers only as a distinct rebuff and as a loss of face in the eyes of the French. (Mohrenheim's subsequent sudden return must have been particularly galling to Giers because it immediately became widely noted in foreign diplomatic circles and stimulated a good deal of speculation as to what lay behind it.)

The background of this sudden decision on the Tsar's part is obscure and intriguing. It is clear that at some time between the 4th and 7th of August, someone—and someone who knew the negotiations were taking place—had got to Alexander and had persuaded him that Mohrenheim should be informed of the negotiations and involved in their formalization. It is difficult to imagine any other reason for Alexander's sudden disposition to slow down the whole course of the transaction than to allow ample time for Mohrenheim to get into the act. Laboulaye himself suspected that it was Giers, *"un peu troublé par la précision que nous voulons donner au second paragraphe de l'échange de vues,"** who had sown uncertainty in the Tsar's mind. But this is not convincing. The finger of probability points to the Empress Dagmar, always well inclined towards Mohrenheim.

However that may be, the unsuspecting Mohrenheim, roused out of the serenity of his summer holiday in the Pyrenees, was at once ordered back to Petersburg. He passed through Paris on the 13th and dined there with Ribot. The latter reported (in the memo he subsequently prepared about their talk) that Mohrenheim, on that occasion, opposed the idea of a formal alliance but recognized the desirability (this was of course Freycinet's thesis) of charging the two general staffs immediately with the task of defining a common action in the event that one of the members of the Triplice should attack. It would be, Mohrenheim had said, a great mistake to fail to do this, because when war broke out (and this could happen any day), communications would at once be cut. It would be wrong, therefore, to let things drag on and to fail to put the two general staffs at work at once. This reaction reflected, presumably, both Freycinet's influence on Mohrenheim and the latter's lack of instructions from Giers.

On the 18th day of August Mohrenheim was back in Petersburg. Lamsdorf noted in his diary that the mere thought of having to receive him and to take him into confidence aggravated Giers' illness. But Giers faithfully went through with the task. To his own amusement (and that of the Tsar, when the latter was told about it), he had some difficulty in interrupting the torrent of words with which his visitor inaugurated the discussion, but he finally managed to break in long enough to explain to him why he had been called home and what was expected of him. Three days later (August 21) Mohrenheim was received in audience by the Tsar. And on the 23rd he was off to Paris once more, greatly excited, bearing with him for transmission to Ribot the original of a note signed by Giers and addressed to himself, setting forth the Russian position.

On the 27th, after a preliminary discussion between Mohrenheim and Ribot, the respective documents were exchanged in Paris. They consisted of a note from Mohrenheim, submitting the letter he had

---

*". . . a bit troubled by the explicitness we would like to give to the second paragraph of the exchange of views. . . ."

received from Giers; and Ribot's reply, acknowledging the receipt of these two communications and confirming the French government's agreement with the two central points of Giers' letter. It was these documents (which, incidentally, both sides took pains *not* to describe as a "treaty") that came to constitute, then and for many years to come, the *political* expression of what was eventually to be known as the Franco-Russian Alliance.

.   .   .

The full texts of the documents exchanged in Paris on August 27, 1891, are reproduced in appendix I to this account. Because of their unique quality as the only written formulation of the political aspect of the Alliance, it will be well to have at this point a glance at certain of their more significant passages.

The letter addressed by Giers to Mohrenheim (dated August 21) began with a highly significant reference to "the situation created in Europe by the evident renewal of the Triple Alliance and the more or less probable adherence by Great Britain to the political objectives that that alliance is pursuing. . . ." This phrase, occurring in the opening statement of the letter, makes it quite clear how deeply the Russians, Giers included, had been affected by the rumors of British adherence to the Triplice.

The two central clauses of the letter, referring respectively to the agreement of the two governments to act in concert on all questions involving threats to the peace, and to the need for consultation on immediate and simultaneous measures (i.e., mobilization) in case peace should be endangered, are portrayed in Giers' letter as reflecting the upshot of his own discussions with Laboulaye, personally. In no way did the language of the letter commit the Tsar or the Russian government as such, or even profess to reflect the Tsar's views. Giers merely asked Mohrenheim to communicate this record of *his* agreement with *Laboulaye* to the French government and to communicate to him whatever decisions that government might come to in this connection.

Mohrenheim, in transmitting this communication to the French government as he had been told to do, significantly altered and heightened its significance, though without authorization to do so.

He began by stating in his covering letter that he was transmitting Giers' communication by order of the Tsar. Nothing in Giers' letter had suggested this. Whether the Tsar would have specifically authorized it is doubtful.

He then included, in his covering letter, a cloudy (and somewhat ungrammatical) paragraph, for the inclusion of which he had no authorization at all (certainly not from Giers)—a paragraph obviously hinting at the possible early conclusion of a military convention. "The ulterior developments," he wrote, "of which not only are these two agreed points susceptible but that indeed should constitute their natural and necessary completion, are ones that it will be possible to treat in confidential and intimate discussions at whatever point may be found opportune by one or the other of the two cabinets, whenever they may find it possible to proceed along this line at an appropriate moment."*

The French might have been excused for seeing in this phrase an authorized indication that the Russians were prepared to proceed in the near future to the negotiation of a military convention. But they must have been aware, as we shall soon see, that this was not the case—not, at any rate, so far as Giers was concerned. (Perhaps they noted that the phrase occurred only in Mohrenheim's letter, not in Giers'.)

Ribot, in his letter of reply to Mohrenheim, did not fail, of course, to express the full agreement of the French government to the two principal points set forth in Giers' letter. In mentioning the situation that gave rise to the need for recording in written form the identity of views of the two governments, he did not, however, mention England in any way; he contented himself with speaking of the "conditions surrounding the renewal of the Triple Alliance." And he then went on to include a paragraph that was invited by nothing said in the content of Giers' letter and that could only have been the reflection of talks he and Freycinet had had with Mohrenheim just before delivery of the Russian note. The Russian government would no doubt agree, he wrote, to the need for "entrusting to special delegates, to be appointed as soon as possible, the practical study of the measures necessary to avert the eventualities [i.e., a threat to the peace or danger of aggression against one of the two parties] mentioned in the second paragraph of the agreement."

In sending the texts of this exchange of notes to Petersburg, Mohrenheim accompanied them with a long personal letter to Giers, in which he attributed to Ribot the strong conviction that one ought to

---

*The writer hopes that this translation faithfully renders the opaque and grammatically questionable nature of the French original, which reads as follows: "Les développements ultérieurs dont les deux points ainsi convenus sont non seulement susceptibles, mais qui en formeront le complément nécessaire, pourront faire l'objet de pourparlers confidentiels et intimes á tel moment, jugé opportun par l'un ou l'autre Cabinet, où ils estimeront pouvoir y procéder en temps utile."

proceed at once to the negotiation of a military pact "in view of the great speed with which, as recent precedents have only too well demonstrated, events can develop in the face of fateful conflicts, and in view of the complete impossibility for the two sides to consult about anything at all if and when they are taken by surprise and have no possibility for mutual contact."[6]

What Mohrenheim did *not* reveal to Giers was that it was he himself who had taken the initiative in advancing these views about the urgency of negotiations looking to the conclusion of a military convention. He did not, in fact, even include in this report the text of the covering letter with which he had transmitted Giers' official communication to Ribot and in which he had included the unauthorized paragraph.[7] Nor did he tell Giers that he had orally informed the French that delegates of "the two competent ministries [i.e., obviously the two ministries of war]" would soon be conferring on the subject of a military convention, and that any communications the French might wish to make about such a convention should be addressed to him (i.e., not to Giers, and not through the French embassy at Petersburg.)[8]

In the light of these circumstances, there can be no doubt that what was being put in hand at this point was a deliberate intrigue by both Mohrenheim and Freycinet to promote the early negotiation of a military convention behind Giers' back and without his knowledge. What is less clear is the extent of the Tsar's knowledge of, and involvement in, this effort.

. . . .

The audience he accorded to Mohrenheim on the 22nd of August, just before the latter's return to France, was the Tsar's last official act before leaving, that very afternoon, with his family for the usual late summer vacation in Denmark. Giers had no opportunity to learn from him what had been said or agreed upon in this encounter. He did, however, succeed in obtaining, from some unidentifiable source,* a copy of Mohrenheim's covering letter to Ribot, transmitting Giers' own note to Mohrenheim. The unauthorized passage therein did not escape attention. Lamsdorf was the first to spot it. He sent the document to Giers with a note pointing out the discrepancy between this passage and the actual wording of the two points. "I venture to think," he wrote,

*The source was presumably Giers' son, then First Secretary of the Russian embassy at Paris.

that Baron Mohrenheim has gone considerably beyond the limits of his instructions. The second point of the accord envisages the possibility of agreement on certain measures should these become *unavoidable* for the two governments "in the event that the general peace should be really in danger, and particularly in the event that one of the two parties should be under threat of attack." But in his covering letter to M. Ribot our ambassador now declares that the further development of the two agreed points is not only possible but *"should constitute their natural and necessary completion."*

Can Baron Mohrenheim really believe that the general peace is now "in danger" or that one of the two parties finds itself at this time "under the threat of" an unavoidable attack?[9]

Giers could not have agreed more strongly. He immediately realized what was up. On September the 3rd he wrote the Tsar (already in Denmark) on the subject. No one in Europe, he noted, was then envisaging, or could desire, a war. It would be imprudent, he argued, to depart from the calm and advantageous situation that the obvious rapprochement with France had produced by going further, as Mohrenheim's letter was suggesting. Such negotiations, especially if entrusted to "special delegates," could scarcely be kept secret. The Russians should, therefore, content themselves with the two points specified in his own letter of the 27th of August to Mohrenheim. To go further would be to run the risk of actually stimulating "certain sudden alarming developments," whereas there was, as things then stood, no reason to expect anything of the sort.[10]

In showing the draft of this letter to Lamsdorf, Giers explained that he was, as Lamsdorf would see,

> obliged to spare Mohrenheim to some extent for a reason you can imagine. I know from experience that any criticism of that individual arouses displeasure in high circles and only ruins the success of any worthy undertaking.

And he showed Lamsdorf, in this connection, a letter from his own son in Paris, in which it was said that Mohrenheim had completely lost his balance—already saw himself as foreign minister—was boasting about his audience with the Tsar—and was going about hinting at the immense importance of the purpose for which he had been called home.*[11]

---

*Aehrenthal, the Austrian chargé d'affaires, seems to have picked up faint echoes of these happenings; for he was able to report (Sept. 21, 1891) that Giers was upset over the pro-French enthusiasms in Russia, that he had complained about this to the Tsar, who had merely laughed the whole matter off; and that Giers had then been known to say that Mohrenheim was the one who

The Tsar returned Giers' letter with his own notation penned on the face of it. The notation was only partially reassuring. "For the moment, of course," he wrote,

> our present agreement with France suffices. The military question is so important that I can, of course, say nothing about it until I can meet personally with you and Vannovski.[12]

Giers was generally pleased with this reply, which he took to be an expression of agreement with his letter. But actually, whether he was aware of it or not, he was not the first person to whom the Tsar had thus expressed himself on this subject. On the first of September, less than a week after the exchange of notes in Paris, Freycinet had dispatched Jules Hansen on a mission to Copenhagen for the purpose of pressing the Tsar to agree to the immediate inauguration of talks between the two general staffs.[13]

In view of the high degree of intimacy between Mohrenheim and Hansen, the former must have been well informed of what Hansen was up to on this occasion, if indeed he, Mohrenheim, was not the initiator of the move.

Hansen left for Copenhagen on the 4th of September, taking with him a memorandum he claimed to have drawn up himself, but that had obviously been approved, if not drafted, by Freycinet. It strongly reflected the view Mohrenheim had been putting forward (and that Giers so flatly challenged): that there was serious danger of an early attack by the Triplice. After outlining the disasters that could be expected to ensue for both parties in the face of such an event in the absence of a detailed understanding between the two general staffs, the author of the memorandum continued:

> To correct that state of affairs, which can become very dangerous and can result in France and Russia being defeated separately, it would seem highly necessary to conclude at the earliest moment a military convention, the essential stipulation of which would be that Russia and France would immediately mobilize all their forces at the first intimation of the mobilization of the Triple Alliance.
> In addition, there must be established an understanding (entente) between the French and Russian general staffs on the subject of the concen-

---

was responsible for this whole situation, which had been "arranged by him to permit him to play a role"—a statement that, whether or not Giers actually made it, was very close to the truth. (Austrian Archives, P.A. X, box 94. Russland, Berichte 1891 IX–XII. Communication, Aehrenthal to foreign office, Sept. 21, 1891.)

trations and simultaneous movements of the respective army corps in the various foreseeable contingencies.

Upon arrival at the Fredensborg palace near Copenhagen, where the Tsar was staying, Hansen succeeded, with the help of his friend (and employer) Rachkovski, the head of the Tsar's personal security detachment, in getting his document into the hands of the Tsar's aide-de-camp, Prince Vladimir Obolenski, who passed it on to his imperial master. The following day (September 5) Obolenski handed to Hansen a note of the following tenor:

> Monsieur Hansen pourra dire à M. de Freycinet que l'Empereur a pris sa demande en sérieuse considération et qu'il s'occupera d'y donner une suite aussitôt sa rentrée à St-Pétersbourg.*

Elated, Hansen at once took this reply back to Paris. The Tsar, it would seem, had thus contrived to give to both Giers and Hansen the impression that their particular approaches had been approved.

Giers, ignorant of Hansen's appeal and pleased, as we have seen, with the response to his own, wrote to Mohrenheim on the 16th of September, putting the latter (as he fondly supposed) in his place. "His Majesty," he wrote,

> having seen the secret letter that you wrote to me on the 27th of August, together with its enclosures . . . has just informed me of his decisions in regard to the important question to which those communications were addressed.
>
> Our august monarch finds that the bases of the agreement drawn up and confirmed by ourselves and by the French government fully meet the requirements of our present situation, and that the military question is too important to be approached without prior study; His Majesty proposes to occupy himself with it at the proper time in company with General Vannovski and myself, after his return to Russia.
>
> For this reason, His Majesty wishes that we should continue to adhere strictly to the program that he outlined for us, and that we should take all necessary measures to see that no premature development is given to the two points that at this stage constitute the expression of our agreement with France.

---

*"Monsieur Hansen may say to M. de Freycinet that the Emperor has taken his request under serious consideration and that he will see to it that a reaction is forthcoming immediately upon his return to St. Petersburg."

It should be noted that the Tsar must have seen Hansen's communication, and given his reply to it, just before he received the letter from Giers. Had he seen Giers' letter, he might have replied more cautiously to Hansen.

His Majesty demands, now as before, the observation of the most *absolute secrecy* with respect to this matter.[14]

.   .   .

On the 24th of September Giers, fancying that he had won this last battle, left Petersburg for Western Europe, where he was to remain, nursing his health, for some two and a half months. The Tsar, and as we have seen, most of the foreign ambassadors, exhausted from the exertions of this strenuous midsummer, had already abandoned the Russian capital. There was, in fact, no one to see Giers and his family off at the station, on their departure for Western Europe, but the faithful Lamsdorf, who hopped on the train, accompanied the party as far as one of the suburban stations, and then returned, feeling very sorry for himself because he had not been invited to go along on the entire journey.

With this, quiet descended for a time on the Petersburg scene. For the moment, all those immediately concerned were glad to have a respite from delicate and intensive diplomacy.

But strong and unsatisfied impulses still gnawed at the various actors on the French side of the drama. Giers and the Tsar, as the French understood it, had agreed to act in concert with France in all questions involving threats to the peace and to discuss the question of immediate and simultaneous mobilization in the event that either of the parties should be directly threatened with aggression. And the Tsar had further agreed to examine, upon his return to Petersburg, the question of the conclusion of a detailed military convention. But for the moment the Russian military leaders themselves remained without specific commitment. In the event of another Franco-German war, Russian mobilization could be, as the French saw it, delayed by the very process of consultation. The state of telegraphic facilities was such that the Germans might well be able to cut communication between Paris and Petersburg in the initial stages of a war, thus further complicating the consultative process.

There was, of course, as Giers argued, no immediate danger of war; nor was there any likelihood that danger of this nature could arise with such suddenness that more binding and effective arrangements could not be arrived at in good time. The fears of British adherence to the Triplice, furthermore, had by now been largely dispelled, particularly in Paris.

But for Freycinet, in particular, this was not enough. His thoughts ran automatically to the internal-political scene and to the probability that someday and in some way what was happening in Franco-Russian relations would have to become known. He must have been well aware that it was not his signature that appeared in the agreement already reached —only that of his cabinet colleague Ribot, to whom his political relationship was something less than one of complete confidence and intimacy. In the case of the negotiation of a military convention, this situation might, as noted above, be reversed. His tenure of office, both as premier and as minister of war, was precarious; in Republican France, such positions usually were. It was important to him that the completion of the military side of the Alliance should take place while he was still in possession of one or both of his cabinet positions. Hence, one must assume, the state of high impatience that caused him to dispatch Hansen to Copenhagen and that was to dominate his conduct throughout the ensuing months.

As for Ribot, it was equally important for him that he should not be seen as impeding, by any lack of enthusiasm, progress towards a further development, namely, the conclusion of a military convention, from which France stood so clearly to gain and in which the premier was so deeply interested. So he, too, while preferring to deal through his Russian counterpart Giers rather than through Mohrenheim, went loyally along with Freycinet's pressures, coming gradually to share the intensity of the latter's impatience as the frustrations of endeavoring to move a dilatory and hesitant Russian regime made themselves increasingly felt.

Chapter 8

THE ULTERIOR RELATIONSHIPS

While these things and others still to be recounted were taking place in the confidential exchanges between the senior personalities of the French and Russian governments, they were not, of course, taking place in an international vacuum; both governments had relationships with other countries that also made claims on the attention of the same senior statesmen. And the point at which our narrative has now arrived—just after conclusion of the first phase of the negotiations for the Alliance and just before the beginning of the second one—is perhaps not a bad point at which to glance at some of these ulterior preoccupations and to see how the Franco-Russian relationship was being affected by them. This exercise, addressed as it is to the entire 1890–1894 period, will necessarily have to reach back a bit in time through the period already treated in this account, and also a bit forward—into the years 1892–1893; but it may throw further light on the events already recounted, and it may be helpful to an understanding of those still to be described.

. . .

The most significant object on the horizon of both France and Russia, over the period in question, was of course the Triple Alliance itself. Formed in 1882 under the initiative and influence of Bismarck, this association of Germany, Austria, and Italy was originally seen by the German chancellor less as a means of defending its respective partners from external attack (of which, at that time, there was little likelihood) than as a device for denying possible alliance partners to a resentful and increasingly powerful France, and for giving a salutary warning to the Tsar—and especially to a tsar who was then showing an increasing vulnerability to Pan-Slav and other anti-Austrian and anti-German tendencies—that Germany also had other strings to her bow and that there were limits beyond which anti-German tendencies could not be pursued with impunity.

The terms of the Triple Alliance were of course never officially revealed during the years treated in this volume; and while the French and Russian intelligence services must, one would suppose, have provided their respective masters with a fair idea of the nature of these terms, the French government, at least, seems not to have been fully and reliably informed of them. The tenor of the various undertakings was, as is customary in such arrangements, formally defensive in nature; and this, at least, the French and Russian governments must have known; but what is defensive to one party is offensive to the other; and it has never been the custom of the envisaged opponent, then or since, to place much confidence in such professions of defensive intent on the part of those who are banding together for military purposes directed against him. The very existence of the Triple Alliance was seen in both Paris and Petersburg as a potential, if not immediate, threat; and in the absence, after 1890, of any restraining obligations on Germany with relation to either France or Russia, this could not fail to constitute the principal factor impelling these two powers into what was (in the same sense) a "defensive" counter alliance.

We have already seen, in the preceding chapters, something of the way in which the Triplice, its perceived dangers aggravated by fears of a possible British adherence, affected the Franco-Russian relationship at one particular juncture—namely, in the spring and summer of 1891. What was involved, however, was not just the reaction of the French and Russian governments to the Triple Alliance as a group, but also their respective relationships to its individual members. These, therefore, will also merit a glance; and one may as well begin with the French.

.   .   .

For the French there was of course, over this entire period, no bilateral relationship more significant than that which they were obliged to entertain with their new neighbor to the east: the newly united imperial Germany. At the risk of some repetition, let us summarize the French attitude.

The determining factor for the French was at all times the German possession of Alsace and Lorraine. This was a situation tolerated in Paris over the years here in question, but never fully accepted. At no time does there seem to have been any disposition on the French side, even after conclusion of the alliance with Russia, to initiate an armed conflict with Germany with a view to recovering the two provinces; but neither was there any disposition to be reconciled to their alienation or to abandon the intention to recover them someday, one way or another. This intention did not by any means preclude the possibility that the recovery of the provinces might one day have to be achieved by force of arms; but it also did not commit the French government to the initiation of such a contest over any particular issue or at any particular time. It did not, in fact, even preclude the possibility (a faint one, to be sure) that a solution might be found by means short of war.

Despite the impressive growth of France's own military strength and despite the progress made towards an alliance with Russia, the French governments of the 1890–1894 period had good reason not to commit themselves to a solution of the Alsace-Lorraine problem by force of arms. In view of what they had learned in 1870–1871 about the power of German arms, any armed conflict with that country had to be regarded as at best a hazardous undertaking. Should it lead to a French defeat, there could be no hope of political survival for those French statesmen who had inaugurated it; indeed, it was doubtful that the Republic itself, as a form of government, could stand such a blow. If, on the other hand, France should emerge victorious, there was the not inconsiderable danger that credit for the victory would go to some senior French military commander, thereby reviving all the Napoleonic and Boulangist tendencies still latent in portions of the French people and threatening the integrity of the Republic in quite a different way.

In these circumstances responsible French statesmen were content, over this entire period, to preserve, outwardly at least, a peaceful and "correct" diplomatic relationship with Germany. But in the meantime, by strengthening France's armed forces and international position (via the Russian alliance), they were doing all in their power to prepare for the ultimate military showdown, whose eventual arrival was generally regarded as probable if not inevitable. They were aided in this restraint by the presence in Paris of a steady, well-balanced, and peacefully inclined German ambassador, Prince Georg Herbert zu Münster, and by the incessant labors of their own ambassador in Berlin, Jules Herbette—an experienced diplomatic professional, devoid of illusions, no friend of Germany, incessantly vigilant in defense of French interests, but cognizant of the fact that his task was to keep things as far as possible on an even keel. This last, in the face of the occasional erratic behavior of Kaiser William II and the periodic outbursts and demonstrations of chauvinistic sentiment in France, was not always easy; but, in the general sense, it was accomplished. As an effort, it sufficed for the moment. It represented no commitment (and about this there were no illusions on either side) for the more distant future.

The majority of the French people, while resentful over Alsace-Lorraine, were peaceably inclined. Had the Germans been more successful in reconciling the people of Alsace and Lorraine to German rule, and had the Kaiser been less cynical and more thoughtfully perceptive in his reaction to French events, willing to listen less to inflammatory military figures in his own entourage and more to the experienced old hands in the German embassy at Paris, it is not impossible that the Alsace-Lorraine problem might someday have lost something of its actuality as a disturbing factor in the relations between the two countries, and even found some sort of peaceful solution.

But behind the scenes the wheels of the two great competitive military establishments, the French and the German, were always grinding along in the invariable manner of such establishments, impervious to any hopeful political possibilities, accepting—if only for the hypotheses of military planning—the inevitability of a war that was otherwise not at all inevitable, and thereby creating a virtual inevitability that, but for their efforts, would not necessarily have existed at all.

Quite different, of course, was the French relationship to the Austro-Hungarian empire. The French had nothing against the Austrians or, for that matter, the Hungarians, except the fact of their association with the Triple Alliance; and even this was a source of sadness rather than anger. They would, in fact, have preferred, in some respects, an Austrian alliance to a Russian one, had this been a real possibility. (Bismarck had seen to it that it was not.) They knew that Austria's membership in the Triple Alliance had nothing to do with *them*—that it was a product of Vienna's fear of the military power of Russia, and its respect for that of Germany. But they were helpless before this situation, and could do no more than accept it.

With Italy, the French relationship was of course more complicated. Here there was a multiplicity of subsidiary problems, including historical conflicts, national, cultural, and religious sensitivities, the frictions of immediate neighborhood, and competing colonial aspirations in northern and eastern Africa. These conflicts would have been there to trouble the relationship, Triplice or none. But the Italian alliance with Germany was viewed in Paris with keen suspicion and resentment, particularly because it was felt that Italy, unlike Austria-Hungary, had alternatives to that orientation—alternatives to which she could, had she wished, have taken recourse.

Italy needed French friendship, if only for financial and economic reasons; and there was, as we have seen, a moment in the spring of 1891 when the French, with a little more patience and foresight, might at least have weakened Italy's attachment to the Triplice, already subjected to heavy strain by Italy's differences with Austria over the Tyrol. Had they recognized this and conducted themselves accordingly, the French might have found for themselves an advantageous alternative to the alliance with Russia; for Italy's abandonment of the Triplice, given a somewhat greater measure of restraint on Russia's part, would have seriously shaken Austria's fidelity to that arrangement and have thus promoted that isolation of Germany that would have served French interests better than a Russian alliance ever could. But the French were not to be had for such an effort. The gleaming fata morgana of Russia's many divisions dimmed French eyes; and visions of military superiority were allowed, as at so many other passages of international life, to take precedence over the possibilities for relieving the military-political tensions that had originally stimulated the arms race. A characteristic French suspiciousness and rigidity in relations with Italy did the rest.

. . .

For the Russians, too, the very existence of the Triplice was a source of resentment and suspicion, particularly because of the inclusion of Austria within it. So long as Bismarck was at the helm, the treaty relationship maintained between Germany and Russia served to temper these negative reactions and to render the Triplice tolerable (if only barely and grudgingly so) in Russian eyes. But with the lapse of the Reinsurance Treaty, the last formal Russo-German tie, this moderating influence fell away, and the Triplice became, for the Russians, a wholly hostile and menacing apparition on the international horizon. With Bismarck gone and no contractual bond to sustain the German-Russian relationship, the anti-German and anti-Austrian tendencies in the Russian political and official establishment, supported by the nationalistic journalists and most of the senior military figures and centering around the Tsar himself, were given free rein. For this, the Germans themselves had a heavy share of the responsibility. It was they, after all, who had taken the initiative in putting an end to the treaty relationship. And while Alexander III was by no means displeased that they had done so, he would, under Giers' urging, probably not have stood in the way of the treaty's prolongation had the Germans offered it.

But how much this would have meant, in reality, is still a question. By the end of the year 1890 an aversion to the young Kaiser had firmly entrenched itself in the ponderous emotional makeup of Alexander III;

and such feelings, once established, were seldom if ever to be changed. What had brought on this acute dislike of the young German ruler is not clearly evident from the available documentation. The writer strongly suspects that the court-to-court gossip so abundantly cultivated in the salons of idle European royalty had carried to Alexander's ears (there is record of at least one such episode) snide remarks made about him by the Kaiser, whose lips abounded in such utterances. Be that as it may, this personal animosity grew, in the early 1890s, to a point where it clearly stamped the Kaiser, in Alexander's view, as a most unattractive and untrustworthy adversary, and began to overshadow (to the disquiet of some of his military and religious advisers) even the more traditional hostility to the heretical Austrians.

On the formal diplomatic level, German-Russian relations remained, like the Franco-German ones, calm and correct. The Russians (including both Giers and the Tsar) liked and respected Bismarck's successor, General Georg Leo von Caprivi, who stood at the helm of German policy from 1890 to the autumn of 1894. Count Paul Shuvalov, who served as Russian ambassador at Berlin throughout this period, though always suspect in the Kaiser's eyes for the good personal relations with Bismarck that he continued to entertain even after the latter's fall, did his best to preserve an outwardly pleasant atmosphere. In this he was seconded, up to 1893, by his opposite number in Petersburg, General Lothar von Schweinitz. The latter, seeing his life's work destroyed in the breakup of the three-emperors relationship, retired, heartbroken, at the end of 1892. But his successor, General Bernard von Werder, who, like Schweinitz, had once been a special military representative of the old Kaiser, William I, at the Russian court,* was also personally acceptable to the Tsar, and did his best to support an acceptable relationship.

Werder was kindly received, personally, by the imperial couple upon his arrival in Petersburg as ambassador; but it soon became evident that his former connections gave him no greater access to the Tsar's person than that enjoyed by other diplomatic representatives in Petersburg; and the historian looks in vain for any sign that his presence there had the slightest effect on the political dispositions of Alexander III.

*This unique institution, by virtue of which the German and Russian emperors each maintained at the court of the other a special military representative who served officially as a personal aide to the receiving monarch, had been established during the reign of Nicholas I. It was allowed to lapse in 1892, when Alexander III recalled the last such Russian representative and failed to replace him —a rebuff to which the Germans promptly responded by recalling his opposite number.

Throughout those early years of the 1890s much attention was given by the world press to the conflicting financial and commercial interests of Germany and Russia. It was commonly supposed and inferred that conflicts in this area were a prominent factor in the existing political estrangement of the two governments. It was true, of course, that since the imposition of the famous "Lombardverbot" of 1887, Russian securities had not been accepted as collateral at the German state bank, and the German financial market had been relatively inaccessible for Russian borrowing; in addition to which the two countries had stood, ever since the early 1880s, in a state of gradually intensifying feud in point of tariff policy, the Germans punishing the Russian estate owners by successive increases in the duties on Russian grain, the Russians retaliating by a correspondingly punitive treatment of German manufactured goods seeking access to the Russian market. By 1892, this conflict had degenerated into a full-fledged tariff war.

In 1890 and 1891 rumors repeatedly found their way into the European press to the effect that negotiations were being undertaken between the two governments with a view to composing these differences. Ribot, to Giers' annoyance, showed much disquiet over such reports, suspecting that the Russians were using the military negotiations with France only as a bargaining lever for the achievement of a commercial agreement with the Germans. Actually, there was at that time no truth in these rumors. But when, in 1892, Vyshnegradski was removed as minister of finance (for reasons both political and of health) and replaced with the strong and active Sergei Yulyevich Witte, a man then very much "on the make,"* things began to happen. By a vigorous combination of increased pressure and greater readiness to negotiate, Witte succeeded in bringing the Germans to the negotiating table; and in early 1894, in circumstances that remain to be recounted, the first German-Russian commercial treaty was concluded, the tariff war being thereby brought to an end. This development was a sensation for the European public of the day; and all sorts of political as well as economic implications were read into it, even by the Kaiser himself.

Most of these speculations were misplaced. While Alexander III gave his personal authorization to the conclusion of the commercial agreement, and while he may, in doing this, have had in mind the desirability

---

*Witte, a man of outstanding capacities, later to become Russia's first premier, had had a successful career as a railway official and had become briefly, in February 1892, minister of transportation. He then succeeded Vyshnegradski as finance minister in August of the same year.

of offsetting any possible leaks to the press about his relations with France, it is impossible to discern the faintest evidence of any restraining effect of this development upon his actions with respect to the Alliance. Even on the economic side, the influence of the commercial treaty was less sensational than the press and public assumed, as had been indeed the case with the preceding tariff war,* but the treaty presumably had some significance as a factor making possible the substantial increase in German-Russian trade that set in after 1895.

Russia's relations with Austria, over all these years, were governed by a wholly different set of impulses. There was no particular animosity between the Austrian and Russian emperors. But within the Russian bureaucratic structure, distrust of, and antagonism towards, the Austro-Hungarian empire was of long standing. This anti-Austrianism was rooted primarily in the religious and military establishments, supported by the semi-independent Asiatic section (much less by the so-called Grand Chancery) of the Russian foreign office. To the Russian-Orthodox Church hierarchy the influence of the Roman Catholic clergy in Poland and of the Uniat (Eastern-rite) Catholics in the Ukraine, all radiating (as the Russians saw it) from the Austrian position in Galician Poland, was a constant object of resentment. This Austrian-controlled part of southern Poland was also an irritant to the Russian military authorities, in whose eyes the territory appeared as a dangerous Austrian military salient, projected beyond the strategic barrier of the Carpathians into what they viewed as Russia's natural strategic domain. They could not forget, moreover, that during the war with Turkey in 1878, the uncomfortable presence of the Austro-Hungarian armed forces along the long Russian supply lines down to the Dardanelles had been one of the factors compelling the Russian government to break off the war in a manner commonly viewed as unfavorable to Russia; and they could see no way of achieving what they had been taught to see as Russia's traditional objectives at the Straits that would not require the prior destruction of Austro-Hungarian military power. These bones of contention were exacerbated by the awareness in Petersburg that Rumania (the use of whose territory was also essential to any effective military action at the Straits) was politically in the Austrian

---

*In his excellent article "Russian Tariffs and Foreign Industries before 1914: the German Entrepreneur's Perspective" (*Journal of Economic History*, 41, June 1981), Professor Walther Kirchner has clearly shown the limitations of customs tariffs, as also of commercial treaties, as factors in the shaping of international trade. The data on which his treatise was based were drawn largely from German-Russian trade of the period under discussion in this book.

camp. And the influence now being increasingly exerted in Vienna, after the *Ausgleich* of 1867, by the violently anti-Russian Hungarians was a particular source of Russian resentment and distrust.

These various irritants would have sufficed in any case to assure a seriously troubled state of Russian-Austrian relations. But beyond them there was one more major source of conflict, more important perhaps at just this time than any of the others because of its origins in the murky but powerful emotional reactions of Alexander III. This was the situation in Bulgaria, about which more will be said presently. Suffice it to note here that Alexander continued to his death to have violent feelings with relation to the situation prevailing in that country. He could not and would not reconcile himself to that situation; and he persisted in the suspicion (for which there is little evidence in fact) that it would not have continued to exist had the Austrians not secretly encouraged and supported it.

All of these disturbing elements in the Russian-Austrian relationship proceeded, it will be noted, overwhelmingly from the Russian side. The Austrians (as distinct from the Hungarians), while occasionally making one or two small contributions of their own to the prevailing tensions, were by and large the passive partners in the relationship and would have been glad to see it improved. This is important, because there is strong evidence that had the Russians been able to overcome some of their traditional resentments and had they then wished to take advantage of the essentially conciliatory attitudes of the Emperor Franz Joseph and of the Austrian foreign minister, Count Gustav Kálnocky, they might well have weakened Austria's fidelity to the Triple Alliance. The Austrians never felt comfortable in this grouping—either with their German partners or their Italian ones, and particularly not in the years immediately following Bismarck's retirement. Austrian military leaders were especially unhappy in their relationship to their German counterparts, of whose arrogant and contemptuous attitude towards them they were never allowed to remain unaware. In general, Vienna would have been prepared, particularly in the spring of 1893, to go far to compose its differences with Petersburg—and this at the expense of its relations with Berlin—had the Russians evinced any inclination to reciprocate the disposition. And Vienna might well have had Giers, sick as he was, as an ally in the effort. It is not likely that any development in that direction would have gone so far as to threaten the breakup of the Austro-German alliance. For that the influence of the Austrian Pan-Germans, and also of the strongly anti-Russian Hungarians, was too great. But, added to the perennial Austrian-Italian differences over the Tyrol, it might have sufficed to weaken the Triple Alliance, if not the Austro-German one.

Petersburg, however, was largely blind to these possibilities. In this, as in all other such moments, it was the Pan-Slav, religious-nationalist, and militaristic tendencies in the Russian political establishment that found their way to the heart of the Russian ruler. And thus whatever possibility there was of exercising at this point, through Vienna, a significantly divisive influence on the Triplice—a possibility that, if exploited, might have changed the future of Europe—was lost.

. . .

Outside the ranks of the Triplice there was no power with which relations were more important for both France and Russia than Great Britain. French interests crossed those of Great Britain at many points— particularly in Africa and Asia; Russian interests crossed them at few points, but highly neuralgic ones. For both powers relations with Britain had an important though not decisive influence on the dispositions and decisions that led to their mutual alliance.

Most of the conflicts that troubled Anglo-French relations in the years in question were of a colonial nature. Of these, the most serious was the acute French unhappiness over the persistence of the British in their occupation of Egypt. Except insofar as they involved Italy, these conflicts had little relationship to France's interests on the European Continent; and Russia, not being an overseas-colonial power, had no appreciable ability to affect them, favorably or otherwise. For this reason France had little to hope from Russia, other than a certain mild and perfunctory support in the Egyptian question, when it came to the solution of most of her problems with Great Britain.

But prior to the conclusion of the Russian alliance these frictions with London had tended to heighten in Paris the uneasy consciousness of France's isolation in the international community and to strengthen the desire to escape from it. And such was the talent of French and British statesmen for rubbing each other the wrong way in personal relations that the French, in particular, must have derived much inner gratification at being able to present themselves to their British opposite numbers, after the Cronstadt visit, no longer as representatives of a recently humiliated and isolated country but as the proud member of a partnership, the military strength of which, while indeed confined largely to the land surface of the continent and thus not really a challenge to Britain's naval supremacy, nevertheless rivaled anything to be found in the way of ground forces anywhere else in the world.

On the other hand, France's tie with Russia was indeed a source of considerable disquiet to the British, insofar as it appeared to strengthen the Russian military hand in central Asia and threatened to encourage the emergence of Russia as a factor in the struggle for naval control in the Mediterranean—a question to which we shall return presently.

As for Russian-British relations, these remained over these years of the early 1890s substantially what they had been for so many years in the past—ones of sharp mutual antagonism and suspicion. Reviewing the archival materials relating to these relations, one is struck not only with the paucity of the information each of the two governments possessed about the other but precisely with their lack of interest in knowing much more than they actually knew. To each of them, the other appeared as a species of malevolent but unmovable object on the international horizon: a factor that of course had to be reckoned with, but not one with which one could communicate to any good effect. Even Giers, sensitive as he was to the complexities of the continental scene, generally appeared remote, resigned, and uninterested when it came to Britain, as though he had long since abandoned any hope of any useful exchanges with anyone in that quarter. One sees reflected in the British documents only the banalities of Petersburg court gossip, as relayed by a bored and skeptical British embassy in that city, and numerous evidences of the almost contemptuous cynicism with which the Russians were treated in the chitchat of the royal salons and the great country houses of England:—bounders, all of them, these Russians, you were usually allowed to infer: always up to their old tricks, never to be trusted, but of course seen through, brilliantly and effortlessly, by whoever happened to be doing the talking.

It was no doubt a consequence of precisely this cynical rejection of communication that each of the two powers overrated, regularly and egregiously (as great military antagonists are so quick to do), both the hostile intentions and the military-political capabilities of the other party. The Russians had visions of the British raising a great army in India, crossing the Pamirs, overrunning Afghanistan, and invading Russian central Asia on a grand scale. The British (and particularly the vice-regal authority in India) entertained the mirror image of these anxieties, picturing the Russians as moving, with similarly massive and irresistible forces, in the other direction. Neither power, of course, had capabilities remotely justifying such apprehensions.

The same lack of realism appeared in the mutual fears relating to the Turkish Straits and the Mediterranean. In 1871 the Russians, taking advantage of the preoccupation of the other major powers with the Franco-Prussian War, had torn up those provisions of the Treaty of Paris of 1856 that had barred them from maintaining naval forces in the Black Sea; and upon the conclusion of the war with Turkey (1877–1878) they had embarked upon the construction of a sizable naval force in that body of water. By the early 1890s they had launched, there, four large armored vessels and a number of gunboats, three of the capital ships having been completed and commissioned in 1889. These craft were, however, still inhibited, by the remaining provisions of the early multilateral treaties governing the regime of the Straits, from passing through those bodies of water and emerging into the Aegean and Mediterranean.

The British were haunted, particularly in the years of the 1890s, by the fear that the Russians might either force the Straits with these vessels or dragoon the Sultan into acquiescing in their passage; after which the Russian ships would emerge into the Mediterranean and associate themselves with the French navy, thereby overshadowing the British Mediterranean force and establishing a Franco-Russian naval supremacy in that sea.

These anxieties were given fresh stimulus in the spring of 1891 when the Turks detained from passage through the Straits two vessels of the Russian "volunteer fleet"—a body of what were nominally commercial vessels but were actually naval auxiliary craft, used primarily (the Trans-Siberian Railway having not yet been built) for transporting men and supplies from Odessa to the Russian forces in the Far East. The incident, as it happened, was peacefully settled; and some months later it became known that the Sultan had issued a decree, satisfactory to the Russians, laying down the conditions under which such vessels might regularly be granted passage. There was no more to it than this; but the whole episode, and particularly the secrecy with which it was treated by both Russians and Turks, set British suspicions once again aquiver. They were not soon to be allayed.

The Russians, on the other hand, entertained the corresponding fears that the British, whose squadron often cruised in the Aegean and sometimes (to impress the Sultan) even held maneuvers in the vicinity of the Dardanelles, would someday force the Straits, destroy the Russian Black Sea fleet, and establish British power at Constantinople.

Actually, both powers were dealing here with a danger that, to the extent that it had any reality at all, was a fading one. The British interest in the Straits, long established as it was and deeply as it had entered into the habitual assumptions and calculations of the European statesmen of that day, was actually beginning to wane as a consequence of the construction of the Suez Canal and the dominant British position in Egypt— factors that, in combination, provided for England a new and more convenient access to southern Asia than anything free access to the Black Sea could have provided.

And the Russian interest in the Straits, too, was no longer quite what it had been in the years before the Turkish war. As the Tsar gradually turned away in frustration, anger, and disgust from the situation in Bulgaria, so his attention became withdrawn from the problem of the Straits, to which there seemed to be no promising answer short of a war for which Russia was not ready. Beyond which, the new relationship with Germany, reinforced by the pressures of the French for a Russian military posture directed primarily against that country, unavoidably diverted official-Russian attention from the more traditional Russian aspirations at the Straits. There were, to be sure, occasional urgings from some of the more aggressive Russian military circles in favor of an attempt to force at least the Bosporus and to establish a Russian military base adjacent to its Black Sea entrance; but these pressures, to the realization of which the French would have violently objected, were successfully resisted by those others, like Obruchev, whose dreams ran to the defeat, in the first instance, of Austria and Germany, and not Turkey. Thus Russian interests at the Straits tended with the years to become increasingly defensive. In January 1882 Giers was able, by agreement with Ribot, to instruct the Russian ambassador at Constantinople, Nelidov, confidentially, that Russia had no aggressive intentions with relation to Turkey and no intentions of encroaching on the integrity of that empire. Her aims in that part of the world, Giers wrote, were only to preserve intact the provisions of the Treaty of Berlin, to maintain the status quo, and to prevent others (read: England and the Triplice) from exercising undue pressure upon the Sultan.

It was, actually, not only the British but also, even more so, the Germans who at this time were affected by the illusion that the Russians were determined to establish themselves at Constantinople and to emerge as a major naval power in the Mediterranean. Holstein and his friends in the German foreign office and diplomatic service were keenly sensitive to this possibility, and saw Germany's interests being vitally threatened by it. The reason for this lay in their anxieties about the position of Italy. They had taken a heavy responsibility upon themselves in preventing the renewal of the Reinsurance Treaty with Russia in 1890. They knew that the soundness of this move rested on the continued intactness of the Triple Alliance; for if that grouping were to break up, Germany, her tie to Russia now destroyed, would face nothing but isolation. They recognized, too, that the weakest link in the Triple Alliance was of course Italy, fragile as she was militarily and politically. They had good reason for this anxiety. The Italian statesmen were never wholly impervious to the reflection that rapprochement with France, if it could be achieved, might yield greater security and prosperity than the tie to Austria and Germany ever could. And it seemed to the Germans that the decisive factor in determining Italy's ultimate orientation, as the years went by, would be Great Britain. If Italy felt protected (and this meant: protected against France) by the British navy, she would probably remain faithful to the Triple Alliance. If, on the other hand, this protection seemed uncertain or insufficient, she might well be moved to seek security in a change of alliances.

It was at this point that the question of the Straits came in. So long as the Russian Black Sea fleet was unable to come out into the Mediterranean, the British navy, notwithstanding the rapid development of French sea power, might be expected, as the Germans saw it, to maintain its supremacy in that body of water and thus to assure the fidelity of the Italians to the Triplice. Should the French fleet be reinforced, however, by the Russian one, then naval supremacy might well pass—or so it was thought in Berlin—to the combined Franco-Russian force; and the Italians might then be frightened into abandoning the alliance.

Moved by this reasoning, the Germans kept up a steady drumfire of pressures on the British throughout the early 1890s, urging them to strengthen their own naval presence in the Mediterranean and to bring their influence to bear upon the Sultan with a view to stiffening his resistance to what were fancied to be intense Russian pressures on him to sanction the release of the Russian fleet.

These fears, too, were greatly exaggerated. The Russians had been the first to insist on the *European* character of the closure of the Straits (meaning that the agreements barring passage of warships through the Straits in peacetime could not be set aside except by agreement among *all* the European powers). Much more defensively minded than the Germans were willing to believe, the Russians had no thought of pressing the Sultan to make a unilateral decision permitting passage of their ships; for this would have established the precedent for a possible similar concession to the British. Nor would the vessels of the Russian Black Sea fleet, equipped as they were only for short-range cruising and untrained in long-range deep-sea operations, have added greatly to the strength of the forces arrayed against the British in the Mediterranean. But of all this, the Germans, inspired by the lively imaginations of their military and naval planners, were not to be persuaded; and the result was that literally hundreds of pages of the *Grosse Politik der europäischen Kabinette* are taken up with accounts of the efforts of the German ambassador in London to press the British along the lines just described—efforts that, it must be added, were not particularly welcome at the London end, and to which the responses of Lord Salisbury and his successors were decidedly tepid.

The French could not, of course, fail to pick up something of all these agitations and to reciprocate them with equally unreal anxieties of their own. The help of the Russian ambassadors at Paris and Constantinople having first been enlisted, efforts were put in hand in 1892 to persuade the Russian government to send a group of ships, presumably from its Baltic resources, to the Mediterranean to form a permanent Russian naval presence in that body of water and to operate jointly with their French counterparts there. Giers, sensing serious political dangers in any such procedure and highly annoyed at the obvious effort to bypass him in the realization of the scheme, successfully opposed it for a time; but after the visit of the Russian fleet to Toulon in the autumn of 1893, the Russians found themselves unexpectedly under obligation to the French naval authorities,* the result being that to please the French a small group of Russian vessels was diverted from the Baltic fleet and detailed for a time to service (but only occasional service) in the Mediterranean. With that the whole excitement seems to have died in a lingering death. There is no evidence that the collaboration of the French navy with these visiting Russian vessels ever achieved any great operational significance.

One cannot leave this subject of the rivalry at Constantinople without mentioning the question of Russian relations with the other Balkan countries; for these loomed large in the eyes of both the Tsar and Giers.

Here, the neuralgic point was, of course, Bulgaria. To the bitter disappointment and frustration experienced by Alexander III during the

---

*Two of the Russian ships, while en route to Toulon as part of the Russian squadron visiting that port in 1893 (see below, chap. 13), collided, unaccountably, at sea. The French went to great lengths to suppress press coverage of the incident, to help the Russians conceal the damage, and to repair the most seriously damaged of the two ships.

reign of Alexander von Battenberg in that country, the final cup of gall was added when, in 1887, the Bulgarian regents elected, as Battenberg's successor, the Roman Catholic Prince Ferdinand of Saxe-Coburg-Gotha. Ferdinand would in any case not have been the Tsar's choice, had the latter been consulted. But for the fact that he was not consulted, he had actually only himself to blame. When the Bulgarians, in 1887, tried to dispatch to Petersburg—before dispatching it to any of the other capitals —a delegation to inquire his opinion and to get his suggestion for a successor to Battenberg, Alexander III declined even to permit it to come. This, however, did not reconcile him to the fact that it then went ahead and chose a new prince without his involvement. On the contrary, he never forgave what he regarded as this slight, and never consented to recognize the legitimacy of Ferdinand's election or to permit any sort of official Russian representation in Sofia. The Sultan, too, out of respect for Russian feelings, also declined to acknowledge the legitimacy of the election, although he was personally well inclined towards Ferdinand.

The French continued, to be sure, to maintain low-level representation in Sofia for consular matters, but otherwise they followed the Russian line. This was easy for them, partly because Bulgaria did not mean much to them, partly because there was, at the end of 1891, an incident involving a French journalist in Sofia that led to a sharp conflict between Paris and Sofia. Thus the French may be said to have given to the Russians in Bulgaria the same sort of perfunctory and minimal support they received from the Russian government in Egypt.

The Germans, still under the spell of Bismarck's furious determination not to permit Germany to be dragged into any involvement with Bulgarian matters, and also reluctant to give unnecessary offense to the Tsar, similarly declined to recognize the legitimacy of Ferdinand's election, made it clear that no German princess would be permitted to marry him, and even (January 1893) rather rudely asked him to leave Bavaria when it was thought that he was looking for a bride there. It was only in London and in Vienna (where Ferdinand was twice received in audience by Emperor Franz Joseph) that benevolence was shown to him; and even there one hesitated to recognize the legitimacy of his occupancy of the Bulgarian throne so long as the Sultan, as the sovereign authority (for Bulgaria was still in theory a Turkish province), was unwilling to recognize it.

In these circumstances, very few Europeans were initially willing to concede to Ferdinand any favorable chances for retaining the Bulgarian throne. But all of them, as it turned out, were underrating him. Behind a socially engaging but otherwise not immediately impressive personality there were concealed very unusual reserves of shrewdness, patience, persistence, and, where needed, of the capacity for dissimulation and ruthless severity—so much so that it may fairly be said that Ferdinand, the grandson of a King of France, deserved a loftier throne than that of Bulgaria. Over the years to which this study is addressed, he wisely bided his time so far as the international recognition of the legitimacy of his position was concerned; but proceeded steadily to consolidate that position and to gain respect in all those capitals—in all, that is, except Petersburg and Berlin —where he was civilly received. While generally relying on persuasion and on the judicious use of money to gain his objective, he did not shrink from the resort to brutality where no alternative seemed available. In 1890 he allowed the Russian protégé, Panitsa, to be executed for subversive activity. And in what was, for him, the eventful year of 1893, he not only succeeded in wresting from the Bulgarian parliament (to the surprise of all Europe) a constitutional amendment permitting him to raise in the Roman Catholic faith any progeny he might have, but then married a Catholic princess (of the house of Bourbon-Parma),* fathered a son and heir, and, finally, deposed his high-powered prime minister, the brutal Stambulov (of whom he was commonly thought to be the puppet), and then disembarrassed himself permanently of that dignitary by measures that, for slyness and ruthlessness, were worthy of the greatest talents of the victim himself.

Thus while Alexander III persisted in his violent opposition to the situation in Bulgaria and indeed based his whole Balkan policy on this one issue, the support for his position was (largely unbeknownst to him) steadily being undermined both in Bulgaria and elsewhere. There was increasing impatience in the other European capitals, and even in Petersburg, as the years went on, with the emotionalism and lack of realism in the Tsar's attitude, which served only to paralyze and immobilize Russian policy in that entire part of the world—so much so that after Alexander's death, in 1894, it was only a year or two before the whole house of cards collapsed and Ferdinand was able to appear triumphantly in Petersburg as the honored guest of Alexander's son. So futile can sometimes be, in international politics, the emotional *entêtements* of aging and opinionated rulers!

Russia's Balkan position over these years of the early 1890s was somewhat eased, to be sure, by contrary developments in Serbia—but only

---

*The Princess was the sister of the future Empress Zita, wife of the last Hapsburg emperor.

somewhat. The abdication of the strongly pro-Austrian King Milan in 1889 had consigned the royal prerogative in Belgrade to the pro-Russian Queen, who, with her thirteen-year-old son, exercised it until 1893 in confused interaction with a body of regents and a flock of squabbling Serbian politicians. The Russians were somewhat encouraged by this, but only with many misgivings; for the politics of Belgrade, in contrast to those of Bulgaria, were an unstable soil on which to found any sort of relationship. Things were better than before, from Petersburg's stand-point—but not *much* better. And to the extent that possibilities for a more active policy might here have presented themselves, Giers' illness, together with the frozen quality of Russia's relations with both Vienna and Sofia, ruled out any imaginative exploitation of them.

Russia's Balkan policy, once so active and so central to all her other concerns, remained, then, over all these years inactive and sterile—a situation that suited the French excellently, since the last thing they wanted was to see Russia again actively engaged in that part of the world. This presumably favored the conclusion of the Alliance. But it repre-sented a certain temporary abnormality in the general pattern of Russian policy. The Balkans were too intimately related to Russia, geographically and otherwise, to be for long the objects of such neglect. And the French might have done well to give greater heed to this reality; for the day would come when it would prove to be of determining importance for the functioning of the Alliance.

. . .

There was one other area of Russian policy where, during the lifetime of Alexander III, the clouds were scarcely larger than a man's hand but where they were destined to grow, almost from the day of his death, with great and fateful rapidity. This was the Far East. Separated from Euro-pean Russia, up to the final decade of the nineteenth century, by months of painful, laborious travel by horse-drawn vehicle—sleigh, carriage, or cart—and otherwise accessible only by fully as many months of travel by sea around the coasts of Europe and Asia (sometimes even Africa as well), the Far East had always had a subordinate place in Russian policy. This situation was symbolized, and initially reinforced, by the sale of Alaska and the attendant liquidation of Russian interests in western North America.

But in the 1870s and 1880s a whole series of factors, including the rapid transformation of Japan into a modern industrial country and the activation of Japanese policy towards the Asiatic mainland—not to men-tion the opening up of Korea to Japanese, European, and American penetration—drew Petersburg's attention to the Far East; and the flowering of the railway age, not least in Russia itself, could not fail to stimulate thoughts of the projection of a railway line across the vast expanses of Siberia.

In the final years of the 1880s this idea was the subject of much discussion in Petersburg; and by the middle of 1890 the decision had been taken, informally and on principle, to proceed with the project. French financial and entrepreneurial circles, hearing of this, became interested in involving themselves in the enterprise; and in 1891 two French senators even went to Petersburg with the thought of promoting such a participation and were received by the Tsar. But Alexander's decision was that the great task should be carried out with Russia's own resources, both financially and technologically; and so it was done.

The return to Russian soil at Vladivostok of the heir apparent, Prince Nicholas, at the conclusion of his journey around Asia in the winter and spring of 1891, was taken as the occasion for the issuance, on May 27th of that year, of an imperial ukaz authorizing inauguration of the construction of the Siberian railway; and a little over a year later, on July the 19th, 1892, the building of the first section—from Chelyabinsk, in the Urals, to Omsk, on the Irtysh River—was put in hand. The remainder of the line, to the border of Chinese Manchuria and again from the eastern border of that territory to Vladivostok, would be under construction throughout the remaining years of the century.

The military section of the French embassy at Petersburg was not slow to recognize the dangers of this undertaking from the standpoint of French expectations in connection with the desired alliance. In a dispatch of November the 6th, 1890, Colonel Moulin, then assistant military attaché in that embassy and the leading French military expert on Russia, expressed his regret at seeing the Russian government launch itself into this undertaking, which, he wrote,

> will swallow up an immense amount of capital without any serious commercial or financial returns, and this in response to no immediate need, and without any justification for it in China's policy toward Russia. The "Chinese peril" has recently been much exaggerated by those who have an interest in the construction of the Trans-Siberian.*

---

*In French: Moulin regretted to see the Russian government "s'engager" in this undertaking, "qui engloutera des capitaux immenses, sans compensations commerciales et financières sérieuses, et sans que la politique de la Chine vis-à-vis de la Russie en réclame la nécessité, ou l'utilité immédiate. Le 'Péril Chinois' a été fort exagéré ici dans les derniers temps par les gens qui ont intérêt à la construction du Transsibérien."

He wished, he wrote, that the Russians had thought less about this and more about the building of strategic lines in the West. A couple of years of effort in *that* direction, in order to give them assurance that they could stand up to the Germans, and they could then safely address themselves to the "Chinese peril."

An interesting statement—this, showing clearly how quick these French military people were to see only the military-political aspect of any such great undertaking, and how blind they were to the economic and social implications of the opening up of the vast Siberian territory. Nevertheless, Moulin's statement was prophetic; for the diversion of Russian resources and attention that the construction of the railway represented was one that, only fifteen years later, would find its denouement in the Russian-Japanese war—a disaster from which the value of Russia, as an alliance partner for France, was never fully to recover.

. . .

One sees, in reviewing these ulterior preoccupations of the two powers, that for the French they added little and detracted little from the motivation impelling them towards the alliance. For them, the expunging of the humiliation of 1871 and the recovery of the two lost provinces were fully as much matters of the future as they were of the past.

For the Russians it was not quite that way. In the case of the military, to be sure, the single-minded preoccupation with the purely military prospects of a war assumed to be inevitable was, particularly since it generally ignored political values, little affected by changes in the real world around them. And foreign policy, which should have been sensitive to those changes, remained, unfortunately, in the hands of two men little able to recognize them: Giers and the Tsar—the one old, seriously ill, and quite unfit physically for the responsibilities he was now bearing; the other, also in a state of slow physical and mental deterioration, his judgment affected by his extreme social isolation and violent emotional prejudices. Both men were still living, intellectually, in the Bismarckian period. Alexander's desire for the alliance and Giers' resistance to it were both the products of their continued preoccupation with the concepts and assumptions of the 1880s. Insensitive to the impulses of the new world now rising around them, they pursued, in the most extreme isolation and secrecy, a project rooted in a world that was rapidly ceasing to exist. Only this secrecy could have preserved their deliberations from the salutary discipline that any extensive exposure to the emerging realities would have brought to bear upon them.

Chapter 9

THE MILITARY
CONVENTION I

The Tsar and Giers, as we have seen, both left Petersburg at the end of August 1891, at the conclusion of the various maneuvers and other excitements of that month, and it was the end of November before either of them returned.

On the Tsar's part, the intervening time had been spent first, through September and October, in Denmark—thereafter, in the Crimea. Aside from Freycinet's secret approach through Hansen, the monarch's activities in Denmark were devoid of political significance—with one exception, which was the necessity of deciding whether he should, on the return from his Danish visit, pass through Berlin and render a return visit to the Kaiser, as normal considerations of protocol would have required him to do. His decision was negative: he and his party would proceed directly, in his yacht, to Danzig. He was able to cite, within his intimate circle, serious reasons for this choice; but it is clear that the decision was one that coincided with his strongest emotional inclinations. He would have been, as he later confessed to Giers, unable to bring himself to confront the Kaiser with *"un visage composé."* He was too greatly exasperated with the Germans *"pour pouvoir faire des politesses à l'Empereur."*[1]

Unfortunately, however, the fact that he *was* faced with this decision became apparent to the press long before the event, with the result that there was much public speculation as to which way the decision would go. This naturally put the Kaiser into an awkward and humiliating position, which he did not fail to resent; and although the Tsar would eventually acquit himself of his *protocolaire* obligation by paying, the following year, a brief and perfunctory visit to the Kaiser at Kiel, this episode of the autumn of 1891 put an end to whatever possibilities for personal confidence and useful communication might by then have remained to the two crowned heads.

As for Giers: after nursing his health at Wiesbaden, where the attentions of a certain Dr. Metzger did (at least momentarily) very well by him, he entered, before returning to Russia, on a small diplomatic *tournée,* partly to get the feel of European diplomatic affairs once again after his recent illness and vacation, but also to steady down any alarmist or extreme reactions in official opinion that might have been caused by the dramatic circumstances of the Cronstadt visit.

His first stop was at Rome, where he assured King Umberto that the Franco-Russian rapprochement was solely a reaction to the renewal of the Triplice. He then proceeded to Paris, where he had talks on two successive days with Ribot, Freycinet joining them on the second of those occasions.[2]

The first of these Paris talks—a courtesy call on Ribot—was brief. Giers gave it as his conviction and that of the Tsar that no early aggressive action was to be feared from the German side. This, he said, was what made them feel that, for the moment at least, the recent exchange of letters (of August 27) sufficed. But this did not preclude an examination, at leisure, of what further steps might usefully be taken at some future point.

There was a formal dinner for Giers that evening, tendered by President Sadi Carnot and attended by most of the French cabinet. The next day the two foreign ministers met again, for more serious and detailed discussions. The talk first turned on their respective interests and policies in the eastern Mediterranean and in Bulgaria. It was agreed that they must concert their policies in that region, and that for this reason they would try to arrange for identical instructions to be sent to their respective ambassadors in Constantinople, particularly with respect to the Egyptian question. As for Bulgaria: since the French had been having serious differences of their own with the Bulgarian government over the treatment of a French correspondent in Sofia, they found no difficulty in assuring the Russians of their support for the continued Russian rejection of Prince Ferdinand's regime, a disposition bound to commend itself mightily to the embittered Tsar.

Freycinet having joined them at this point, the question of Franco-Russian relations then finally came up for discussion.

Giers introduced the subject by assuring the French that the initiative for the opening of discussions with Laboulaye on the possibility of a written agreement was his own.*

*For the reasons already given, it is the writer's opinion that it is most improbable that this was the case. It is more likely that it was agreed between the Tsar and Giers that Giers would claim this responsibility for himself in his contacts with the French, precisely in order to save the Tsar from any commitment.

Freycinet then exposed his reasons for believing that one ought to proceed at once to the negotiation of a military convention. According to the French records, Giers allowed himself to be persuaded of the need for such a convention, and agreed that it should cover the following points:

1. reassertion of the obligation of mutual assistance in the case of aggression—an obligation already implicit in the existing exchange of notes;
2. agreement to mobilize immediately if either Germany or Austria mobilized, even in the absence of a declaration of war; and
3. agreement on the measures to be taken by both sides to assure the success of any ensuing military effort.

Giers himself was to explain to the new French ambassador at Petersburg a few days later that while he had initially had "hesitations" about the need for an early military convention, these hesitations had been dissipated by the force of Freycinet's arguments.[3]

Once again, one can only be puzzled by this statement. Giers, as we have seen, had left Petersburg in September under the pleasing impression that he had been successful in persuading the Tsar that the exchange of notes with Ribot had sufficed for the moment and that there was no need for going further in the direction of a military convention. He had conveyed this position in writing to Mohrenheim. The latter had informed the French of it. There had been no subsequent opportunity for Giers to confer personally with the Tsar on this subject, or any facilities for doing so at long distance. Even if he had been persuaded to the contrary by Freycinet's arguments (which is unlikely), it would not have been normal for him to reveal this to the French on the spot, in the absence of any authorization to this effect from the Tsar. One must look elsewhere, therefore, for a plausible motive for this behavior. The official record will not help us here, but the indirect evidence may.

Giers was well aware, when leaving Russia in late September, that Mohrenheim was trying to undercut him in the matter of the military convention by inducing the French to deal exclusively with himself in their pursuit of the matter. Giers had presumably been informed through his son of Hansen's mission to Copenhagen, and of the Tsar's surprisingly encouraging response to Freycinet's inquiry. But now, here in Paris, Giers found himself obliged to talk with the French leaders in Mohrenheim's and Freycinet's presence. And it was no doubt clear to him that if, in this situation, he opposed outright the idea of a military convention, this would only play directly into Mohrenheim's hands by confirming for the French what Mohrenheim had been intimating to them all along: that the only real obstacle to progress towards a military convention was Giers, and that their best hope, therefore, was to get at the Tsar directly, through Mohrenheim and Hansen. But if they should follow that course, then Giers would run the risk of being entirely removed from the channel of communication and thus losing control of any negotiations that might ensue. Better, in these circumstances, for him to profess sympathy with Freycinet's desires and to encourage the French to work through him, even if he should later have to find reasons for delaying the talks and restricting their portent. In pursuing these tactics he could be sure of having silent allies in both Ribot and the Russian military leaders Obruchev and Vannovski. These last two, as he must have known, had no greater confidence in Mohrenheim than he himself did, and were likewise in danger of being bypassed if communications ran directly from the French through Mohrenheim.

All this suggests that Giers had good reason for pretending to be persuaded by Freycinet's arguments in favor of a military convention. Whether he really was so persuaded is another question. His subsequent conduct does not suggest that he was.

While thus acquiescing, on principle, in Freycinet's views about the need for a military convention, Giers took care to suggest that the matter might best be pursued, initially, through the new French ambassador at Petersburg, it being understood that a high French military figure would be sent, at the proper time, to assist in the discussions.

He then also gave to the French his explanations about Russian relations with Germany. He explained both the background of the Tsar's decision not to visit Berlin on his return from Denmark and the reason for his own intention to stop off there on his return from Paris.

In connection with these explanations, he is quoted in the French accounts as saying that while war with Germany might be long delayed, he did not think it could be indefinitely avoided. Whether the French correctly understood him on this point is again uncertain. If they did, the statement is a very important one. For Giers' opposite number, Ribot, held the same opinion, as his private documents reveal; and experience has shown that nothing operates more inexorably to assure that a given war will take place than the preconceived belief, on the part of responsible statesmen, that it is indeed inevitable.

It seems unlikely, given Giers' temperament and inclinations, that whatever he actually said on this subject was meant as starkly as the French understood it. The probability is that what he intended to voice, on that occasion, was no more than a resigned pessimism, flowing from an assumption—not that war *couldn't* be avoided, but that, governments being what they were, it *wouldn't* be.

. . .

Stopping off at Berlin on his way back to Petersburg, Giers had talks with Caprivi, the German chancellor (whom he had always liked and respected), and with the foreign minister, Baron Marschall. He did what he could to soothe German feelings over the political fireworks of the Cronstadt visit and over the Tsar's recent failure to visit the Kaiser when passing through Germany. And he made a particular effort to persuade the Germans of the peaceful intentions of the French statesmen with whom he had just been talking. But the Germans, while polite, were cool, noncommittal, and obviously not to be easily reassured—particularly with relation to the French. To Giers' assertion that the quest for revanche was the enthusiasm of only a small and not greatly influential minority in France, their reply was that if the French leaders were really opposed to a policy of revanche, they could have the courage to say so publicly.[4]

Despite this grumpy German response, Giers returned to Petersburg stimulated and well satisfied by this renewal of his personal diplomatic activity. He felt that he had poured oil on troubled waters, that he had corrected to some extent the overdramatic speculations aroused in Western Europe by the Cronstadt visit, and that he had succeeded in recovering firmly into his own hands the secret Franco-Russian exchanges concerning a possible military convention. His satisfaction over these achievements was heightened by the fact that rumors of the first of these successes had reached the Russian capital even prior to his return, so that he found himself being widely congratulated on what he had achieved. The *Grazhdanin*, the most reactionary of Petersburg papers and in some respects the closest to the Tsar, praised him liberally. Even the sour old Pobedonostsev, Oberprokuror of the Holy Synod and at one time a violent enemy of Giers' policies, received him kindly and paid him compliments on what he had done. Only the Tsar, to whom Giers rendered his first personal report on December the 1st, had no word of appreciation for these services. In place of it, he presented to Giers a portion of a package of pipe tobacco he had received as a gift from the Sultan. "Very kind of him," observed Giers, dryly, to the sympathetic Lamsdorf, upon returning to the foreign office. "This [pointing to the tobacco] is my Order of Saint Andrew."[5]

. . .

While Giers and the Tsar were away, in that autumn of 1891, the French had been addressing themselves to the question of a replacement for Laboulaye. The choice fell upon a senior career diplomatist of that time, the marquis (Gustave) de Montebello, then serving as ambassador at Constantinople.

Montebello (1838–1907) came of a family with a relatively short but substantial tradition of military and diplomatic service.* His father, also a diplomat, had been foreign minister in the late 1830s and had served some years later, in the time of the Tsar Alexander II, as ambassador at Petersburg. The son, Gustave, prior to assuming his post at Constantinople, had served as diplomatic secretary (and occasionally chargé d'affaires) at London, and then (1882–1886) as ambassador at Brussels.

Giers and Lamsdorf did not at first think very highly of Montebello. He was, observed Lamsdorf, "an unexceptional person, pleasant to do business with, since he is of high social status, and not an intriguer," but "quite incapable of conducting a conversation about really important matters." This impression may have been derived in part from the fact that Montebello was generally overshadowed by his wife, reputedly a woman of much wit, intelligence, and social charm. But his dispatches reveal him as an experienced and sensible diplomatic professional, encountering (as so many other diplomatists have encountered before and since) greater difficulties with his own government than with that to which he was accredited, but meeting these difficulties thoughtfully, patiently, and with that self-effacing prudence that is the true hallmark of the diplomatic profession. In time, Giers learned to appreciate his qualities.

Montebello appeared in Petersburg just at the time of Giers' return from Western Europe. He paid his obligatory *protocole* visit to the minister on the 5th of December, 1891. While serious matters were not discussed on that occasion, Giers did tell him that he would soon be

---

*Montebello's grandfather, Jean Lannes, a man of humble origin, had worked his way up in the French army, under Napoleon, to become a marshal (1804) and to have conferred upon him the title of duc de Montebello (1808). The title was inherited by his son, but was modified to that of marquis in the case of his grandson.

talking with him about the question of a military convention.*[6]

Some days later (December 10) Montebello presented his credentials to the Tsar, at Gatchina. The latter received him kindly, professed the hope of renewing the good personal relations that had existed between their respective fathers, praised the leaders of the existing French government, and expressed the hope that these latter would remain long in office. But he mystified Montebello by making no mention of the secret agreement of the preceding summer or of the outstanding questions connected therewith.[7]

Montebello, startled by this omission, went immediately to Giers, to tell him of his astonishment and disappointment. Giers labored to soothe him. The Tsar, he said, *was* like that. He was too timid to broach so delicate a subject on the first occasion. He, Giers, had reported to the monarch in detail about his talks in Paris. He had spoken with him, in particular, about (a) the measures to be taken in case of German mobilization; (b) the same in the case of a sudden German aggression; and, (c) the question of a convention detailing the technical-military points of the entente. The Tsar had considered that the first two of these points had been covered, at least implicitly, by the recent exchange of notes. As for the third, he had reiterated the suggestion that the French should send a high-ranking officer, Miribel or Boisdeffre, to Petersburg at their convenience.† He had seen, Giers reported, no reason for haste; he considered, in fact, that hasty action might even involve certain dangers.‡

Giers stressed, once again, the need for secrecy. One had to be particularly careful about this if the military were brought into the picture. The military sometimes had *"la tête un peu vive."* He and the Tsar had not revealed to the senior Russian officers the facts concerning the agreement of the preceding summer. Obruchev had once tried to draw him out about this, but he had resisted.§ Nevertheless, if the French would send

---

*One may gather from this statement that Giers had by this time already been given clearly to understand by the Tsar that the latter desired to go ahead (although with deliberation and not forcing the pace) to explore the possibilities for a military convention.

†Montebello observed, in this connection, that he had heard that the Tsar had certain personal objections to Boisdeffre. "Not at all," Giers replied. The source of this rumor had been, he said, Mohrenheim, who had been offended by certain discussions Boisdeffre had had with Obruchev in Paris. This no doubt had reference to the discussions that had actually taken place in the Dordogne.

‡The Tsar, Giers said, *"ne croyait pas qu'il y eût lieu d'y mettre une précipitation qui pourrait n'être pas sans danger."*

§The reader may recall that Obruchev had tried, in the summer, to find out what Boisdeffre knew about possible exchanges between Giers and Laboulaye. It is clear that even after the exchange of notes of August 1891, Obruchev was kept in the dark by Giers and the Tsar.

an officer in whom they had confidence, the Russians would not decline to talk with him. A plausible pretext for his presence in Petersburg could surely be found.

Giers added that he had given to Mohrenheim only a very brief account ("in a few words") of his own talk with the Tsar on this subject. The ambassador, he explained, was subject to certain *"élans de jeunesse"* that sometimes caused him to say a bit more or a bit less than the facts would warrant. (In this way the French were warned that they, too, should not take him into confidence.)

Montebello asked whether it would not be better that instead of a high French officer coming to Petersburg, a Russian one should be sent to Paris. Giers could not agree. If discussions took place in Paris, he said, it would be awkward to have them proceed behind Mohrenheim's back; but it would be still more awkward to let the ambassador be informed of them.

. . .

The French, as it turned out, would have been well advised to take a bit more seriously than they did the Tsar's intimation that he saw no reason for haste in the pursuit of these matters. He had serious reasons for this disposition.

Giers, for one thing, had surely urged him to not let himself be rushed; and this was an urging that coincided only too well with Alexander's own indolent temperament. Giers will have pointed out that the Cronstadt visit had already caused more public stir than was desirable; and he will have argued that the atmosphere should be given a chance to cool off. But beyond this, the recent exchange of notes had already provided the assurance that Russia would not be left, in a future war, to fight the Germans alone; and this, after all, was the main thing. His own recent visits to Paris and Berlin had convinced him that there was no immediate danger of war; thus there was no urgency. While he could concede that a military convention might eventually have its uses, there was no need for haste in the negotiation of it.

Another factor giving the Tsar reason for hesitation may well have been the Russian famine. As early as the previous summer reports had begun to come in of crop failures of great seriousness in a number—some seventeen, it was said—of the agrarian *gouvernements.* By early autumn it was clear that famine conditions were developing in many of these districts. In the course of the autumn, the government had been obliged to devote some 80 million rubles to famine relief. Much of this had been squandered by administrative inefficiency. More was now required. Vyshnegradski, the finance minister, was in despair. These unforeseen expenditures were draining the reserves of the state treasury. The situation had already necessitated an embargo on the export of grain, with the natural adverse repercussions on the trade balance (since grain was the principal export item) and on the rate of the ruble. Beyond that, it had become necessary for the government to commandeer much of the operation of the strategic railways in the western districts for the movement of grain and other foods to the famine-stricken *gouvernements,* thus limiting, at least for a time, the facilities available for potential military mobilization in that sensitive area of deployment.

Alexander III, yielding to the characteristic disinclination of Russian rulers of all ages to admit the existence of any sort of catastrophe (even a natural one) within the Russian realm, tended to deny that there was any such thing as a famine. "There are no famine sufferers," he observed crossly to some officers who came to him offering to give up their annual regimental dinner in order to devote the funds to famine relief. "There are merely regions that are suffering from a poor harvest."[8] He continued, to the end, to make light of the crisis.

But the reports brought to him by the ministers of finance and the interior immediately upon his return from the Crimea, at the end of November 1891, were such that he must have been well aware of the existence of a serious situation in the respective provinces, and must have been equally well aware that the costs of famine relief were placing a heavy strain on the budget and making it difficult to adhere to the demanding schedule of military expenditures.

These adverse effects of the famine on the state financing were heightened, just at that time, by another serious reverse in the program of Russian foreign borrowing. We have already had occasion to note the shock produced, and the strain imposed on Russian credit, by the sudden withdrawal of the Rothschilds, in May 1891, from the major loan transaction (450 million rubles, at 3 percent) that had been under negotiation between them and the Russians. In the wake of those events, during the course of the following summer, the Hoskier-Paribas group stepped unwisely into the resulting vacuum and organized a consortium (in which the Rothschilds were not included) that launched, on October the 15th, 1891, a Russian 3 percent bond issue—an outright loan, this time, not a conversion. In doing this, the bankers were evidently counting on the hysterical popular pro-Russian enthusiasms of the recent Cronstadt period to assure the success of the venture, although it was clear that the actual interest rate (the bonds were to sell initially at a price of 79.75 percent of par, which would have yielded only 3.75 percent to the investor) would scarcely be competitive. The issue, in the amount of 500 million francs (125 million rubles), was oversubscribed in advance; but this must have been by people whose motives were primarily speculative, for when the issue was launched, on October the 15th, the market for the new bonds at once began to collapse. Within a few days the prices had fallen to a point that threatened not only the success of the issue itself but the market for Russian securities throughout Europe generally. In order to prevent a complete panic, the Russian treasury was forced to move in and to buy back approximately two-thirds of the entire issue. Not only did this materially diminish what the treasury was able to derive from the loan itself, but Vyshnegradski was forced to sell off several tens of million francs' worth of other Russian assets abroad to make possible these repurchases. In the face of this fiasco, all further large-scale Russian borrowing abroad was precluded for what appeared to be an indefinite time to come. (It would in fact be another two years before another major Russian loan could be floated in France.)

When Giers and the Tsar returned (at the end of November 1891) from their respective long absences from the Russian capital, Vyshnegradski had just succeeded, by herculean efforts, in stabilizing the market for Russian securities generally on the European exchanges, but only at the heavy cost we have just had occasion to note. Coming on top of the famine and the forced suspension of grain exports, this disaster constituted a heavy blow to Russia's public finance and brought great anxiety and dismay to her minister of finance.*

How much this series of reverses affected Alexander III and what effect it may have had on his attitude towards the French desire to get on with the negotiation of a military convention is difficult to say. It was not his habit to take very seriously the financial difficulties reported to him by his minister of finance. When the latter had tried to persuade him, in the preceding summer, to visit Berlin, pointing out that Russia, in the face

---

*Poor Vyshnegradski, who had strongly opposed the anti-Semitic measures that had played so large a part in the withdrawal of the Rothschilds from their loan project in the spring of the year, was never to recover from the combination of these two blows. He was an able man, who had worked valiantly and successfully, ever since 1886, to restore Russia's shattered finances. He now saw his plans ruined and felt wholly disavowed by the Tsar. His health broke down in the ensuing winter; and in August 1892 he was replaced by Witte.

of her various financial difficulties, might have real need for a renewal of her erstwhile close financial and commercial relations with Germany, the Tsar had swept this argument aside. "Russia has lived through things worse than this, and by God's grace has nevertheless survived" had been his reaction.[9]

By the beginning of December 1891, on the other hand, he cannot have been wholly unaware of the seriousness of the internal situation. And since the official Russian instinct, in times of difficulty, is invariably to conceal as far as possible from external observation the true extent of one's troubles, he may well have experienced a vague feeling that it might be better to let the financial storm blow over a bit before involving oneself too extensively in delicate dealings with another government, especially one that might well have the effect of calling attention to one's financial embarrassment.

It was in these circumstances, then, that the French and the Russians moved into the eventful year of 1892. The Russians had agreed to talk about a military convention, and the Tsar had allowed it to be known that they would, at some convenient time, consent to receive a high French military figure for the purpose of getting on with the pertinent discussions. But, oppressed as he was with more internal difficulties than he liked to talk about, he had shown himself in no hurry to pursue the matter. This left the French, particularly Freycinet and the General Staff, in something of a quandary. These latter were, for different reasons, impatient to get on with the negotiations but were still wondering, as of the onset of the new year, just how to go about it.

How all this looked, at that point, to the only two men on the Russian side who (with the exception of the Tsar) were fully informed of the situation—namely Giers and Lamsdorf—is vividly revealed by an entry in Lamsdorf's diary for January 31/February 11, 1892. Giers had had an interview that day with the deputy minister *(upravlyayushchii delami)* of the navy, Admiral Chikachev. There had long been pressure, on the French side, for the regular stationing of a Russian naval squadron in the eastern Mediterranean. The Russians had resisted this pressure— for the very obvious reason that they simply did not have the ships. Now, however, Mohrenheim and the Russian ambassador at Constantinople, Nelidov, were again agitating the issue, advocating the idea of a joint Russian-French naval visit to Crete or to Piraeus. Telegraphic intercepts had revealed that Mohrenheim, although again devoid of authorization to do this, was pushing the proposal in his talks with the French.

Giers and Lamsdorf were both firmly opposed to the whole project. "The French," Lamsdorf observed, in the diary entry in question,

> seem to wish to make use of us with all the unceremoniousness of pushy friends. They are constantly moved by the secret purpose: to compromise us by useless and imprudent demonstrations. They are also preparing to besiege us with proposals for an agreement about joint military actions in case of attack by a third party. Once caught in their nets, we shall be betrayed and sold at the first convenient opportunity. Who can guarantee the stability of the present [French] government? Yet their successors might well wish to adopt a different policy. I have been saying to the Minister that our rapprochement with France, as an answer to the Triple Alliance, seems to me to have been successful and very clever. The Cronstadt demonstrations, our agreement [with the French] on questions of principle, and his [Giers'] journey to Paris:—this was all very well; we could not remain isolated and unprepared; it was necessary to restore at least the semblance of a balance of power in Europe. But why overdo a good thing? We need peace and quiet in view of the miseries of the famine, of the unsatisfactory state of our finances, of the uncompleted state of our armaments program, of the desperate state of our transportation system, and finally of the renewed activity in the camp of the nihilists. In order to calm things down, at least for a time, we need to repair as far as possible our relations with Germany; and the only effective way to accomplish that is by a visit by our monarch to William II.

It is clear from these observations that the French, with their desire to get on with the negotiation of a military convention, were not likely to meet with a very enthusiastic response at that time on the part of Giers or of Lamsdorf or, for that matter, of the Tsar. But their military diplomacy did, nevertheless, spring into action; and it appears to have been the Russian military leaders who, intentionally or otherwise, stimulated them to this renewed activity.

On or about Christmastime, 1891, Colonel Moulin, formerly deputy military attaché and now military attaché of the French embassy at Petersburg, had a talk with either Obruchev or one of his closest collaborators.* (Moulin, it may be noted, was a protégé, confidant, and close collaborator of Boisdeffre. A man of long Petersburg experience, aided by a recently acquired Russian wife, he had excellent connections in the Russian capital.) What this Russian interlocutor had to say was good news. For the Russian described to him certain plans for strengthening

---

*Moulin referred to his opposite number, in this report, as a collaborator of Obruchev. It may, of course, have been Obruchev himself. A more likely possibility is that it was General Dragomirov, then commanding officer at Kiev, an old friend of Obruchev.

the Russian garrisons in the western districts and went on to mention one feature of these plans that, as both parties recognized, was of particular interest to the French. It was the strengthening of the northernmost of the major Russian forces in that area, the force based on the region of Vilno-Bialystok. It was now, this interlocutor said, the Russian intention that in the case of war with Germany these forces would not remain on the defensive, as previously planned, but would at once take the offensive against the German forces in East Prussia. This did not mean, it was explained, that the general plan of directing the initial major blow against Austria rather than Germany had been abandoned. The Russian high command still considered that it would be impossible to employ in offensive operations against Germany the main body of the Russian army, stationed in and around Warsaw, while leaving the Austrian army intact on its southern flank. The Austrians, therefore, would have to be tended to first. But it was now envisaged (and it was this that was new) that the Vilno-Bialystok force would adopt something more than a passive and defensive stance, as had previously been envisaged, in the first stages of a war with Germany. This was, from the French standpoint, significantly encouraging; and Moulin hastened to write a report of the conversation and to submit it to Montebello.

Montebello, also impressed, sent Moulin's report along to Ribot under cover of a personal letter of the 9th of January, 1892, and drew attention particularly to the point just noted.[10] He went on, then, to say that while circumstances were not favorable at the moment for bringing up with the Tsar the question of a military convention, and while he could not tell just when the favorable moment might arise, it was important that when that moment did arise, the French should be in a position to take instantaneous advantage of it. For this reason, he thought it not too early to begin with the drafting, in Paris, of the text of such a convention, his thought being that he should have this French draft at hand, so that he could, when the favorable moment arrived, get it at once and directly into the Tsar's hands, before any of the latter's aides could see it and comment on it. The monarch would thus have opportunity to digest its contents in peace, his reactions still uninfluenced by the hesitations of any of his advisers.

This information, with the accompanying suggestion, struck a lively and responsive chord in Paris. The chief of the French General Staff, General Miribel, at once set to work, presumably with Boisdeffre's assistance, on a paper outlining the French view. The document was not, as it has sometimes been described by historians, the draft of a convention, but rather a statement of the considerations of principle upon which such a convention should be based. As completed and dispatched to Montebello on the 4th of February, the paper was highly technical and somewhat difficult to read. Montebello therefore took it and rewrote it, dispatching the revised draft back to Paris for approval. A few more modifications of language (mostly minor) were introduced at the Paris end; and on the 29th of February the final document was sent back to Petersburg, with instructions to Montebello to show it to the Tsar.[11]

The paper was addressed, as explained in its first sentence, to the contingency of a defensive war provoked by an attack by the forces of the Triple Alliance against one or both of the two powers—France and Russia. The principle on which the two powers were to proceed was that both should respond immediately, with all disposable forces, to repel such an attack. This being the case, mobilization should begin, on the part of both of them, immediately and simultaneously, and should be pursued without interruption from the very first hours of mobilization by the forces of the Triple Alliance. The aim should be to make it impossible for the enemy to gain a decisive advantage over either one of the two defending parties in the first days of the war.

It was then pointed out that the forces on both sides were numerically almost equal, the French and Russians having a small edge in actual numbers of manpower, the opponents—however—in speed of mobilization.

There followed a paragraph on the necessity of concentrating from the start on the principal opponent (Germany). For this purpose the French, it was said, would direct five-sixths of their first-line ground forces (approximately 1,300,000 men) against Germany, leaving only 360,000 to face the Italians. They hoped that the Russians would at once deploy, out of the 1,600,000 men they were supposed to have available, at least 700,000–800,000 men against Germany. These men should be concentrated as fast as possible on the German frontier "in such a way as to facilitate an advance that would permit them to make contact as quickly as possible with the German concentrations in order to deprive them from the outset of all possibility of shuttling their forces between east and west."

The paper ended with a detailing of the forces that, it was thought, each of the powers likely to be involved in such a war could be expected to put up in the initial stages of a war. The figures were as follows:

Germany:	1,550,000 men, to be in position in the frontal districts by the 14th day of mobilization.
Austria:	800,000 men, two-thirds of whom should be on the Russian border by the 16th day, the remainder sometime between the 20th and the 25th days.
Rumania:	100,000 front-line troops.
Italy:	360,000, in place by the 15th day.
France:	1,550,000, by the 14th day.
Russia:	1,600,000 men, of whom "a notable portion" were to be concentrated on the frontier in short order, the remainder as soon as possible thereafter.

So much for Miribel's paper. It will stand a word or two of comment.

The general thrust of the argument is clear: to oppose the known Russian concept of initial concentration against the Austrians, and to bind the Russians to commit the main body of their available forces, in the first days of the war, against Germany. Russia, to this end, was to concentrate 700,000–800,000 men on the German frontier and to move them at once against the opposing German concentrations.

What was demanded of the Russians, with this in mind, was a great deal. The Russian standing army, as of the end of 1890, had totaled approximately 950,000 men, including officers. Of these only about 730,-000 were in combat units, and of these only about 476,000 were stationed in the four western military districts (Vilna, Warsaw, Kiev, and Odessa) of European Russia. Figures mentioned in the French archival papers suggest that there were something on the order of a further 700,000 Russian reservists (out of a theoretical total of 1,620,000) who could be called up at once and brought into the line within the first few weeks after the outbreak of war. But the Russian facilities for moving these reservists up to the front were notoriously poor, and the French, in their paper, did not even venture to suggest a figure for the dates of their arrival.[12] It follows from this that the Russians were being asked to throw a force representing the totality of their standing garrisons in Eastern Europe, plus roughly half of the immediately available reserves, against the Germans in the first days of a war, leaving a wholly inadequate number with which to confront the some 900,000 Austrian and Rumanian forces, not to mention the manning of the enormous southern and eastern frontiers of the Russian empire. The Russians could hardly be expected to accept this without remonstrance.

. . .

Before pursuing the fate of Miribel's newly edited paper, now on its way by courier to Petersburg in the first days of March 1892, note must be taken of certain changes then occurring on the French internal-political scene by virtue of a new parliamentary crisis—changes that were not to be entirely without effect on Franco-Russian relations.

The causes of this particular crisis were trivial and too complex to warrant explication here. As so often happens in legislative bodies, a minor point of contention (in this case the proposed place on the agenda of a question involving relations between church and state) suddenly and unexpectedly disrupted the existing parliamentary majority, with the result that Freycinet found himself, on the 18th of February, obliged to give up the premiership. Another cabinet was formed two days later under the leadership of the moderate-Republican senator (former minister of public works, and later to be president of the Republic) Emile Loubet. But President Sadi Carnot, well aware that the delicate exchanges with the Russians might be unfavorably affected by too abrupt a change of faces at the French end, saw to it that even in the new cabinet Freycinet and Ribot should retain their respective portfolios of War and Foreign Affairs, so it was only the premiership that Freycinet relinquished.*

Nevertheless, the shock in Petersburg was considerable. When the news of the cabinet's fall first became known, Giers and Lamsdorf received it as yet another demonstration of the chronic instability of political conditions in France. "With whom," asked Lamsdorf, rhetorically, in his diary,

> are we now to deal? When I saw the Minister, at 10:30, he, like myself, expressed satisfaction over our recent prudence. The notes exchanged in August 1891 . . . do not compromise us; but what if we had yielded to Baron Mohrenheim's insistence and had signed a military convention in anticipation of a war with Germany, etc., etc.? "No," said Giers, "we have really done a great thing. But the Tsar doesn't realize it, and ascribes everything to himself."

*Clemenceau's paper, "La Justice," alleged that Mohrenheim had interceded on behalf of the retention of Ribot. The Austrian ambassador, Count Alexander Hoyos, confirmed this to his government, adding that Mohrenheim had also pressed for Flourens's return to the foreign ministry in the event that Ribot could not be retained. Carnot and Ribot were said to be highly displeased over this interference.[13]

The Minister is not entirely displeased with what happened in France: it will keep Mohrenheim and Nelidov from trying further to ingratiate themselves [with the Tsar], which they endeavor on every occasion to do. It will now be possible for the Tsar to convince himself how dangerous and imprudent it is to get yourself involved with countries that have no permanent government, such as present-day France.[14]

These Russian hesitations were, of course, partially relieved when the news came in that Freycinet and Ribot were to retain their ministerial positions. The French, in fact, were under the impression that this had been all that was needed and that there would now be no further anxieties on the Russian side. This, however, was not entirely true. The Tsar, rather uncharacteristically, appears to have been soon appeased. But Giers and Lamsdorf, as we shall see, continued to ponder thoughtfully the lesson of Freycinet's sudden disappearance from the premiership; and it did not encourage them to press on with the negotiation of a military convention.

The new premier, Loubet, incidentally, was a close friend of the then President, Sadi Carnot; and with his assumption of the premiership he must, like Carnot, have been initiated into all the details of the negotiations with the Russians. There is no available evidence that the Russians were ever officially informed of this fact; but they must have assumed it, knowing that it would scarcely have been possible to keep the French premier ignorant of so momentous a development of France's external commitments as the negotiation, for the first time in the history of the Third Republic, of a military alliance.

.   .   .

While all this was happening in Paris, Montebello, having received (in the first days of March) the revised and final draft of the French military memorandum, was faced with the problem: how to get it into the hands of the Tsar? It was not practicable for him to seek a private audience with the Tsar for the purpose. The Tsar did not normally grant special audiences to ambassadors. Even if he could be induced to make an exception in the present instance, the visit would almost surely become known and would give rise to undesirable speculation in the press and elsewhere.

Faced with this situation, Montebello came to the decision that it was impossible to bypass Giers; better yield to necessity and attempt to make him one's ally in the effort. So he went to see the foreign minister on Monday, the 7th of March, handed him the French document (copied out in his own hand but without signature), and asked him to lay it before the Tsar on the next convenient occasion. This Giers agreed to do.

Montebello added (probably with a view to putting a bit of pressure on the Russians) that ten days hence—on the 17th—he would himself be leaving on a visit to Paris. He would be prepared, he said, to take back to Paris whatever reaction the Tsar might have.

No sooner had Montebello left than Giers and Lamsdorf threw themselves, with great curiosity, into the perusal of the French document. Their conclusion was that the main argument of it was unlikely to be acceptable, as it stood, to the Russian military leaders. "The commitment they are demanding of us," Lamsdorf noted in his diary that evening,

> would give the French a carte blanche for adventures and for the provocation of conflicts in which it would be hard to distinguish who had really started the affair; and then we would be obliged to support them with an army of 800,000 men! The mere existence of such a commitment would place us at the mercy of the French government, which at any moment could change and could fall into the hands of fanatical radicals, who, without pangs of conscience, whether out of fear or of calculation, could sell us out to the Germans. Of course, the strategic side of this project is something only the military can judge; but its political side appears to be very dangerous. The Minister is of the same opinion. We, presumably, would destroy Germany for the benefit of the French, and they then, even in the best of circumstances, would leave us to finish things off with the Austrians and with the other Eastern powers as best we might, giving us no help at all.[15]

The decision, however, was not Giers' to make. So he took the paper along when he went, the following day, for his weekly report to the Tsar at Gatchina, and laid it, without comment, before the monarch.[16] To his surprise and consternation, the latter, even before reading it, pronounced himself firmly in favor of the principal recommendation around which the French paper was built. "We really do have to come to an agreement with the French," he said. "We must be prepared to attack the Germans at once, in order not to give them time to defeat France first and then to turn upon us. . . . We must correct the mistakes of the past and destroy Germany at the first possible moment." With Germany broken up, he argued, Austria would not dare to move.

Giers, gathering his courage in the face of this unexpected statement, put the question: "But what would we gain by helping the French to destroy Germany?"

"Why, what indeed?" replied the Tsar. "What we would gain would be that Germany, as such, would disappear. It would break up into a number of small, weak states, the way it used to be."

What Giers replied to this utterance on his master's part is not recorded. "Our monarch thinks," he later grumbled to Lamsdorf, on returning from Gatchina, "that when he has taken care of the great Germany, he will be the master of the world. He spoke such nonsense, and revealed such savage instincts, that nothing was left for me to do but to hear him patiently out."

Lamsdorf himself reflected further on the Tsar's statement when writing in his diary that evening; and he took issue squarely with the monarch's view. "Germany," he wrote, most prophetically,

> when her independence is at stake [i.e., in case of a world war], will scarcely break up. It is more probable that she will be welded together by such a struggle. One can foresee, in the case of a German defeat, the end of the [German] empire and the triumph of republican and socialist principles, but a return to the old order is unthinkable. France, in the event of her success, satisfied by the revenge she has thus achieved, will have no further use for us; and we will then be faced with the immediate neighborhood of a great hostile nation all along our extended, open border.

Returning, however, to Giers' audience with the Tsar: It was agreed that the Tsar would study the French document and let Giers have, at their next weekly meeting, his view as to what should be done about it. But Giers, before departing, took occasion to remind him of the danger of public revelation of such an agreement as the French were asking for. The French, he thought, were quite capable of revealing it if this should suit their purposes. Did one really wish, Giers asked, to place such a power in the hands of so unstable a government? It was with this parting question (which he thought had made some impression) that he left the monarch to study the French paper.

.   .   .

Giers will not have failed to consider, in pondering this interview with the Tsar, that the latter's readiness, even before reading the document,* to accept the French thesis (of the necessity of an immediate Russian attack on Germany at the very outset of a war) could only have reflected some ulterior influence brought to bear upon him since Giers

---

*Or *presumably* before reading it. One wonders, in view of Alexander's readiness to comment on it before reading the copy Giers brought to him, whether another copy had not already been got to him through other channels.

had last seen him. Someone, in other words, must have got to him with arguments very similar to those advanced in the French paper.

This appears indeed to have been the case. General Mikhail Ivanovich Dragomirov, former tutor to Alexander III in military science, close friend and colleague of Obruchev, and a man strongly anti-Austrian and anti-German in his views, had been in to see the Tsar in late February. He had claimed afterwards, in a talk with Moulin, that he had found the monarch already persuaded of the necessity, in case of war, of an immediate attack by the northern Russian army group against the German forces.[17] Giers will have wondered, as does the historian, whether it was not rather Dragomirov himself who persuaded the Tsar of this necessity, and whether Dragomirov's view did not reflect prior exchanges between French and Russian military circles of which none of the civilian figures were aware.

· · ·

However this may have been, when Giers came to Gatchina for his next weekly report, on the 15th of March, the Tsar professed to have acquainted himself with the French paper. He was agreed, he said, to the principle of simultaneous mobilization and mutual assistance in the first stages of a war. For the rest, he wanted to study the paper further, after which he wanted it sent to Obruchev for his perusal and reaction. Then, when he himself returned from a forthcoming visit to Denmark, a French officer could be sent to Petersburg to discuss the matter further with his Russian counterparts.[18] (Just when this return was envisaged is not clear; it was probably at some time in the month of June.)

Giers transmitted this information to Montebello on the 16th; and the latter left, the following day, for Paris.

· · ·

It may be worthwhile recalling to mind, before one goes on to trace the further development of the Russian commitment to go to war against the Germans, as proposed in the document just described, that there was at that time simply no political issue outstanding between Russia and Germany that could remotely have justified, or called for, a settlement by force of arms. Neither power had any territorial designs on the other. Neither had any specific objectives with relation to the other that only a successful war could be expected to achieve, unless it be the Tsar's rather wistful assumption that a defeated Germany would fall to pieces and cease to be a bother to him. And Bismarck, in his final years in office, had repeatedly warned the German military leaders not only that Germany had no designs on Russian territory but that if they got themselves into a war with Russia they would have no rational objectives and would never find a favorable place to stop.

Why, then, all this talk of war, as though the inevitability of it were generally recognized? The Russian military leaders were no doubt influenced by the assumption, already firmly established in their minds, that a war with Austria was not only desirable from their standpoint but ultimately inevitable. Germany, they reasoned, would have to be eliminated one way or another before they could hope to deal successfully with the Austrians. But in a more general sense this assumption of the inevitability of a German-Russian war, and the concentration of attention in both military establishments on the preparations for such a war, arose simply from the internal compulsions normally engendered by the cultivation of large armed forces—by the mutual anxieties, that is, which such a competition invariably arouses, and by the preoccupation of both the governments and the public with the dangers that it appears to present. So powerful are such compulsions, at all times and in all places, that the absence of any rational motives for a war, or of any constructive purpose that could be served by one, is quite lost sight of behind them. The assumption of the inevitability of a war is allowed to rest exclusively on the fact that "we" and "they" are both preparing so intensively for it. No other reason is needed for the acceptance of its necessity.

Chapter 10

THE PRELUDE TO NEGOTIATION

It was, the reader will recall, on March 16, 1892, that Giers informed the French ambassador, the marquis de Montebello, of the Tsar's reaction to the memorandum the French had submitted on the question of a military convention. The monarch had agreed in principle, Giers reported, to the main thrust of the paper. The document was now to be sent to the Russian military authorities for study and comment. This would take some time. The Tsar would be leaving a bit later in the spring to attend a family celebration in Copenhagen.* He would scarcely be able to give the matter further attention before his departure. When he returned, presumably sometime in June, the French, Giers had said, could send a senior military figure—either the chief of the General Staff, General Miribel, or his deputy, Boisdeffre—to Petersburg, to pursue the matter further.

It was with this information, which to him seemed reasonable enough, that Montebello left Petersburg on March the 19th on a trip to France, the purpose of which was to fetch his wife, who had not yet appeared on the Petersburg scene, and bring her back to Russia with him. It was this information that he must have reported orally to Ribot immediately upon his arrival.

Just what Alexander III meant when he allowed it to be said to the French that they might send an officer to Petersburg to discuss with the Russian military authorities the matters raised in their recent communication is uncertain. It seems clear that there had recently taken place a major alteration in his thinking. He now professed himself persuaded that Russian military aspirations should no longer be addressed to Austria-Hungary alone—that Germany, too, must be defeated and the new German empire broken up. But what this required, in the way of further military arrangements with France, is a question he seems not fully to have thought through. He must have known, one would suppose, that the French would take the permission to send an officer as a sign that he was ready to discuss

---

*This was the golden wedding anniversary of Dagmar's parents, the King and Queen of Denmark, which fell on May 26, 1892.

the conclusion of a full-fledged formal military alliance. But it is possible that what he had in mind was only a set of technical discussions between the two general staffs, designed to facilitate the coordination of their efforts in the event that either country seemed to be threatened with German aggression—discussions possibly leading to some sort of agreed memorandum of the conclusions and arrangements, but not to a formal international agreement, and least of all to one that would be binding upon himself, or even upon his foreign office.

He was, in any case, in no hurry to get on with the matter; and there is no evidence that this question preyed very seriously on his mind during the remainder of the spring of 1892.

. . .

One might have supposed that the concession Alexander had made, in authorizing the dispatch of a French officer, would have satisfied the responsible French statesmen, and that things might have ridden along peacefully enough over the ensuing few weeks on this understanding. As it was, the moment marked, for Montebello, the beginning of an ordeal that was to hound his life for months to come: an ordeal flowing from his uncomfortable position—caught in the middle between a great impatience at the Paris end to get on with the conclusion of a military convention, and a set of circumstances at the Russian end highly unconducive to any forcing of the pace beyond the limits of the schedule the Russians themselves had proposed.

It had been, to this point, primarily Freycinet who, by trying to bypass the patient Giers and to take his case directly to the Tsar through Mohrenheim, had attempted to force the pace. Now it was Ribot's turn to take this lead. Shaken, apparently, by the recent cabinet crisis, he was anything but confident, now, of the security and long endurance of his own position as foreign minister. He was aware that in the light of Freycinet's failure to reach the Tsar independently and of the recent change in Freycinet's position, the matter could now be carried successfully forward only through the channels of which he, Ribot—and he alone, as foreign minister—was the custodian. He was conscious, finally, of the immense political credit that could accrue to whoever could establish his name as that of the architect of the Russian alliance. Thus he was frantic to bring the convention into being during the shrinking period of his own likely tenure of office. He therefore bombarded the unfortunate Montebello, over the spring and early summer of 1892, with pleas and injunctions to expedite the matter at all costs.

Montebello, on the other hand, discovered, upon his return to Petersburg in early April, that there had occurred in his absence an event that was destined, as it happened, to complicate the Franco-Russian relationship for years to come. Giers, namely, had fallen seriously ill (March the 23rd). The full seriousness of the illness was not at first apparent. The trouble was initially diagnosed only as an erysipelas of the ear—an ailment which, however painful, could normally have been surmounted in the space of two or three weeks. But, actually, this was only the beginning. Fifty-four years of faithful governmental service, added to the normal ravages of age, had taken their toll of the strength of this venerable statesman. What was left, for the three and a half remaining years of life, was a physically helpless figure, mentally quite alert, but racked with a succession of illnesses, often and for long periods bedridden, never able to reassume the full burden of his official duties, yet never permitted, so long as Alexander III was alive, to abandon the position to which the latter had appointed him.

For Montebello this presented a dreadful situation. He could not, except on the major protocol occasions, see the Tsar. To ask for a special audience would be not only to risk a rebuff but, in case the request was granted, to invite public attention to the audience and to stimulate press speculation as to its purpose. As for the Russian military leaders: it was not normal procedure for an ambassador to deal directly with them; nor were they always themselves in easy and regular contact with the Tsar. Giers' condition was now such that he was often—in fact usually—unavailable. Yet such was the secrecy of the military negotiations that there was no one else in the Russian foreign ministry to whom Montebello was at liberty to mention the matter at all. And here, at the same time, was Ribot, veritably hounding him with demands—some pleading, some peremptory—that he get on with the negotiations.

The first of these demands came only a few days after Montebello's return to Petersburg. It was full of anxieties and questions. Rumors were circulating, Ribot wrote, that Russian-German relations were improving, and that the Russians, in the light of the failure of the recent Paris loan, were again turning to Berlin for financial assistance. Was it not true, he asked, that the Russians had entered into talks with the Germans, looking to the conclusion of a new commercial agreement to replace the one that had expired in 1890? And if so, was this not jeopardizing the negotiation of the military convention?

Much of this was nonsense; but if its unsubstantiality was evident to Ribot, this did not deter him. How could one, he asked rhetorically, remain passive in the face of such a state of affairs? Was this not dangerous? Might one not lose, in this way, the momentum of the preceding summer? Had not the time come for Montebello to go directly to the Tsar?[1]

Once again (for it was not the first time) Montebello had patiently to explain why he could not go directly to the Tsar. Would it not be better, he asked, if he, using Giers' illness as an excuse, went directly to the war minister, Vannovski, or to General Obruchev?[2]

"No," was the stern reply. He *must* see the Tsar. What if the visit did become public knowledge? What possible reason could there be to conceal the existing intimacy between France and Russia? Would such concealment not simply confirm the doubts now making themselves heard about the firmness of the relationship? People were already coming to him with curious and disturbing reports: that the Tsar had refused to receive Montebello's letters of credence—that it had been found necessary to send Flourens to Russia to get the Tsar to change his mind.[*3]

Knowing of no way to comply with Ribot's instruction, Montebello sought out Vannovski, the war minister, anyway, and told him of his plight (circa May 3). Vannovski expressed bewilderment. He reviewed once again the arrangements of which the French had been informed. Everything was moving along, so far as he could see, on schedule. The Tsar was shortly leaving for Denmark. When he returned, the French could send their officer. The Tsar did not want them to send him any earlier because he wanted to be on hand himself when the discussions took place. What more did the French want? What were they complaining of?

Montebello, though secretly agreeing, pressed Vannovski to try to arrange for him an audience with the Tsar upon the latter's return; but Vannovski came back at him with the very same arguments he himself had already used with Ribot; and the frustration was complete.

In this same conversation with Montebello, Vannovski, who had evidently recently spoken with the Tsar, gave an interesting account of the latter's words. The Emperor, according to this account, recognized the necessity of a joint Franco-Russian war effort; otherwise the adversaries might dispose of each of them separately. But the purpose of their alliance, Alexander insisted, must remain a peaceful one. Although for

---

*The source of this ridiculous rumor was presumably Flourens himself. He had indeed been in Petersburg in that spring, where he was received, albeit coolly and briefly, by the Tsar. But the purpose of this audience (which was arranged for him, incidentally, at his request, by Montebello) was merely to present to the Tsar a medal commemorating the French exposition in Moscow of 1891. This did not prevent Flourens from spreading it around Paris, after his return, that he had come back with an important personal message from Alexander III to the French President.

purely defensive purposes Russia's existing forces might suffice,[4] it would unfortunately be several years before her military preparations (for active operations against Germany) could be completed.

A fortnight later (May 23), Montebello was able to report to Paris some more encouraging news. Vannovski and Obruchev, he had learned, having studied the French paper, had submitted to the Tsar their own draft of a convention. The Tsar had now passed the whole file on to the sick Giers for his reaction. This, of course, would take a little time; but it meant, he (Montebello) thought, that things were moving along as well as could be expected.[5]

Ribot replied two days later with a letter expressing grudging pleasure over this news but continuing to press for immediate action.[6] However, before that letter reached Petersburg the Tsar had left again for Denmark; and shortly thereafter Giers moved to his Finnish dacha. There was no alternative now for the hard-pressed Montebello but to observe further patience.

. . .

The information Montebello had wired on May 23rd, to the effect that Vannovski and Obruchev had come up with the draft of a military convention, was not entirely accurate. He would have been less pleased about it had he known the whole story.

Vannovski and Obruchev (most importantly, the latter) had indeed studied the French document during the month of April and had submitted to the Tsar, at some time in early May, Obruchev's comments on it, drawn up in the form of a long and formal memorandum. In view of the importance of this document as an illustration of the thinking of the Russian General Staff on the eve of the conclusion of the military convention, a translation of it, made from the original that reposes in the Russian diplomatic archives, is included as appendix II to this study.[7] For present purposes a summary will suffice.

Obruchev's first point was that in view of the fact that the process of mobilization by the leading European powers was now normally measured "not in weeks but in days and hours," mobilization by the French and the Russians, "in the light of the inevitable approach of war," must take place simultaneously. Mobilization, Obruchev wrote, "can no longer be considered as a peaceful act; on the contrary, it represents the most decisive act of war." This meant that at the moment of mobilization, "no further diplomatic hesitation is permissible. All diplomatic decisions must be taken in advance. . . ."

The second point was that given the extreme state of military tension in which Europe then found itself, any significant limitation of an armed conflict was unlikely. Nor would such a limitation be in Russia's interest. Any localization of a conflict between Russia and her Western neighbors, or Turkey, could end as the Russo-Turkish War had ended: one of the great powers, that is, having preserved its military strength while Russia exhausted hers, would enter the active political arena at the end and would dictate the terms of peace, as Germany had done in 1878. Here, again, the diplomats were advised to resist the temptation to try, at the last moment, to localize the conflict or even to limit its effects.

Thirdly, Obruchev emphasized the advantage of a military convention over a treaty of alliance, because such a convention would not require parliamentary ratification in France. The Russians would thus have to deal only with the executive authority in France, and could avoid involvement with "the political parties, the squabbling of which is given free rein in the Parliament."

Fourthly: given agreement on the *simultaneity* of French and Russian mobilization, one had to consider what should be the *occasion* for the undertaking of it. Here, too, the Russians must guard against being suddenly left alone at the beginning of a war. If the convention did not guard against this, the Germans might suddenly make attractive offers to France with a view to persuading her to remain aloof from the struggle; and given "the extremely peace-loving disposition of the mass of the French people and the cleverness of German diplomacy," this might really work. A coalition might be formed against Russia, which would then have to defend itself from all sides. In order to preclude any such possibility, the convention must provide for simultaneous mobilization of the French and Russian armies in the case not just of an attack by Germany but of such an attack by any of the powers of the Triple Alliance. People on the diplomatic side might criticize such an obligation because it would commit Russia to go to war with Germany and Austria even in the case of an attack on France by Italy; "but only by the acceptance of such an obligation could we balance out the obligation laid upon France to mobilize and to go to war in case of an attack on us if only by Austria alone."

Obruchev's last point was a firm rejection of the desire of the French, implicit in their recently presented paper, to specify in any final document the exact number of the forces each of the parties was to put up on a given front. The Russians, Obruchev insisted, must not accept any such obligation. They had to reserve to themselves the right to employ their forces where the necessity presented itself. Too much was at stake for them to permit them to bind themselves as the French wished them to do. "In the face of the readiness of entire armed peoples to go to war, no other sort of war can be envisaged than one of the most decisive sort—a war that would determine for long into the future the relative political positions of the European powers. . . ." In the face of this situation the Russians could bind themselves only to immediate mobilization, reserving their right to direct the main thrust of their military operations "against the nearest of the powers of that [the Triple] Alliance," as they might see fit.

So much for Obruchev's paper. There are two or three points of it that will bear particular notice.

The first of these was the unhesitating acceptance of the inevitability of war and the complete absence of any indication of a desire to avoid it. On the contrary, the paper was marked, at two points, by rather arrogant injunctions to "the diplomats" to keep out of the way at the last moment, and to do nothing to try to prevent or localize the conflict, lest this mess up the plans of the military. In view of the tendency of a belief in the inevitability of war to create that very inevitability, this is a significant point.

Secondly, it is clearly apparent, from the last of Obruchev's theses, that the Russian military had by no means given up their determination to deal first with their Austrian opponents in this envisaged war, while going primarily on the defensive, at this stage of the game, against the Germans.

And finally, one must ponder the significance of the fact that in this entire document no attention whatsoever was given to the question of the objectives of the war it envisaged, any more than had been given in the exchange of notes of the previous summer. This was simply not mentioned at all. There is no evidence, in fact, that it had ever even been discussed between the two governments. It had been mentioned, very briefly, in Obruchev's talk with Boisdeffre in the summer of 1891; but the latter, after reaffirming the well-known desire of France to recover Alsace and Lorraine, had brushed off the rest with the observation: Let us defeat them first; the rest will be easy.

This omission has interesting implications.

First, it raises the question as to how two armies were to join their efforts when neither of them knew what the other was fighting for. But secondly, it raises the question as to whether either government had any very concrete idea of what, precisely, it would itself be fighting for, quite regardless of whether there was any understanding with the other party.

In this last respect, the paper marked a significant change in the European concepts of warfare generally. This was a change that was to have great significance for the approaching twentieth century. In the dynastic wars of the past, the various powers had normally fought for specific objectives: to seize or protect a given province, to guard one's overseas trade against this or that sort of harassment, to settle particular dynastic conflicts and others; and military operations had been conducted on a limited scale with a view to the achievement of these objectives.

Now, as one sees from Obruchev's paper, victory was to be either total or overwhelmingly decisive; and it was, in this sense, regarded as an objective in itself. The idea now was that you would defeat your opponent —his armies and his people—so decisively that his will would become crushed or insignificant; your will, correspondingly, would become supreme. Total war, in other words, and total victory. Then, as Boisdeffre said, the rest would be easy.

In the case of the Russians certain specific objectives had, to be sure, been suggested, at least in the privacy of their own counsels. There was the long-standing desire of the Russian military, supported no doubt by the Tsar, to expel the Austrians from the area of Galician Poland that they had acquired through the eighteenth-century partition, and to take this region in some way under Russian military-political control. And in the case of Germany, there was also the Tsar's recently conceived idea that he would like to "break up" that country. But how, to what extent, and into what fragments was it to be broken up? The situation of Germany prior to 1870 had been a highly unstable one. It could not now be restored anyway. What *status quo ante* was there, then, to be restored? One suspects that all the Tsar really had in mind was to put this upstart of a young Kaiser in his proper place. But what *was* his proper place? Did it never occur to Alexander that a breakup of Germany would probably mean the total demise of the Hohenzollern dynasty as one of the reigning houses of Europe? And suppose this were to be achieved, what would be the effects of these supposed victories on the Hapsburg dynasty in neighboring Austria? Could anyone seriously conceive that the position of *that* dynasty, weakened as it now was by the Mayerling tragedy,* would not be shaken to the core by such a series of blows, ending with a third great military defeat within the reign of a single emperor, and then, on top of that, the collapse of imperial-dynastic rule in neighboring Germany? And if the position of the Hapsburg dynasty, too, were to be shattered, what would be the consequences for the only remaining European empire, the

---

*The death by suicide of the Austrian crown prince Rudolph.

Russian—also multinational, like the Austro-Hungarian, and faced not only with the centrifugal impulses of modern romantic nationalism but with an embittered and violent revolutionary movement?

It seems incredible that these questions should not have been apparent to Alexander III. Had he not been brought up in the atmosphere of the "Three Emperors' League"? Had he not himself signed the treaty known as the "Dreikaiserbund"? And had not the Germans—the two Kaisers, and Bismarck, and Schweinitz—all tried repeatedly to impress upon him the importance of the solidarity of the three emperors from the standpoint of the survival of their respective dynasties? In Alexander's complacent acceptance of the prospect of a breakup of imperial Germany under the impact of a Franco-Russian military victory over that country, one can see the first clear evidence of that strange political blindness to the real potential sources of internal disintegration in Russia that not only affected him in the final years of his reign but were to affect so strongly his son Nicholas, and to carry both the Russian empire and its ruling dynasty to destruction twenty-five years later.

But what, then, of Obruchev himself? Unlike Alexander III, Obruchev was not complacent; he did not live isolated in a palace; he did not combine slyness with intellectual laziness. Could he not see these menacing possibilities?

The question gains interest from several circumstances. Obruchev was no ordinary general. He had no reason to love either the Romanov dynasty or Alexander III personally. He was neither a nobleman nor a courtier. He was, in the full sense of the term, a classless intellectual. His family, albeit partially military by origin, had in it a strong liberal-revolutionary streak. His brother was a revolutionary. He had himself, as we have seen, once chosen the celebrated literary-political oppositionist, Chernyshevski, as a literary collaborator—and suffered professionally for doing so. As a military figure, he had been reared in the spirit of his great patron, the former liberal war minister Dmitri Milyutin—a man often suspected of wishing to make of the Russian army a school for the education of a new generation of young Russian manpower, with a view to fitting them for effective service to the Russian state, but not necessarily for service to the autocracy as such. Not only that; Obruchev, married to a Frenchwoman and accustomed to spending his vacations in France, was closely connected with the French Republic; and there is no evidence that he took any umbrage at French republican institutions.

Obruchev was a Russian liberal nationalist of the late-nineteenth-century school. This was a school dedicated, certainly, to the advancement of the interests of the Russian state. But these interests were not necessarily identical with those of the dynasty. In fact, it may be questioned whether the two were always compatible. It was sometimes charged, during the decades to which this study is addressed, that the Russian liberal-nationalists, in pressing for a war in Europe, were actually pressing, whether consciously or otherwise, for those fundamental political and constitutional changes in Russia itself which they felt were long overdue, which they thought a war could not fail to produce, and which would mean the end of the autocracy, if not of the dynasty. Could it be, then, that Obruchev, in promoting the end of the Hohenzollern dynasty, was also consciously promoting the end of the Romanov one as well, or was at least aware that precisely this was what a war with Germany might lead to—and was indifferent to that danger? There will presumably never be an answer to this question. But it will be well to bear it in mind as the further course of this inquiry progresses.

These various questions stand as examples of the dangers that lay latent in the concepts of total war and total victory—the dangers of a war fought without preconceived objectives, fought only with the assumption that when triumphant military victory had swept away all recalcitrance from before one's eyes, one would know, in the light of one's own great virtue and wisdom, exactly what to do. It was in this primitive spirit that the great powers were to enter upon World War I. It was in the same spirit that they would fight World War II to the end.

. . .

So much, then, for the nature of the memorandum from Obruchev's pen that Vannovski transmitted to the Tsar at some time in the early half of May 1892. The Tsar returned it to him, some days later, with the statement that he would like to have Giers' reactions to the political aspects of the matter. Vannovski therefore sent the memorandum (May 19) on to Giers, who pondered it and replied (May 25) with the following letter:

Dear Pyotr Semyonovich:

Having read with attention the secret memorandum on the project for a military agreement with France, which I am returning herewith, I come to the conclusion that the proposed measures would place us in a most unfavorable position, limiting as they would the freedom of decision of His Imperial Majesty in the serious question of war and peace.

It is a question, after all, not just of mobilization as the French understand it when they speak of concentrating forces within a fourteen-day period, but of our immediately attacking two of our most powerful adversaries at the slightest indication of mobilization by the Italians along the French border! Such an obligation on our part would be at best in the highest degree premature and most disadvantageous to us in the political sense.

I shall feel in duty bound to take the first convenient opportunity to submit for His Majesty's consideration my views on this matter.

With sincere respect and devotion, your

N. Giers[8]

Giers had no opportunity, however, to submit these views to the Tsar before the latter's departure for Denmark, where he was to attend his parents-in-law's golden wedding anniversary and to enjoy another of his highly appreciated Danish vacations.

. . .

In the light of the above record, a confusing note is introduced by a passage in one of Hansen's books.[9] Hansen here alleges that at the time of the Tsar's arrival in Denmark, Freycinet, three months having transpired since his own abandonment of the premiership and no progress having been made so far as he knew,* in the matter of the Alliance, charged Hansen with writing a letter (apparently in his, Hansen's, own name) to the Tsar at Copenhagen. The letter was to be sent through the hands of Rachkovski, head of the intelligence unit in the Russian embassy at Paris and (whether or not Freycinet knew this) Hansen's secret employer. (Rachkovski, it appears, often accompanied the Tsar on his foreign travels and served on these occasions as the commander of the latter's personal security guard.) In this letter Hansen claims to have proposed (obviously on Freycinet's behalf) the dispatch to Petersburg of a senior French officer *"pour traiter directement avec le Ministre de la Guerre de Russie et le chef de l'Etat Major,"* and requested the Tsar's consent to this proposal. To this letter Hansen received, he writes, a telegraphic confirmation, dated June the 5th, that the letter had been delivered; and

---

*In the original: *"Trois mois s'étaient écoulés sans amener aucun changement."*

on the 10th, he claims, there came a *"réponse définitive et affirmative."*

What is one to make of this curious claim? It apparently had some substance; for Hansen quotes verbatim the text of Rachkovski's first telegram of the 5th. But the whole story is explicable only on the supposition that Freycinet, after his fall from the premiership, had no longer been taken entirely into confidence by Ribot on the progress of the exchanges, and had never been informed, in particular, of the Tsar's earlier-expressed agreement to the dispatch of a French officer. In any case, the episode clearly reveals that Freycinet, perhaps because he was aware that the exchanges with the Russians had now gotten out of his hands, was back at the old game of trying to establish direct contact with the Tsar whenever the latter was in Denmark, with a view to promoting direct communication between the two war ministers, over the head of the respective foreign ministries.

. . .

Two events of the first days of June, immediately following the Tsar's arrival in Denmark, drew the attention of the European press and public to the problems of Russia's relations with France and with Germany. Of these, the first was the unexpected appearance of the young Russian grand duke Konstantin Konstantinovich, nephew of Alexander III, at a great French patriotic gathering in Nancy, on the border of Lorraine. The gathering was attended by the French President, Sadi Carnot; and this unexpected appearance of a Russian grand duke, which seriously upset the protocol arrangements for the President's visit, was not at all agreeable to the latter. The incident was further dramatized by the fact that the grand duke, his identity having become known, found himself the center of a tumultuous friendly demonstration, obviously reflecting the belief of the crowds that his presence signified the association of Russia with France's aspirations for the recovery of Alsace and Lorraine.

The background of this episode is still obscure. The Russians subsequently allowed it to be understood that the Tsar had authorized the grand duke's visit; and it may of course be that Mohrenheim, using his irregular facilities for communicating with the Tsar at Copenhagen, had indeed wangled some sort of authorization. In any case, what little information is available on the subject suggests that the visit was inspired by Mohrenheim, under the influence of the indefatigable Flourens; and the German embassy had it that the grand duke, who had had no desire to make himself the center of such a demonstration, never forgave Mohrenheim for pushing him into it.[10]

The episode may have had its uses from the Russian standpoint, however, for it helped to balance out the other event referred to above. This last was a visit by the Tsar to the German Kaiser, several days later, on the occasion of some sort of naval function at Kiel. This gesture (urged on Alexander by his Danish relatives, among others) was simply a return for the visit the Kaiser had paid to Alexander at Narva, nearly two years before. It could hardly have been avoided without giving serious offense to the Germans. The visit was brief, the Tsar coming from Copenhagen by night in his yacht, spending the day with his German cousin, and leaving again in the evening for the return to Copenhagen. The two crowned heads contrived to give the impression, throughout the day, of being in animated and amicable conversation; but the Russians later made it known that no political matters had been discussed, and there is every reason to suppose that this claim was quite correct. Alexander hoped, no doubt, that this would be the last time the two of them would ever meet; and indeed it was.

. . .

A day or two after the Kiel visit, Giers and Vannovski, still in Petersburg, came together to discuss the Obruchev paper. Vannovski had received Giers' note of May the 25th, but neither had yet made his views on the paper known to the Tsar. It soon came to light in the course of their discussion that Vannovski knew nothing of the exchange of notes with the French of the preceding summer. The Tsar had never told him of it. Giers, finding it impossible to explain his position without reference to this exchange, now took the liberty of filling him in on what had transpired, and had no difficulty in persuading him of the correctness of his own position on the question of the military convention. Vannovski, after all, had never himself favored the conclusion of any written agreement with the French.

Fortified by Vannovski's agreement, Giers then wrote to the Tsar, informing the latter of what he had said to Vannovski—namely, that the earlier exchange of notes was sufficient, and that nothing more in the way of a written agreement was necessary. It would be quite in order, he wrote, that any views the Russian minister of war might have on the technical questions raised by the French memorandum should be communicated to the French government; but the Russians had no need to bind themselves by any formal convention. The agreement of the summer of 1891 had created, he considered, a "firm foundation" for whatever common military action they might wish to pursue with the French.

This letter, sent by courier to Copenhagen, was returned some days later (June 26), bearing the Tsar's handwritten notation: "I entirely share your opinion, and fully approve all that you said to the Minister of War."[11]

The only logical conclusion that can be drawn from this notation is that Alexander III still envisaged, at that particular moment, that the French officer who was to be sent to Petersburg would be coming simply for technical discussions with the Russian General Staff, from which there might emerge useful understandings among these various officers, but nothing in the way of a formal international agreement.

. . .

There is one curious feature of this communication by Giers to the Tsar that will bear mention. Giers was able on this occasion (and to his great delight, one may be sure) to cite in support of his view dispatches from the very Mohrenheim who, as we have seen, had been advocating with such enthusiam, only some months earlier, the immediate conclusion of a military convention. In a dispatch of mid-April 1892, Mohrenheim was now urging that Russia should adopt a waiting attitude with respect to any significant development of the political intimacy with France. If, he observed, the political situation should become worse, it would be better for Russia to remain uncommitted; if, on the other hand, things should improve, there would always be time to move towards a formalization of the relationship.[12] Similar warnings from Mohrenheim were forthcoming some weeks later, in May.[13]

What had produced this sudden and complete change? One possibility is, of course, that Mohrenheim's attitude was influenced by Freycinet's retirement from the premiership. But a more likely explanation is that Mohrenheim, knowing that the discussions were now proceeding through channels to which he had no access, had lost his enthusiasm for their success. Least of all did he wish to see either Giers or Obruchev, with neither of whom he was on good terms, get the credit for achieving the alliance of which he himself would have been so happy to appear as the architect.

All that, however, is speculation. What stands out from the episodes just described is that as of the onset of summer 1892, the Tsar, his ministers of war and foreign affairs, and his ambassador in Paris, were all on record as opposing the idea of concluding a binding military convention with the French at that time. It will be useful to bear this in mind as one proceeds to the examination of the events of the further weeks of that summer.

Chapter 11

THE MILITARY CONVENTION II

The officer selected by the French government to be sent to Petersburg in response to the Tsar's statement that they might "send an officer" after his return from Denmark was, not unsurprisingly, General Boisdeffre. The annual public "maneuvers" (actually, they were more in the nature of a public military show) at Tsarskoye Selo were originally scheduled to begin on the 7th of August.* Ostensibly, Boisdeffre was being sent to attend them; this was to be his cover. But the Russians suggested that he should arrive a week in advance—that is, about the 1st of August—in order that there should be time for further discussions before the maneuvers would begin.

Much to the consternation of the French, the Tsar put off his return from Denmark to mid-July. (He actually arrived in Petersburg on the 18th of that month.) Meanwhile, there was much confusion between the French and Russian governments as to what it really was that they were preparing to do. Being under the erroneous impression (gained by Montebello from his talk with Vannovski in May) that what Obruchev had presented to the Tsar was the draft of a military convention, the French assumed that all the senior Russian officials in question were fully persuaded of the need for concluding such an agreement and had already prepared a draft of the convention. Ribot even had dreams of its being negotiated and agreed upon among Giers, Vannovski, and Montebello before the Tsar's return, and of the latter's giving it his blessing in time for him, Ribot, to submit it to the French cabinet before Bastille Day (July the 14th), at which time the members of the cabinet normally dispersed for the summer *villégiatures*. [1] This scenario left no place for any involvement of the two general staffs in the negotiations—an ironic omission in view of the fact that the only man on the Russian side who professed to see any need at all for a written convention was the chief of

*They began, actually, only on the 12th.

171

the General Staff, Obruchev, and the only man on the French side who could conceivably have negotiated it was the deputy chief of the French General Staff, Boisdeffre. It also envisaged in effect a public announcement of the conclusion of the agreement at the French end; for the members of the cabinet, once informed of it, would never be able to keep their mouths shut about it. This, of course, was something to which the Tsar was violently opposed. Meanwhile Giers, whom Ribot had envisaged as the one with whom one would negotiate the convention, lay seriously ill and suffering in his Finnish dacha, a full fifty miles distant from the Russian capital, and he was strongly opposed, anyway, to the conclusion of any convention at all.

Some, though not all, of these misunderstandings were dispelled before Boisdeffre arrived (August 1) in Petersburg, but not before the unhappy Montebello had been obliged, by Ribot's needlings and instructions, to pay an uninvited visit to the ailing Giers at the latter's Finnish retreat. He had first tried to see how far he could get with the acting foreign minister, Nikolai Pavlovich Shishkin, saying that he needed to see Giers and wished to go to Finland for this purpose. When Shishkin, citing Giers' health as the reason, strongly urged against it, Montebello had even gone so far as to hint broadly at the nature of what was on his mind, voicing distress at his apparent inability to bring to a conclusion, as he described it to Shishkin, "a matter to which the agreement of the Tsar and the Minister of War had long since been given, and for the completion of which only a line and a signature from Giers were needed."*[2] Shishkin must have sensed what this was all about; but, being well aware that he had been deliberately kept in ignorance of it, he merely said that he was not informed of the matter and considered that he had no right to hear anything further about it.

So far as his own feelings were concerned, Montebello had no need to be thus dissuaded. Nothing could have been less agreeable to him than to have to invade a sick man's privacy in this way. But Ribot had left him no choice.

What was involved was many hours of travel by rail and canal boat. Being uninvited, Montebello contrived a pretext for being in the vicinity of Giers' cottage on the day in question; but the pretext was a flimsy one,

---

*This statement by Montebello shows clearly how egregious was the misunderstanding under which he and his principals were laboring. They still believed, even at this late date, that the document Obruchev had produced in May was the draft of a military convention and that the Tsar had approved it.

Charles de Freycinet, French minister of war

Alexandre Ribot in his later years

Mme. Ribot, American-born wife of Alexandre Ribot

General Raoul le Mouton de Boisdeffre

General N. N. Obruchev

The marquis (Gustave) de Montebello,
French ambassador in Russia from 1891

Antoine de Laboulaye,
French ambassador
in Russia, 1886–1891

Baron Arthur
Mohrenheim,
Russian ambassador
to France from 1884
through the early 1890s

Royal and aristocratic summer guests at the Fredensborg Palace. Of these persons at least twelve were either then reigning royalty or destined to become such. Reading from left to right, and omitting the children and the dog:

1. Prince George of Greece   2. Tsar Alexander III   3. (Behind Tsar Alexander III) the Prince of Wales   4. Prince Christian   5. King George of Greece   6. The crown princess of Greece   *7. Princess Maude and Princess Louise of England   8. Crown Prince Frederick of Denmark   9. Queen Louise of Denmark   10. Princess Ingeborg of Denmark   11. Prince Wilhelm of Denmark   12. Princess Louise of Denmark   13. Prince Valdemar of Denmark   14. Prince Karl of Denmark   15. Princess Marie (wife of Prince Valdemar)   16. Grand Duke Michael (presumably Mikhail Mikhailovich, first cousin of Alexander III)   17. The duchess of Chartres   18. Alexandra, then Princess of Wales   19. Prince Hans (presumably of Denmark)   20. Empress Dagmar   *21. Grand Dukes Yuri and Nicholas   22. The duke of Chartres   23. King Christian of Denmark   24. Princess Victoria of England

*There are two persons numbered 7 and two numbered 21

and no one was fooled. The ambassador described the experience immediately after his return in a long personal letter to Ribot.[3] It was exactly a year now, almost to the day, since his predecessor, Laboulaye, had been at the dacha; but how different now the circumstances! Laboulaye had been there by invitation, and had stayed the night. It was while pleasantly seated on the veranda, watching the passage of the occasional barge or other craft along the quiet waters of the canal, that he and Giers had pursued the first tentative feelers for a written agreement. And it was Giers who had made the opening move.

Now, it was another thing. Arriving, unannounced, at the door of the dacha, Montebello was greeted by an astounded Mme. Giers, herself also ill and en déshabillé. Giers, to whom the ambassador's presence was, of course, reported, invited him to the sickroom.

"I found him," Montebello later reported to Ribot, "prostrate in the bed where he has been for two weeks, suffering from horrible rheumatic pains that deprive him entirely of the use of his limbs. He gave the impression of a man gravely afflicted and discouraged. Tears came to his eyes as he told me of his moral and physical impotence. 'I am glad you have seen me,' he said, 'so that you can confirm that I am really ill; no one wants to believe it.' "

"The fact is," Montebello added, "he is worse off than he himself cares to recognize."

It was obviously impossible, in these circumstances, to do any serious business. Montebello was obliged to return empty-handed, exhausted by the journey, which had consumed an entire twenty-four hours. But he tried at length, in the letter reporting the journey, to reassure Ribot. The Tsar, he emphasized, regarded the exchange of notes of the preceding summer as a binding engagement, assuring that if war broke out, the Russian forces would join those of the French. What was needed now was only refinement of the technical details of common action; this, Boisdeffre would arrange. Why, then, the hurry?

To support this argument, Montebello appended to his letter a memorandum just handed to him by the military attaché, Colonel Moulin, who had been talking with Obruchev. The latter, Moulin reported, had drawn up a paper in preparation for Boisdeffre's arrival. The paper was being submitted to the Tsar that very day (July 16). In addition to stressing the need for a convention and the importance of immediate and simultaneous mobilization of the two armies, it envisaged the mobilization of 1,600,000 men on the Russian western front: 700,000, plus the standing garrisons, against each of the major prospective opponents. This went far to meet the French demands.

. . .

All would, then, have been well, so far as Montebello could see. But the very day of Montebello's visit, July 16, brought the news of another and potentially more serious complication, this time in Paris. *Le Figaro*, it seemed, had come out on Bastille Day with an article entitled "Alliance ou Flirt?" The anonymous author began by professing to see signs (this was surely in part a reflection of the Kiel meeting) of a certain rapprochement between the Russian emperor and the German and Austrian ones. In general, he then continued, it seemed that the longer one waited, the smaller became the chances for a Franco-Russian alliance. As evidences of this there were adduced a number of Russian developments: the death of Gresser;* Giers' illness; the illness of Vyshnegradski† and the fall in the rate of the ruble; the drought and its various consequences. On the French side, mention was made of parliamentary conflicts; of anarchist attentats; and of socialist agitation. The conclusion drawn from these considerations was that, desirable as an alliance might be, a flirt that led to no marital union was imprudent and not desirable at all.

The real source of this article has never been revealed. Ribot claimed he had reason to suppose that it was inspired by adversaries of the treaty. The foreign diplomats in Paris suspected Flourens.‡ However that may have been, it came as a severe shock to the Russians. They at once suspected that the French government was behind it, and that someone outside the governmental establishment—some journalist, obviously— had been let in on the secret of the negotiations. This suspicion was clearly reflected in an apparently governmentally inspired editorial in the Petersburg *Grazhdanin.* The impression did nothing, as one can imagine, to prepare a favorable reception for Boisdeffre.

*Gresser was head of the Tsar's personal palace guard. He had been considered to be strongly pro-French.

†Vyshnegradski, the finance minister, had also fallen ill during the winter of 1892, had been obliged to go off to the Crimea for treatment and convalescence, and was never to resume active exercise of his office. Highly respected in Western Europe for his professional competence, Vyshnegradski figured as the strongest opponent of the Tsar's anti-Semitic measures, so offensive to the Western bankers. His discontent with the Tsar's persistence in these measures may well have had something to do with his retirement.

‡The article was answered from the governmental side by an anonymous article in *Les Débats* (August 17, 1892) pointing out that the French government was not constitutionally bound to give information to the Parliament *in all cases* concerning the negotiation of treaties—a clear hint, for those who wished to note it, that something was up. The article was probably written by Francis Charmes, former political director at the Quai d'Orsay, and a close friend of Ribot.

The latter's scheduled departure for Petersburg being now not far off, Ribot, Freycinet, and the two generals, Miribel and Boisdeffre, came together (on or about July 27) to agree on Boisdeffre's instructions. It cannot have been an easy task. Each of the politicians had his own political future in mind. (Some days later, Boisdeffre, arguing with the Tsar over the question of secrecy, would maintain that the continuance in office of both Ribot and Freycinet would depend on their ability to claim credit for achieving the Alliance.) In addition to which, the two statesmen differed in their approach. Ribot, having gained effective operative control over the negotiations, was anxious to bring them to an early and successful conclusion and was not inclined to be sticky about the terms. Freycinet, having lost control over the negotiations and having less to gain politically from their success, was now more concerned that the record should show him as the prudent, vigilant party, protecting French interests in the face of the reckless zeal of an impetuous colleague.

The imminence of serious negotiations and the necessity of drawing up an actual draft of the convention to be used as the basis for discussion with the Russians forced the French statesmen to confront, on this occasion, the thorny question of the relationship of the two secondary partners of the Triple Alliance—Italy and Austria—to the proposed Franco-Russian agreement. If Germany were to mobilize or to initiate hostilities in some way, even if these measures appeared to flow from some German-Russian crisis and to be directed primarily against Russia, then it was clear—and on this there was no disagreement—that France would have to follow suit. Otherwise the Germans, having disposed first of the Russians, could turn their entire strength against a France now devoid of allies. But what if the mobilization against Russia should be carried out, initially, not by Germany but by Austria alone? Should France, in this situation, be obligated to mobilize against a Germany that had *not* mobilized at all, and that had, in fact, shown no disposition to attack her? The exchange of notes of the previous year had been vague on this point. It was now necessary to come to grips with it.

Freycinet insisted that France must not accept such an obligation. To do so would be to place her in the position of an aggressor vis-à-vis Germany. It could involve her in a conflict with Germany at a time when Russia, challenged on her Balkan front, was already locked into a desperate struggle with Austria and could give little aid to France. France, in other words, must reserve the right to remain aloof from any purely Austro-Russian quarrel, so long as Germany did the same.

There was a fine French logic in this view. As a matter of practical possibility, however, the other French statesmen were initially not much impressed with Freycinet's thesis. The Austrians, they thought, were unlikely to take any step so drastic as mobilization against Russia unless they had assured themselves in advance of German support. Freycinet nevertheless successfully insisted that they must at least see, as a starter, whether the Russians would not accept such a reservation. If they refused to do so, one could always reconsider.[4]

To this, the others yielded, with the result that when Boisdeffre set out for Petersburg, on July the 29th, he had in his briefcase the draft of a military convention, the first two substantive points of which were as follows:

1. In the event that the forces of the Triple Alliance or of Germany alone should come to mobilize,* France and Russia, at the first news of such a development and without the necessity for any prior consultation, will immediately and simultaneously mobilize the totality of their forces and will deploy them as close as possible to their frontiers.
2. Should France or Russia be actually attacked by the forces of the Triple Alliance or by those of Germany alone, these powers would commit against Germany the totality of their forces not absolutely indispensable for further commitment on other fronts.

These points were followed, in the French draft, by others—one of them calling upon the French to put up 1,300,000 men, and the Russians 800,000, against Germany in the first days of the war; another ruling out any separate peace; and a third obliging each party to sponsor the interests of the other "as though these were its own" in any subsequent peace settlement. This last stipulation, incidentally, was intended to mask (as is usual among military allies) a complete lack of clarity concerning the political development of an intended military victory.[5]

. . .

Boisdeffre arrived in Petersburg on Monday, the 1st of August, armed not only with this draft but with an instruction (on which Ribot

---

*The reader will note the significant omission of any language obliging the French to mobilize if the *Austrians alone* should do so. These two clauses would have been easier for the lay reader to understand if, in each case, after the words "the Triple Alliance," there had been added "including Germany." It was really this, the implied "Austria alone," not the explicit "Germany alone," to which the Russians objected.

had no doubt insisted) requiring him to report all his results to Montebello and to be guided by the latter in his talks with the Russians. The line of communication was now, with Freycinet no longer premier, firmly in the hands of Ribot and Montebello.

Boisdeffre met, that first evening, with Obruchev, and gave him orally a résumé of the main points of the French position. The result was not encouraging. Obruchev objected firmly to the phrase "or Germany alone"—to the implication, that is, that France should not be bound to mobilize if the Austrians, acting alone, mobilized against Russia. He left no hope that this would be acceptable to the Russians. Beyond this, he advised Boisdeffre not to be in a hurry to achieve results. "Certain people," he said, had suggested to the Tsar that the French were trying to force Russia's hand.* He mentioned, in this connection, the *Figaro* article, which lent a certain sustenance to this charge.

All in all, Boisdeffre came away from this first encounter saddened and uneasy. All the past problems of Franco-Russian relations seemed, at this point, to be arising once again to bedevil his mission.

The next day, Tuesday the 2nd, Boisdeffre went for his first meeting with Vannovski. This was much worse. Vannovski left it to him to bring up the subject of a convention, and, when he did bring it up, only threw cold water on it. Vannovski professed to see no reason for a written document at all. Why not leave it with a verbal understanding? He denied that the Tsar had expressed approval of the French paper presented to him in March. He intimated that the Tsar now had little interest in the whole subject. He brought up the *Figaro* article so offensive to the Russians. He pointed to the difficulties the Russians always had in dealing with unstable and insecure French governments. He declined either to discuss the draft convention Boisdeffre had brought along or to present it to the Tsar.[6]

Boisdeffre was naturally offended and disturbed by this treatment. If this was to be the minister's attitude, he said to Obruchev the following day, Obruchev could tell the Tsar that he, Boisdeffre, would ask for his recall, and that would be the end of the project of an alliance.[7]

The only explanation for this cold reception of Boisdeffre by the Russian war minister is that the latter, who had never personally favored another written agreement with the French under any circumstances, was still under the impression produced (see chap. 10) by the Tsar's notation

*This, one must suppose, was a reference to Giers and Lamsdorf—possibly also to Vannovski.

on Giers' letter, voicing disapproval of Obruchev's plans for a military convention. The same, as we shall see shortly, was also true of Giers. Neither of the two ministers appeared to have discussed the matter with the Tsar since the latter's return to Petersburg; or, if they did, Alexander did nothing at that time to correct the impression, under which they were laboring, that he was averse to another written agreement.

It was full of anxiety over this hostile reception by Vannovski that Boisdeffre went out to Peterhof, the following day (August 3), to attend the name's-day fete of the Empress. But there, to his relief and bewilderment, he was cordially and kindly received by the imperial couple. And there, too, he had opportunity to see Obruchev, who, after letting him blow off steam, advised him just to be patient. All, said Obruchev significantly, was not lost.

Thursday, August the 4th, was, for some reason, an idle day. But on Friday Boisdeffre again saw Obruchev, who suggested to him, most delicately, that it might be best if, before Boisdeffre resumed his discussions with Vannovski, he and Obruchev had further private talks. Should they come to an agreement, Boisdeffre could submit their agreed position to Vannovski as his own proposal. Vannovski would then ask Obruchev for his opinion, and Obruchev would express himself favorably.

Boisdeffre was only too delighted to follow this delicate procedure, which was designed to save Vannovski's face while permitting the other two of them to get on with an agreement. Boisdeffre and Obruchev— friends, anyway, of many years' standing—thus proceeded to meet for two days running (August 5 and 6). Minor concessions were demanded and conceded on both sides. And they agreed, in the end, on a text of a convention, with the single exception of the first article proposed by the French, with its phrase "or Germany alone." On this point Obruchev was adamant.

While all this was taking place, the Tsar, apparently feeling compunctions over the fact that Giers was being left out, summoned Giers' deputy in the foreign office, Shishkin, who had been told nothing of the whole affair, briefed him on the state of the negotiations, and asked him to pass the information on to Giers. Shishkin, virtually trembling with agitation at being thus suddenly admitted to momentous secrets, at once carried out this order, presumably by courier.

Giers was surprised and appalled. He too had comforted himself for six weeks with the impression, gained by the Tsar's notation on his letter, that his imperial master had agreed that no further written agreement, committing the two governments, was necessary or desirable. Yet here was the Tsar, obviously permitting negotiations for just such an agreement to proceed.

On Monday the 10th, greatly disturbed, but feeling it necessary that Shishkin, now that he had been taken into the Tsar's confidence, should be fully briefed, Giers sent off the following letter to Lamsdorf, the only other person in the foreign office who had knowledge of the matter:

> *My dear count:*
> M. Shishkin has communicated to me all that His Majesty instructed him to tell me about the Boisdeffre mission. Evidently, His Majesty has begun to back off from his former view, notwithstanding his complete approval of my last report to him. As far as concerns myself, I can only stand by the firm conviction that I had the honor more than once to express to him. We must not accept new obligations, and a letter by the Minister of War would have the same significance as a formal military convention.* Kindly brief M. Shishkin on all details of this matter, with which you are as well acquainted as I am, if not better. I earnestly beg you to go over the whole dossier once again with Nikolai Pavlovich. With your characteristic tact, and with that judiciousness of judgment that has always been such a help to me, ponder together with him the nature of the reply I am in duty bound to give to our Imperial Master in this serious —and more than serious—matter, which one is now attempting to deflect onto a course so crassly in conflict with the policy that has been followed from the very outset of the present reign.
> With a thousand assurances of my sincere friendship,
>
> Giers[8]

Poor Nikolai Karlovich! This was the best he could do. But it was too late. He had fallen victim to the axiom that whoever would influence the decisions of the very great at the crucial moments must contrive somehow or other to be on hand. The architects of such decisions seldom wait for the

---

*The Tsar had evidently given Shishkin the impression that the proposed agreement was to take the form of an exchange of letters between the two war ministers—an arrangement analogous to the exchange of notes between the two foreign ministers, through the agency of Mohrenheim, the previous year. When Obruchev became charged with the negotiations, the two general staffs evidently stepped into the picture in place of the war ministers.

opinion of the absent adviser, particularly when they suspect his inclinations to be adverse to their own. Two days before Giers prepared this letter (dictating it to his son because he was too ill to wield a pen), Boisdeffre had already taken to Vannovski the draft of a military convention—the same, presumably, that he and Obruchev had worked out, though represented as purely his own. Vannovski had agreed to study it.

The following day Vannovski and Boisdeffre met again, alone, over dinner. It was, this time, a different Vannovski that Boisdeffre encountered. From now on, Vannovski said, it would no longer be necessary for Boisdeffre to deal with him. Obruchev would now be in charge of the negotiations; it was with him that Boisdeffre could now communicate.

If this concession solved half the difficulty, the other half was solved the following morning, August the 10th, the day that Giers drafted his letter to Lamsdorf, when Montebello received a telegram from Ribot authorizing him to yield on the question "of Germany alone." President Sadi Carnot, Prime Minister Loubet, and he himself, had all agreed, Ribot wired, that it was unnecessary for France to reserve freedom of action for the event of an isolated, unilateral Austrian mobilization. To do so would only be to incur for France the risk of having to stand idly by while Russia locked herself into a war with Austria, and then to be faced, at a later stage, with the necessity of fighting Germany alone.

Freycinet, it was made clear, had not agreed to this concession; but Ribot professed confidence that he could be brought around in the end, if only for the sake of simplifying the discussions.

This obstacle being now removed, Boisdeffre and Obruchev had no difficulty in drawing up, that very day, a final agreed text, to be submitted to the French government through Montebello, and to the Tsar through Vannovski. Although it was to be many more months, as we shall see, before this document would receive the final and formal approval of the two governments, it was this text, which ostensibly as a supplement to the exchange of notes of 1892, was eventually (with only minor changes) to constitute the basis for what came to be known as the Franco-Russian Alliance.

The body of this agreement, as signed on August 10, 1892, by Boisdeffre and Obruchev, read (in this writer's translation from the French version sent to Paris by Boisdeffre[9]) as follows:

1. If France is attacked by Germany, or by Italy supported by Germany, Russia will employ all her available forces for an attack on Germany.

If Russia is attacked by Germany, or by Austria supported by Germany, France will employ all her available forces for an attack on Germany.

2. In case the forces of the Triple Alliance or of one of the partners of that Alliance should mobilize, France and Russia, at the first announcement of that event and without necessity for prior agreement, will immediately and simultaneously mobilize the totality of their forces and will move them as close as possible to their frontiers.

3. The available forces to be employed against Germany shall be: on the French side, 1,300,000 men; on the Russian side, 700,000–800,000 men.

These forces will enter into combat with full strength, in such a manner as to oblige Germany to fight simultaneously in both East and West.

4. The general staffs of the armies of the two countries shall concert, at every stage, their efforts to prepare and to facilitate the measures here envisaged.

They shall communicate to each other in time of peace all information that may come to their knowledge concerning the armaments of the Triple Alliance.

The ways and means of corresponding in time of war shall be studied and arranged in advance.

5. France and Russia will not conclude peace separately with the Triple Alliance.

6. This convention shall have the same duration as the Triple Alliance.

7. All the clauses numbered above shall be held rigorously secret.

The first thing to be noted about this document is the curious juxtaposition of the two first numbered clauses, and the implicit contradiction between them. Normally, one would have treated first the contingency of a hostile mobilization—then, that of an actual attack. Here, the order is reversed. But beyond that, the reader will note that the obligation on the two parties to *mobilize* their forces applies without reservation as a response to mobilization on the part of *any* of the parties to the Triple Alliance, whereas the obligation to *go to war* applies only to the contingencies of an attack on France by "Germany, or Italy, supported by Germany," or, conversely, an attack on Russia by "Germany, or Austria supported by Germany." The obligation *to go to war* was not to apply, that is, in the case of an attack launched by Italy alone or by Austria alone.

But if either Italy or Austria were to mobilize, even acting alone, Russia or France, as the case might be, was to be obligated to respond by a *general mobilization* (that is, by "the totality of their forces"). *General mobilization,* in other words, if either Italy or Austria mobilized; but resort to hostilities only if, in case the provoking attack came from either Italy or Austria, it was supported by Germany.

What sense, one must ask, did this make? It appeared to allow for the possibility that in the case of an isolated mobilization by either Italy or Austria, the respective Franco-Russian partner might carry out a general mobilization but not go to war. Yet there were no two men more firmly of the opinion that mobilization actually meant war than Obruchev and Boisdeffre. We have just had occasion to note (chap. 10) Obruchev's statement, in his memorandum for the Tsar, to the effect that "the undertaking of mobilization can no longer be considered as a peaceful act; on the contrary, it represents the most decisive act of war." And Boisdeffre would be saying to the Tsar, only a few days after signing this document:

> ". . . to mobilize is to declare war. To mobilize is to force your neighbor to do the same. . . . To permit your neighbor to mobilize a million men on your border without yourself mobilizing is to deprive yourself of every possibility of movement."[10]

In the light of these statements, one can only regard as disingenuous the curious juxtaposition of these two clauses by the authors of the agreement. Boisdeffre admitted this when he wrote, in his report to Freycinet on the negotiations: "This second article, as phrased, is not entirely in accord with Article I."

What, then, was the reason for this inconsistency? Boisdeffre gave the clue to the answer when he added the following words to the sentence just quoted: ". . . but the general [Obruchev], despite my observations, demanded *absolutely* his Article I—the one that he had most closely at heart."[11] It was, then, the Russians who insisted on it. And one can only surmise that it represented a weak, and unsuccessful, attempt to meet Giers' objection that it simply would not do for Russia to obligate herself to go to war just over some isolated fracas arising between France and Italy. Under this wording, Russia was not formally obliged, by Article I, to do this. But Article II obliged her, by implication, to do it anyway; and this, one must suppose, was enough for the generals.

Yet the question remains: Whom was this obfuscation intended to disarm? Could it really have been Giers? Obruchev knew him well. Giers was not that unobservant. One can only suppose that Obruchev had in some way or other obtained the Tsar's approval of it in advance, after convincing him that this language was adequate as a way of meeting Giers' objection.

As for the other provisions of the convention: Obruchev, as will be seen, gave way on the question of detailing the number of the forces each of the sides was to put up to confront the Germans. He even accepted, in the end, the French figures for the proposed Russian contingent. The obligation to exchange information and means of communication was new, and presumably reflected more detailed matters that had come up in the discussions between the two generals. The clause barring a separate peace merely masked, as is usually the case with great military alliances, a total lack not only of agreement but even of realistic exploration on the question of war aims and of the political development of the desired victory. Here (probably because there was a mutual awareness that this was the situation), a clause binding each of the parties to defend each other's interests at a peace conference was dropped in the final version.

· · ·

This, then, was the Boisdeffre-Obruchev military convention, as agreed upon, on August the 10th, 1892, by the two generals—the one (Obruchev) chief, the other deputy chief, of their respective general staffs.

The text of the document was at once wired to Ribot, in the special code (one may be sure) that Montebello had for this purpose.[12] Freycinet being at that moment absent from the city, it was examined by Ribot and Carnot, and also, presumably, by the new premier, Loubet. They all found it acceptable. Ribot, to be sure, was initially concerned about the difference between Articles I and II—about the obligation thereby placed upon France to mobilize if the Austrians alone did so, and thus in effect to mobilize before the Germans did. But he consoled himself with the reflection (prophetic as it turned out) that an Austrian mobilization would surely bring about a Russian one, and that in this case "neither France nor Germany would be free to remain aloof from the conflict."[13] A note explaining all this was at once dispatched by messenger to the absent Freycinet, with the proposal that Boisdeffre be authorized to sign the document, it being understood that it would not have final validity until signed by the two ministers of foreign affairs. To this Freycinet gave, or appeared to give, his agreement. And Montebello was at once instructed to proceed along this line (August 13).[14]

In Petersburg, meanwhile, things had been moving along with great rapidity. The annual maneuvers at Tsarskoye Selo were about to begin. Vannovski, Obruchev, and Boisdeffre, as well as the Tsar himself, had all moved out there to be on hand. Informed of the French government's approval, Boisdeffre and Obruchev signed the document on the 14th, in two copies, and these were handed to Vannovski the following day. One copy was given back to Boisdeffre. The other was taken by Vannovski, on the 15th, to the Tsar. The latter, after examining it, said that he approved of it *"dans son ensemble,"* but that in view of the political connotations of certain of the provisions, he wanted Giers to be consulted.

Giers, as we have seen, had already written to Lamsdorf, asking the latter to suggest the wording of the reply he might make to the message the Tsar had sent him through Shishkin. This Lamsdorf did, and at some point Giers sent off by courier his reply (it was no doubt Lamsdorf's draft) to the Tsar. He pointed out that he had not yet seen the draft of the convention, and did not know its terms. If it represented only the record of an exchange of opinions, he saw no great objection to it. But if it involved an obligation on the Russian side to take any sort of specific positive measures, that, then, would be something that would limit the Tsar's freedom of action in matters of war and peace; and this he could not approve. To accept in advance obligations not called for by the existing political situation would be "extremely dangerous, and all the more so because no one could foresee in what circumstances a war might develop."[15]

Upon receiving this communication, Alexander, to whom it was obviously seriously disturbing, responded by dispatching Obruchev all the way to Finland, to see Giers, to explain to him the rationale of the document, and to solicit his approval.

It must have been no easy thing for Obruchev to make this awkward journey, to make it just at this busy time, and to make it, in spite of his high position, secretly. All this, however, he contrived to do (one wonders by what means of transportation). He arrived at Giers' dacha on the 16th. What actually passed between the two men is not easy to determine. Obruchev obviously had very little time. He appears to have read aloud to the sick man the text of the convention. Giers, for his part, seems to have gained the impression (partly, no doubt, from what Obruchev said) that the convention was something to which the Tsar, overriding his (Giers') own contrary opinion, was already on principle committed, and that what was wanted from him (Giers) was therefore only his technical-critical comment on the language, not his general attitude towards the whole project (on which subject he had already made his views amply clear). Evidently, then, he heard Obruchev out; but there is no evidence that he actually read the document himself; and in view, no doubt, of the absence of adequate security facilities at the dacha, plus the fact that he himself was scheduled to leave two or three days later for France (where he hoped to obtain medical treatment for his illness), he declined to keep a copy of it. He simply said that before giving his final judgment on it, he wanted to have an opportunity to examine it *à tête reposée.* [16]

The following day he addressed a letter to the Tsar summarizing his reaction. Obruchev, he pointed out, had been at the dacha only a very short time. Their talk had therefore been hasty—"which is of course most inconvenient in such a serious matter." Obruchev, he wrote, had read the draft to him, pointing out the changes he had introduced. He, Giers, had found these changes well founded. But it remained his conviction that an exchange between the two general staffs was acceptable only if it did not contain any binding obligation that would limit the Tsar's freedom of action. Obruchev, he said, was in agreement about this. "He and I came to the conclusion that even if his exchange of views with General Bois-deffre was set forth in a *letter,* it must retain completely the character of a *draft.*" And if the Tsar were to express to Boisdeffre any approval of the draft, that approval must be given only in principle* and on the understanding that the clauses should be subject to further study. This, he felt, was particularly necessary from the political standpoint[17]

There is no further documentary evidence of the Tsar's reaction; but it is clear that he accepted at least Giers' insistence that the document must continue to be considered a secret and nonbinding draft, pending final approval by both governments. And this decision was in some way communicated to Boisdeffre.

. . .

The four days following Obruchev's visit to Giers in Finland were hectic ones. The first two were taken up with the military show at Tsar-skoye Selo. Then—everyone was leaving. In these circumstances, everything had to be wound up in a hurry.

---

*Alexander, annoyed with this insistent admonition on Giers' part, noted in the margin, opposite this phrase: "I personally spoke to Boisdeffre to this effect."

On the final day of the maneuvers, after the last of the troops had vacated the dusty parade ground and the last bars of martial music had died away, the Tsar received Boisdeffre in audience. The question arose of the identity of those who would be consulted, at the French end, for approval of the document. The Tsar indicated his willingness that Carnot, Ribot, and Freycinet should be included, but no one else. Boisdeffre thought it would be necessary, at some point, to consult the cabinet. The endurance in office of Ribot and Freycinet, he pointed out, might depend on their ability to claim credit for creating the Alliance. The Tsar was not to be moved. Let the cabinet know, he said, that we have an entente; but keep secret the existence of the military convention.

The Tsar then went on to say that Russia, for various reasons including the famine and the attendant cholera epidemic, needed at least two years of peace. (He obviously feared that if the existence of the military convention should become known in Western Europe before these two years were up, this might lead the Germans to launch a preventive attack, and this fear surely played a dominant part in his determination to see secrecy observed.)

Lamsdorf gained the impression, almost certainly from Moulin, that Boisdeffre left Petersburg deeply depressed, confessing to those close to him that his mission had been a total failure. "It was essential for France," Lamsdorf observed in his diary, "to gain the possibility of basing itself on a publicized agreement with Russia."[18]

Boisdeffre's own report scarcely bears out this version of his state of mind upon departure. It is true that in his final talks with Obruchev he expressed great disappointment over the Russian refusal to permit any public revelation of the conclusion of the convention, even going so far as to say that in view of all this, and of the fact that there had been no governmental ratification of the agreement, "we are right back where we were before." But from his talk with the Tsar, even though the latter seemed adamant on the question of publication, Boisdeffre seems to have come away not unduly discouraged. The French could regard the convention, he now reported to his principals in Paris, as firmly and definitely adopted. He was convinced that the Tsar, in his own mind, considered himself already fully committed. And Montebello was even more confident.[19]

On the following day (the 19th of August), Boisdeffre left for Paris, to which place he was immediately followed by Obruchev, the latter on the way to his annual vacation in the Dordogne. The Tsar, too, left very shortly for further (and more serious) maneuvers in Poland. Poor Giers, having meanwhile been transported to Petersburg, was dispatched, a few days later, in a special railway car, via Germany and Switzerland, to Aix-les-Bains.

. . .

With these exits of most of the major actors from the Petersburg scene, the drama of the creation there of the military convention came virtually to an end, at least for the year 1892. Attention now shifted to France, where, in the final days of August and the first days of September, a minor but not insignificant epilogue remained to be enacted.

Even before Boisdeffre could arrive in Paris, Carnot and Freycinet had begun to have second thoughts about some of the wording of the document. Their anxieties related particularly to Article II. Was there not, Carnot asked Ribot in a letter of August 20 (while Boisdeffre was still en route), some obscurity in the wording of that clause? Would not a limited Austrian mobilization *"du côté du Danube"* require general mobilization on the part of France and the general movement of the French army to the frontiers? "Could not some word be found to avoid, for certain eventualities, the danger of France's appearing in the role of the aggressor?

Freycinet, who had felt this uneasiness from the start, was also disturbed over Article VII, which provided that the entire content of the convention should be held rigorously secret.

Ribot, in the face of these waverings, felt obliged to wire Montebello, warning him not to press Giers for ratification until the French could get their thoughts in order.[20]

Boisdeffre arrived in Paris on the 23rd. In the ensuing days Freycinet developed his proposals for modification of the language of the proposed convention. Only two of these proposals were of any significance. He wanted it clearly stipulated, in Article II, that the French would be obliged to mobilize only if one of the members of the Triple Alliance were to effect a *general* mobilization of its forces. In other words, he wanted it made clear that if, for example, the Austrians were to take limited measures of precaution, such as the mobilization of two or three army corps, in connection with some incident arising in the Balkans, the French would not be obliged by the wording of the convention to effect a general mobilization and to advance a major portion of their ground forces to the German frontier. This was a reasonable suggestion, the meeting of which would have involved the addition of only a word or two to Article II.

Secondly, Freycinet was worried about a possible conflict between the provision in Article VII, to the effect that the convention should be held in strictest secrecy, and the letter of the French constitution, which could be held to require parliamentary approval, at some point, for any such agreement. He proposed that the clause be altered to provide simply that the agreement could not be revealed publicly without the consent of both parties.

These proposals were discussed at length among Carnot, Freycinet, Ribot, and Boisdeffre. Carnot shared Freycinet's anxieties about signing a clause that could be construed as being in conflict with the French constitution; and Ribot, one suspects, was unwilling to take the political responsibility for opposing Freycinet on these points. Ribot, judging from certain of the statements in his historical memoir concerning these negotiations, was already affected by strong doubts as to how much longer the Loubet cabinet could remain in office. He was no doubt further mindful of the fact that if and when his role in the whole affair became known to a new set of cabinet officials, he might have to defend his present conduct not only before them but, if worst came to worst, before the parliament as well.*

Carnot and Freycinet presumably had similar anxieties; and it was probably this that explained their decision to try to renew the discussions with the Russian government (for which the circumstances could not have been less auspicious), and to get the latter's consent to Freycinet's proposed alterations in the Boisdeffre-Obruchev draft. In any case, a letter was at once dispatched to Montebello, instructing him to take up these proposed amendments with Vannovski.[21] And Boisdeffre, now in Paris, was authorized to approach similarly the itinerant Obruchev, just then in France, and to try to get his support.

Obruchev was appalled and alarmed to learn what was being done. Under no circumstances, he said, must one even think of approaching Vannovski with such proposals—at least, not before the ground had been prepared. The proposed change in the clause about secrecy, in particular, was enough to cause the Tsar to back out of the entire deal. Certain of

---

*Evidence is lacking as to just what caused these anxieties on Ribot's part. At one point he even referred to the possibility of a cabinet crisis in the coming November. One is moved to wonder whether it was not concern over the developing embarrassments of the Panama Canal affair, destined to become a matter of public controversy before the month of September was out, that was weighing on his mind.

Freycinet's proposals could have been accepted, he said, had they been put forward when the document was under discussion at Petersburg; but it was now too late. Why couldn't they have let him know before?[22]

It was, as it turned out, also too late to call off Montebello; but the latter, sensing danger ahead, wisely refrained, when asking for an interview with Vannovski, from explaining what it was he wanted to see him about. Obruchev, meanwhile, had addressed a letter to Vannovski, explaining what was up and voicing his own hesitations. For reasons of security this letter was forwarded through the French courier service to Montebello, who was instructed to transmit it to Vannovski. This he did, when asking for the interview. Vannovski, who fully agreed with Obruchev's anxieties, was able to dispose of the matter by not receiving Montebello personally, but by simply acknowledging in writing the latter's communication, thanking him for transmitting Obruchev's letter, saying that he had no reply to make to Obruchev, and expressing his doubts that the Tsar would be able to occupy himself with the matter prior to his forthcoming departure from Petersburg. Thus Freycinet's proposed amendments to the draft convention were not at that time officially communicated by the French government to the Russian one. Ribot, alarmed by Obruchev's reaction, at once instructed Montebello to desist from any further effort at the Petersburg end, and authorized him to come home on leave of absence, which he had been anxious to do.

This, however, was not the end of the French effort to get the convention formally approved. The attack was now to be directed against Giers, who, already in France at Aix-les-Bains, was, at least geographically, conveniently at hand. As it happened, President Carnot was just at that time departing on an official visit to the Savoie to commemorate the centennial anniversary of the annexation of that province by France. It was therefore hastily arranged that Freycinet and Ribot should attach themselves to his party and should take advantage of the President's brief stop at Aix to visit the ailing Giers.

This was then done. On the 5th of September Giers, stretched out on a chaise longue in his salon in the Villa Nicoulaux, received the two French statesmen. The latter, somewhat to their own embarrassment, found themselves accompanied by Mohrenheim, who, having prudently arranged to take his own "cure" in Aix at this time, and being no doubt wildly curious as to what was going on, had contrived in some way to attach himself to their party.

Not knowing how much Mohrenheim knew, or was supposed to

know, about the military convention,* the two French statesmen were reluctant to speak about it in his presence; so Freycinet contrived to take him away to another part of the room and to engage him in a separate conversation while Ribot talked with Giers.

This talk, necessarily brief, did little to advance the purposes of the two French visitors; but it was not without interest. Giers described the visit that had been paid to him, at his dacha, by Obruchev, after the latter and Boisdeffre had agreed on the text of the convention. He confirmed that he had seen no objection to the tenor of the document as read aloud to him, on that occasion, by Obruchev, but that he had wished to see the actual text and to have an opportunity to study it, before giving it his formal approval. If he could do this, for which he had as yet had no opportunity, he was sure the matter could be finally disposed of in half an hour.

Ribot stressed the danger of postponing too long the final signature of the document. Who could tell, after all, what incidents might occur in the Parliament, and what new delays these incidents might occasion?

"Ah yes," Giers replied. "This is our constant anxiety. We are always in fear of a change of ministry in France. This already held us up for a long time." But now, he went on to indicate, the situation was more reassuring. French politics (and in this he could not have been more wrong) seemed more calm and stable. He did not think any new crisis was impending. The influence of the Pope in calming the French Catholics and in reconciling them to the Republic had been useful. And Europe, too, was peaceful. Germany had been obliged to recognize that there was no possibility of separating France and Russia. This had made her more peacefully inclined. And as for the Russians themselves: they wished only for peace. The Tsar had finally become convinced that Russia had nothing to gain by following an active policy in the Balkans. To be sure, he had not always been that wise, Giers added. It was he who, when still only heir apparent, had headed the movement that had "sent agents into Rumania and Bulgaria" in the aftermath of the war with Turkey.† But the Tsar now recognized that "we"—the Russians—had been at that time too sanguine and too demanding in "our" relations with these small peoples.

By way of concluding the discussion, Ribot observed that he,

---

*Actually, Mohrenheim had been told that a document of this nature had been negotiated at the military level, but he had not been informed of its content.

†See Kennan, *Bismarck's European Order*, p. 126. Obruchev had himself been one of these "agents."

confined by the schedule for the President's visit, could not remain and talk with Giers further about "the details of the project" (meaning, of course, Freycinet's proposed alterations), but that Freycinet would do so. Giers, he later recorded, had seemed to be agreeable to this suggestion.[23]

In this last impression Ribot was, however, mistaken. When, three days later, Giers received a note from Freycinet, asking when he might be received to continue the discussion, this was answered by a note from Giers' son Nicholas, now in attendance upon his father, saying that the latter was too ill to conduct any further official discussions and was obliged to ask to be excused.

With this reply, the French found themselves, for the moment, up against a blank wall. The Tsar was absent from Petersburg. So was Montebello. Vannovski was clearly unwilling to occupy himself with the matter. Giers professed himself too ill to conduct further business.

What would have occurred, all this being the case, had the French political situation remained calm, must remain a matter of conjecture. But actually, the French political situation was destined soon to become anything else but calm. Freycinet, to be sure, did not desist from his insistence that his proposed amendments must eventually be taken up with the Russians. But no sooner would the French statesmen return to Paris than they would find themselves confronted on the domestic-political horizon with clouds so menacing that for weeks and months thereafter even the promotion of the alliance with Russia, to which both Ribot and Freycinet had looked as the crowning external undertaking of their governmental careers, lost its preeminent place in their concerns and their attention.

. . .

So much for the story—to the end of 1892—of the Franco-Russian military convention. And a curious story it is.

On the Russian side, it is clear that the ministers of foreign affairs and war were both firmly opposed to the conclusion of any agreement of this nature. Once the Tsar had apparently given his blessing to the negotiations, these men went loyally along, so far as they felt they had to, with what they viewed as his decision, Vannovski backing out of the negotiations entirely, Giers taking refuge behind his illness and trying not to reveal to the French the full extent of his disagreement with his imperial master.

As for the Tsar, it would seem that he vacillated to the end. He was never averse to the idea of some sort of understanding between the general staffs, but he clearly hesitated to commit himself too deeply in the face of the opposition of the two ministers most directly concerned. He had accepted an implicit commitment of sorts, at least to discussions at the general staff level, when he granted permission for the French to send an officer. But on the question of a formal military convention committing the two governments, he was evidently still uncertain. As late as June 1892, he had professed agreement with Giers and Vannovski that the exchange of notes of 1891 sufficed for all existing purposes and that there was no need of any further written document. Yet he permitted Obruchev, in the first week of August, to negotiate precisely such a document. True, he dug his heels in and would not let the convention be formally signed before Giers had given his opinion on its political aspects. But he *had* permitted the document to be signed. And he *had* let it be known to the French that he approved of it "in principle."

The only conclusion to which one can come is that at some time between the 20th and the 25th of June, when (presumably) he made his approving notation on Giers' letter, and the first days of August, when Boisdeffre and Obruchev entered upon their discussions, someone got to Alexander with arguments that persuaded him of the need for a military convention. This could only have been Obruchev, who, as Moulin reported to Montebello, had seen the Tsar on the 16th of July and presented to him some sort of paper concerning the forthcoming negotiations. But there is also the possibility that the *Figaro* article—"Alliance ou Flirt?" —much as it may have irritated those around him, did actually cause him to feel that if he did not soon yield to the French pressures for a convention, the French might indeed abandon the whole project, place the facts (as Ribot had threatened to do) before the Parliament and the public, and search for other solutions to the problem of their security.

One thing is clear: it was, on the Russian side, the Tsar, and the Tsar alone, acting under the influence of the sanguine Obruchev and perhaps other unidentifiable influences as well, who promoted the negotiation of the agreement.

Chapter 12

PANAMA AND MOHRENHEIM

Throughout the negotiations for the Franco-Russian military convention two conflicts of interest and attitude between the two governments had exceeded all others in importance. One, of course, was the fact, already so often noted, that Russia's military interests related primarily to Austria-Hungary and the Balkans whereas those of France related to Germany. The other was the question of how, when, and to what extent the public was to be made aware of the existence of any agreement that might be arrived at. In this last respect, the difference of view went deep.

The two French ministers who had closest knowledge of the negotiations and were most intimately involved in the conduct of them, namely Ribot and Freycinet, were in a delicate position. They functioned within the framework of a parliamentary system. They were responsible to a parliament; they could fall from power instantly if they lost its confidence. The effort to conclude a military alliance with Russia was, in their eyes, the most momentous of all their undertakings as ministers of the government. It was the one from which, to the extent it should become known, they could expect to receive the greatest credit in the public eye. They never doubted that at some point the Alliance *would* become known—indeed, must become known. They could not themselves expect to remain indefinitely in office. Someday—and probably on some not very distant day—others would succeed them. These others would then have to be informed of the existence and terms of the Alliance. So, ultimately, would the Parliament. This was not a question of *whether,* but of *when.* Ribot and Freycinet naturally wished most fervently that all this might become known not after they had left office but while they were still clothed with it; for it would be a great feather in their caps, politically, and might enable them to overcome much of the opposition they were then encountering in other fields of policy. It was indeed a question whether they could long remain in office at all, unless they could produce for the French public some such major achievement of statesmanship. It was not without understanding for their position that Boisdeffre, in talking with the Tsar on August 18, 1892, had pointed out to the monarch, as we have seen, that the very endurance in power of these two men might depend on their ability to claim credit publicly for bringing the Alliance into being. It was indeed a lot to ask of them that they, functioning as they did within a parliamentary framework, should refrain from playing the greatest single political card they held in their hands.*

This, on the other hand, was precisely what the Tsar was demanding. He was demanding it in the most insistent and uncompromising way. He was convinced that any leakage of the news of the existence of a Franco-Russian military convention could easily provoke the Germans into launching the very attack against which the convention was supposed to guard. He had been persuaded—presumably by Obruchev and Vannovski—that another two years were needed, at the least, before Russia could even contemplate with any reasonable degree of confidence a military conflict with the Germans and Austrians together. And Giers was never slow to remind him that were he to give final approval to the convention without the strictest requirement of secrecy, control of the timing of an outbreak of war could easily pass out of his hands entirely. All the French would then have to do in order to provoke the inauguration of hostilities by the Germans at a moment most convenient from the standpoint of French interests would be to reveal the existence of the convention. This, presumably, was precisely why Alexander, in his talk with Boisdeffre on the occasion just mentioned, demanded that knowledge of the convention be restricted on the French side to Ribot, Freycinet, and the President, Carnot, and warned that if the existence of the agreement were to become public knowledge, he would consider it as automatically annulled.

In the face of these circumstances one might be permitted to suppose that the attitude of the Tsar towards the Alliance in the ensuing months and years would be intimately affected by the development of the domestic-political situation in France, and particularly by the endurance or nonendurance in office of the two ministers just referred to. With this assumption in mind, let us now go back a bit in time and have a glance at what was happening in French political life in the period following

---

*The German ambassador at Paris, Count Münster, reported to Berlin (at a somewhat later date) that Ribot had been heard to say that he had certain accomplishments for which he could not take credit but which gave him the right to become premier. (*Grosse Politik*, vol. 7, no. 1523, pp. 239–240.)

Freycinet's relinquishment of the premiership and the establishment of the Loubet cabinet in March 1892.

. . .

The France of 1892 stood, politically, under the shadow of several developments that, if they did not—as it turned out—actually shake the foundations of republican rule, nevertheless appeared for a time to offer a serious threat to its stability.

There had been, at just that time, a rise in radical-socialist and anarchist-terrorist activity. The spring of the year 1892 had been marked by a series of challenging strikes and anarchist attentats. Coming as they did in the wake of the Boulangist excitements of recent years, these disorders led to uncertainty in the minds of many people as to whether the Republic, hampered by its constitutional and legal restraints, would in the end be able to stand the strain. They had the further effect of causing the Radicals, heretofore despite their name a moderate-liberal party, to lean farther to the left in order not to be outflanked in that quarter, and to take a line of sharper hostility to the Opportuniste establishment than that which they had taken in earlier years.

At the same time, there was ferment, too, on the right wing of the political spectrum. Among the monarchist and clerical factions fifteen years of frustration and exclusion from power had bred no small measure of desperation and much questioning as to whether the line of total rejection of the Republic that they had been following for so many years was really the right one. Of outstanding importance, in this connection, was the fact that the policies of the Vatican, under Pope Leo XIII, were now undergoing a delicate but unmistakable revision. The French Catholics were beginning to receive, for the first time, encouragement from that quarter to reconcile themselves to republican rule and to participate constructively in the political life of the Republic. The *ralliement* (see chap. 1, pp. 3–4) found support, of course, among many of the French Catholics; but among others it aroused alarm and resistance, causing them to cling with redoubled tenacity to their hatred and rejection of the Republic. And in this they were seconded by many of the surviving Boulangists, still seething with bitterness over the political failure and subsequent exile and suicide of their admired leader, and no less determined than the die-hard monarchists to unseat the entire republican form of government.

In the face of these smoldering discontents, the political atmosphere of France at the outset of 1892 was one of much nervousness, uncertainty, and potentially explosive political opposition. And it was in this situation that there now ripened (for it had been long abuilding) a new political crisis, destined to put the entire existing political establishment under the most severe sort of strain, and to have, as well, a significant impact on Franco-Russian relations. This was the Panama scandal.

"L'affaire Panama" has engaged the labors of a number of excellent historians and historian-novelists, concerned to disentangle its multitudinous skeins and to reduce its complexities to comprehensible dimensions.* But it is questionable whether anyone, confining himself to the limits of a single book, could do full justice to the incredible welter of suspicions, accusations, reticences, blackmailings, evasions, and dramatic moments that went to make up this extraordinary episode. This writer, in any case, has no such pretensions. A word or two of recollection may be nevertheless useful to the reader at this point.

The Compagnie Universelle du Canal Interocéanique, chartered by the French Parliament in 1879 to build a canal across the Isthmus of Panama, got down to the actual process of construction in the years 1882–1883. It soon became apparent that the capital with which the company had been founded, much of it raised by publicly sold bond issues, was quite inadequate to the purpose at hand, particularly because the founder, the octogenarian Ferdinand de Lesseps (already famous as the builder of the Suez Canal) was determined to run the canal through at sea level rather than elevating a portion of it with locks, and this sea-level option proved to be much the more expensive way of doing it. After four years of operation, the company had run through almost the entirety of its original capital; yet the project was nowhere near completion. There seemed at that point to be no alternatives but bankruptcy or further borrowing; and the decision was taken, most disastrously, for the latter.

With a view to concealing the dimensions of the trouble and to preserving some measure of financial credit, the company had by this time already begun to dispense startlingly large sums of money for "public relations" purposes—a concept that, in the customs of the day, meant handsome handouts to numbers of individuals in the press, in government, in the financial world—individuals who, it was thought, could be useful in concealing the company's financial plight and improving the

---

*Among these, outstandingly: Jean Bouvier, Les Deux Scandales de Panama (Paris: Collection Archives, 1964); Adrian Dansette, Les Affaires de Panama (Paris: Perrin, 1934); D. W. Brogan, The Development of Modern France (1870–1939) (London: Hamish Hamilton, 1940); and Maurice Barrès, Leurs figures (Paris: Emile Paul Frères, 1917).

prospects for further borrowing. In 1888 this practice was raised to new levels of desperation. The only favorable prospect for a new bond issue seemed, at that time, to be one with lottery features—an arrangement that had strong appeal to French investors. Such an issue, however, could be launched only with the consent of Parliament. An authorization bill was therefore placed before that body at the beginning of 1888. But many of the legislators were by this time more or less aware of the company's plight; and it was generally recognized as doubtful whether, in normal circumstances, the necessary majority could be obtained. The result was that donations—bribes, if you will—now began to flow into the pockets of a considerable number of the parliamentary deputies, with the obvious intention of influencing their votes.

The company, meanwhile, had already become known for its extraordinary largesse, and had attracted a multitude of new claimants. Among these, most unfortunately, were—or would appear to have been—certain of the senior statesmen on the executive side of the government, who either put pressure on the company to satisfy the appeals of individuals in whom they themselves were politically interested or solicited funds for themselves that they proposed to use (or so, at least, they said) for secret purposes of state, the nature of which could not initially be revealed. These appeals and solicitations, too, were seldom resisted.

A year later, in 1889, the company went into bankruptcy, dragging with it the interests of a host of creditors. The investigation conducted by the receiver revealed a veritable chamber of financial horrors: so many abuses, or suggestions of abuses, that the receiver's report had to be submitted to the government with the recommendation that legal proceedings be instituted against the officers of the company. In June 1892, the state prosecutor approached the minister of justice with a demand for indictment of the directors. This, as it became public knowledge, set up behind the scenes a desperate panic among the many persons who had reason to fear that the forthcoming judicial procedures would reveal the names of those who had benefited from the company's generosity in ways that were either outright illegal or, if revealed, could be damaging to their reputations. Of these, there were hundreds—in the executive branch of the government, in the Parliament, in the press, and in business circles.

Towards the end of the summer of 1892, the whole story began to break in the press. This touched off a stampede of *sauve qui peut* efforts, not excluding some more or less refined efforts at blackmail. The more people felt their own reputations endangered, the more they sought to protect themselves by threatening to reveal what they knew about others. By early autumn the entire bubble was clearly ready to burst, releasing its unsavory contents, with effects then incalculable on the personal fate of many compromised individuals and on the political life of the country.

The opening gun in what might be called the explosion of the Panama scandal was fired by the famous anti-Semitic editor and publicist, Edouard Drumont, in September 1892, with the publication in his *La Libre Parole* of a series of sensational anonymous articles (actually written by a former financial agent of the Panama Canal company) entitled "The Inside Story of Panama." These articles, invoking the names of a number of prominent personalities, set tongues wagging and the accusations flying for fair. The government, fearful of any further opening up of this dreadful can of worms, delayed as long as possible the instituting of proceedings against the company but was finally obliged, on November the 19th, 1892, to consent to the indictment of three of its directors. In mid-November, the Austrian ambassador at Paris, forewarned of the indictment, reported to his government that "a scandal of gigantic dimensions is imminent."[1] He was right. The ensuing judicial proceedings led, as they were bound to do, to further revelations. Within a short time, other proceedings were instituted—this time against certain former cabinet ministers. The Parliament, meantime, found itself forced, amid much agony, to set up its own commission of investigation (the so-called Brisson Commission) to examine the conduct of a number of its own members. The banker, Joseph Reinach, deeply involved in the Panama company's financial affairs, committed suicide in dramatic and mysterious circumstances, while his *compagnon*, the financial adventurer Julius Herz (who had apparently been blackmailing him), hastily fled to England.

The simultaneous pursuit of the three sets of investigations mentioned above, coming on top of the frantic investigatory efforts of the gentlemen of the press, produced by mid-January 1893 a state of excitement, anxiety, panic, and scandal in the French political establishment that defies description. Among those whose names became involved, justly or otherwise, were eight former premiers, including Floquet, Freycinet, and Rouvier, plus a number of former cabinet ministers.

The effects of all this on the government in office were not long in coming. In November 1892, the minister of justice, Ricard, caught unhappily between the requirements of true justice, which demanded the indictment of the officers of the Panama company, and the political interests of the cabinet, which were bound to suffer from any such airing of the affair in court, floundered in the resulting dilemma, and had to be sacrificed. This caused the fall of the whole cabinet (November 27). Loubet, the prime minister, stepped down from the premiership to the position of minister of the interior. Ribot took over as premier in his place, but retained the foreign ministry. Six days later, it became necessary to drop the finance minister, Rouvier, even more heavily compromised than Ricard by the revelations now pouring forth from the press columns and the gossip mills of the capital. And some weeks later, in mid-January 1893, Ribot found himself obliged to reorganize the cabinet once more, dropping, this time, both Freycinet and Loubet, and himself, while remaining premier, yielding the post of foreign minister to Charles Paul Develle, politician of left-republican coloration and former minister of agriculture. Freycinet's position at the War Ministry, which he had occupied with much distinction for four years, was taken over by an interim appointee, General Jules Loizillon, a wholly unknown figure.

By this time, in midwinter 1893, the scandal was at its height. The press was roaring. Further revelations were expected. The situation of the Ribot cabinet (a minority cabinet, actually) had become precarious in the extreme. It lasted, actually, only for another two agitated months. On March the 30th, after a particularly harrowing round of confrontations over Panama, it collapsed entirely. Ribot retired. The premiership was taken over by a little-known figure: Charles Dupuy, a man whose principal qualification for this high office, as in the case of Develle, was only his lack of involvement in the Panama affair.

With these developments, both of the French statesmen who had been active in the negotiation of the Alliance—Freycinet and Ribot— were eliminated, at least for some time to come, from active political life.

. . .

The effect on Giers and the Tsar of these precipitate upheavals in French political life is a subject on which little direct information is available. (Lamsdorf's diary—at least, the available published version of it—unfortunately omits the year 1893.)

In the case of Giers it is not hard to picture the reactions. The state of his health not permitting an earlier return to Russia, he had remained in Western Europe, first at Monte Carlo, then at San Remo and Florence, over the entire winter of 1892–1893—that is, throughout all these events. (He returned to Russia only in April 1893.) He obviously read the French newspapers; and his son Nicholas, now counselor of the Russian embassy at Paris, presumably kept him informed of such of the Paris gossip as did not appear in the press. Giers must, therefore, have followed closely all the details of these happenings; and they can only have confirmed him in his strong reluctance to see Russia allied with so unstable a democracy as that which the France of 1892–1893 appeared to represent. There is nothing in his subsequent behavior that would suggest anything else.

In the Tsar's case, things are more complicated. One would suppose that he, too, would have reacted to these developments in a manner that would have precluded anything like the ratification of the military convention for years into the future. The bewildering rapidity of changes in incumbency at the head of French affairs had, as we have seen, long been a source of impatience and complaint on his part. It was he who, at the very outset of his reign, at the time of his coronation in 1883, had admonished the special French ambassador attending that event: *"Ayez de la stabilité, de la stabilité."* Yet here were three drastic cabinet changes within four months. And what changes! It was Alexander himself who had recently insisted that knowledge of the military convention should be restricted at the French end to Ribot, Freycinet, and Carnot. Now, two of these three were suddenly gone; and unknown men, in whose discretion he had no reason for confidence, had appeared in their places. These latter would presumably have to be initiated into the details of the negotiations. Who could say whether they would be either inclined or disposed to keep the secret?

And this was not all; for there was another dimension to the scandal, touching even more intimately on Russian interests. This was the rumored involvement, almost from the start, of the Russian ambassador at Paris, Baron Arthur Pavlovich Mohrenheim.

We have already seen (chap. 4) that Mohrenheim, stationed in Paris since 1884, had never been, in Giers' eyes a suitable Russian representative. A Roman Catholic of Galician-Polish origin, the descendant of a parvenu grandfather (a supplier of provisions to the Russian army), he had never enjoyed the confidence or liking of his colleagues or his underlings in the Russian diplomatic service. Many of these latter were of course Russian noblemen, not partial to either Catholics or parvenus, much less Polish ones. But these prejudices did not alone account for their aversion to Mohrenheim, or for that of many others. For Mohrenheim, although well educated and not unintelligent, was known for his high-stepping slickness and compulsive volubility rather than for his integrity. His underlings viewed him with concealed contempt, doubting his financial probity and suspecting him of frequently having his hand in the embassy till. His prodigality (and that of his wife) in the use of money, coupled with his habit of contracting extensive debts (the Russian government was occasionally obliged to bail him out), was a matter of common gossip in diplomatic circles. Indeed, he owed his appointment to the Paris post, and his long retention of it, largely to the favor of the Empress Dagmar, to whom he, then serving as minister in Copenhagen, had been useful at the time of her marriage to the then Russian crown prince, the later Alexander III.

Mohrenheim was an intensely ambitious man, wildly jealous of Giers. The events of the summer of 1891—the fact that he was called home, was taken into confidence about the negotiations for the Franco-Russian entente, and was permitted to appear as the signer and author of the crucial diplomatic note by which the entente was established (and all of this by personal order of the Tsar)—induced in him a state of elation and self-importance so exalted as to disbalance to some degree his equanimity and good judgment. It is clear that in the ensuing period, he entertained high hopes of soon displacing the ailing Giers and becoming his successor. A serious attack of influenza, in the late autumn of 1891, seems further to have affected his equilibrium.

While reports had not been lacking, even in earlier years, about evidences of venality and of questionable financial practices on Mohrenheim's part, the autumn of 1891 had produced a new and more serious crop of them. It was rumored in Petersburg that he was showing signs of a sudden and, in view of his normal state of financial distress, inexplicable affluence. It became known that the Paris *Le Gaulois*, a monarchist paper well known for its enthusiastic advocacy of a Franco-Russian alliance and long reputed to have benefited from Russian subsidies, had set up a nationwide financial subscription in his favor, ostensibly by way of recognition for his efforts on behalf of Franco-Russian relations; and that he, when consulted, had done nothing at all to discourage the undertaking. Moreover, word reached the Russian foreign minister that he had contrived to benefit financially from certain of the French loans to Russia launched by the consortium of the Danish-French banker Emile Hoskier (a great friend of his), and particularly from the ill-fated loan of the autumn of 1891.* Vyshnegradski, the finance minister, even complained

---

*Hoskier, as noted above, was related by marriage to the former French ambassador in Petersburg, General Félix Appert. Appert's wife, well connected at the Danish court, was Hoskier's sister. Young Giers adduces in his memoirs evidence to show that Mohrenheim had been receiving wholly improper cuts not only on this loan but on each of the others promoted by Hoskier.

to Giers that Mohrenheim, by his shady speculations, had actually impaired the success of that loan.

Evidence does not suggest that Ribot, in contrast to Freycinet, was ever at any time taken in by Mohrenheim, ever saw him as a likely successor to Giers, or viewed him as a suitable channel for communication with the Russian government. He could not, in any case, have been under such illusions for long. A personal and confidential letter addressed by Ribot to Montebello on January the 14th, 1892, contained the following passage:

> M. Mohrenheim has recovered from his attack of influenza; but he has aged markedly. His deficiencies become more evident by the day. He has consistently made the mistake of meddling excessively in our internal affairs and of failing to control his tongue. Since his recent illness he has permitted himself particularly unfortunate indiscretions. At one time he spares no praises for the French government; at another time he is quick to assert that we are on the verge of catastrophe. He has complained to me that Paris has lost enthusiasm for the Franco-Russian entente, that only the provinces remember Cronstadt, that since the visit of M. Giers everything has been spoiled, etc. If he continues to use this sort of language to many other people and if he presents things to his government in the false ways in which he sees them, I fear that serious harm could be done over the long run.[2]

These observations were followed by a request to Montebello to try to find out through Giers what Mohrenheim was reporting, and to warn Giers (than whom no one could have been less in need of such a warning) about the *"erreurs d'optiques"* of his representative in Paris.

With respect to the nature of Mohrenheim's reporting at this juncture, Ribot's suspicions had not deceived him. Only shortly before, it will be recalled, Mohrenheim had been pressing for the early conclusion of a military convention, and this even at the cost of a virtual insubordination to his own foreign minister. It has been noted above that with the onset of the year 1892 his tune appears to have changed entirely. He now began not only to speak unfavorably of his former collaborator, Freycinet, but also to depict the state of French political affairs in the darkest colors and to cite this sad state of affairs as reason why the Russian government should refrain, at least for the time being, from any and all negotiations or discussions looking to the conclusion of a military convention. By May 1892, in fact, his reports were containing warnings along this line so dire that they could have been written by Giers himself. "Nothing could be worse and more dangerous," he wrote on May 5, "than to let them [the French] hope that they could depend in all circumstances on the help of a Russia bound [to them] by formal and unbreakable agreements;"—a thought so agreeable to the Tsar at that time that the latter wrote opposite this passage, in the margin of the report: "They know and sense this very well indeed." Mohrenheim went on, then, to express (to Giers' own amazement) the view that his foreign minister had been expressing all along, namely: ". . . I doubt that we would be risking anything in retaining as long as possible our freedom of action."[3]

Mohrenheim could cite, of course, sound objective reasons for such a position. There were indeed the strikes and the anarchist attentats, to which reference has already been made. There was indeed the underlying instability of French political life. Nevertheless, the change of tune was so abrupt and so striking that one looks for an ulterior motive. There are limits, of course, to the usefulness of speculation on such matters; but it may be well to remember that Giers' visit to Paris in November 1891 had made it clear to Mohrenheim that Giers intended to keep any negotiations for a military convention strictly in his own hands. Giers, on the other hand, was a sick man. It was doubtful how long he could retain his ministerial position. If he, Mohrenheim, had a chance of becoming Giers' successor, it would obviously be better that the negotiation of such a convention should be delayed until he could take the matter into *his* own hands and receive the credit. It was, surely, not only on the French side that personal considerations of this nature played a part in the maneuvering that preceded and attended the negotiation of the Alliance. Actually, of course, whether Mohrenheim knew it or not, the Boisdeffre-Obruchev negotiations, coming only three months later, would put an end to whatever reality dreams of this nature might otherwise have had.

Mohrenheim's difficulties in connection with the Panama affair did not begin in earnest until the end of the year 1892. On the 25th of November the Boulangist editor and parliamentary deputy Jacques Delahaye, upon whose demand the parliamentary (Brisson) commission of investigation into the Panama charges had been originally set up, charged in testimony before the commission that 500,000 francs extracted from the funds of the Panama company had been used for the subvention of the *Moskovskie Vyedomosti,* the influential Moscow paper edited and published (until his death in 1887) by the famous editor-publisher Mikhail Katkov. The scientist Elie de Cyon,* longtime

---

*This highly curious personage, whose Russian name was Ilya Fadeyevich Tsion, was described, and his doings were treated in some detail, in the first volume of this series: Kennan, *Bismarck's European Order,* particularly in chapters 4 and 16. Scientist, journalist, and political commentator, Cyon, who lived in Paris from the mid-1870s to the early 1890s, was a strong supporter of the idea of a Franco-Russian alliance. But he had a great talent for making enemies, among whom Mohrenheim occupied a prominent place.

friend of Katkov and occasional correspondent of the *Moskovskie Vyedomosti* in the 1880s, at once sprang to the defense of Katkov's memory, writing letters to newspapers both in Paris and in Petersburg pointing out, correctly, that the charge related to the year 1888, whereas Katkov had died in the summer of 1887. Cyon was careful, however, not to commit himself with respect to events subsequent to Katkov's death. In a piece written towards the end of December for the *Nouvelle Revue*, he even made the characteristically ambivalent statement that he would never have ventured to guarantee the incorruptibility of the *Moskovskie Vyedomosti* had the charge related personally to the later editor, Katkov's successor, S. A. Petrovski.[4]

Thus far, then, it was only Katkov's successor and the unknown French intermediaries on whom suspicion had been thrown. But in early January, with the pot of Panama revelations now burning briskly, blows of a different nature began to fall. On January 4 a highly reactionary Boulangist sheet, *La Lanterne*, relayed a report from a Budapest paper, based on a story from its Paris correspondent, one Szekely, the exact nature of which is obscure (this writer has been unable to find a copy of this issue of *La Lanterne*) but which evidently expanded on the charges about the *Moskovskie Vyedomosti* and threw suspicion of some sort on both Freycinet and Rouvier, as well as on an unnamed ambassador.[5]

Szekely was immediately expelled from France and returned to Budapest. At the same time similar expulsion orders were carried out against certain German and Italian journalists—a circumstance that led to suspicions that the French government was trying to portray the charges against Mohrenheim as part of a campaign by the powers of the Triple Alliance to damage Franco-Russian relations.

One week after Szekely's expulsion, the allegations against Mohrenheim were supported in a much more explicit and authoritative manner. It was already a matter of public knowledge that a list existed, compiled from the respective check stubs, of legislators and officials who had received personal bribes—or at least subsidies—from the Panama company; and, further, that there was one instance in which the name of the beneficiary had been deleted from the list and replaced with an "X." There was much speculation as to the identity of "X."

Now, on the 12th of January, another Paris paper *(Le Petit Journal)* ran the text of an interview with a certain Arton, former agent and lobbyist for the Panama company, who had taken a leading part in the distribution of the secret subventions. Arton, in this interview, asserted that the real beneficiary of the mysterious check had been "the ambassador of a very great power friendly to France—a dashing gentleman, actually, whose financial embarrassments, long a matter of common knowledge in Paris, had continued to the present day."* The intermediary through whose hands the money passed on its way from the coffers of the company to the ambassador had been, Arton claimed, "un savant étranger, bien que très parisien, un physiologue—un docteur."[6]

The two veiled references were, unmistakably, to Mohrenheim and Cyon, respectively.†

Cyon, stung to the quick, reacted explosively. He fired off letters to both French and Russian newspapers protesting his innocence and asking to be allowed to testify before the Brisson Commission. Being indeed innocent, he was generally successful in these efforts to clear his name. The paper published a retraction, and the charge was soon dropped from the public prints.

Mohrenheim, too, reacted explosively, albeit in the end less successfully. He at once stormed down to Ribot's office in high dudgeon, protesting the fact that charges of this nature had been permitted to appear in the French press and demanding that the French government take action to clear his name. He also at once wrote to Giers, demanding the same thing of the Russian government—even asking that the Order of Saint Vladimir be at once conferred upon him as a mark of his government's confidence in him.

Just how all this was reported to Petersburg we do not know; but on the 19th of January Shishkin, the acting foreign minister, told Montebello that he had discussed the matter with the Tsar; that the latter did not hold the French government responsible for the episode—was grateful to that government, in fact, for the measures it had taken, including the assurances given to Mohrenheim that everything would be done to protect foreign governments and their representatives from the abuse of their good names.‡ The Tsar, Shishkin reported, suspected a plot to discredit relations between the two countries. He had asked that the French gov-

---

*In the original French: "le bénéficiaire réel du chèque est à Paris l'ambassadeur d'une très grande puissance amie de la France, fort galant homme du reste, dont les embarras financiers, jadis très connus à Paris, n'ont pas pris fin depuis. . . ."

†The charge was quite absurd. Mohrenheim and Cyon detested each other and held each other in extreme suspicion. Cyon would never have done such a thing for Mohrenheim; and the latter would never have placed himself in Cyon's hands by accepting from him a service of this nature.

‡Ribot actually introduced before the Parliament a bill making it illegal to publish material impugning the good names of friendly powers or their representatives.

ernment do all in its power to uncover the source of these attacks and to keep him informed of the results.[7]

On January the 25th Ribot, questioned about all this before the Parliament by the Boulangist deputy Lucien Millevoye, replied: "Quite recently the name of the ambassador of a friendly power was mentioned most unfortunately in connection with certain outrageous polemics—polemics in connection with which shame alone should have inhibited its mention. . . . We have protected the ambassador of a friendly power immediately and firmly, as was our duty. These were calumnies—outrages, in fact—that we could not tolerate."[8]

Mohrenheim would no doubt have been less pleased by this statement had he known that Ribot had only shortly before received another document, this time one apparently sent to him by Szekely, from Budapest, detailing the grounds for the story he had originally sent from Paris.* In this document, dated January 21, it was related that Szekely had met in Paris, apparently in early January, one Grossier, proprietor of a very reactionary French press wire-service, and a relative of the former premier, Charles Floquet. Grossier had told him that the sensation of the day had been the confession by Rouvier, also a former premier, to the chief prosecutor that he, in company with Freycinet and a third individual, whose name Grossier had said he would never reveal, had obtained from the Panama company 200,000 francs, which they had turned over to Mohrenheim. The intermediary through whom the money had been sent to Mohrenheim had been Herbette, brother of the French ambassador at Berlin. Szekely went on to say that he had at first been skeptical and had subsequently questioned Grossier sharply on more than one occasion, but that the latter had stuck to his story and had encouraged him to publish it. Furthermore, shortly after he had sent the story, Arton had himself confirmed the details of it. Until the French government or the accused parties specifically denied the truth of the story, which they had not yet done, Szekely would not, he wrote, retract his statements.

Just when Mohrenheim saw Szekely's document is not clear. The evidence suggests that by early March, at least, it had come to his attention, for at some time during that month he sent a copy of it to Ribot

---

*It is stated in the book by René Girault *Emprunts russes et investissements français en Russie 1887–1914* (Paris: Publications de la Sorbonne. Librairie Armand Colin, 1973), pp. 216–217, that Ribot received, on January 21, 1893, a letter from Szekely, the tenor of which, as summarized by Girault, follows closely that of the document referred to above. I am assuming, in view of the identity of the dates, as well as the content, that this was the document Girault referred to.

under cover of a letter that reflected great agitation of spirit.[9] In this letter he expressed surprise that Grossier had not been arrested, and demanded that Rouvier and others should come forward publicly to assert his own innocence.*

Shortly thereafter things assumed an even more disturbing turn. On March 16 *Le Gaulois* came out with a story, reproduced in several other papers, to the effect that Ribot had learned that the identity of the famous "X" was known to one of the unfortunate directors of the Panama company, M. Cottu, now convicted and in prison; that M. Cottu's appeal of his sentence was about to come the following day before a court of appeals; that Cottu was expected at this session, in his own defense, to name the beneficiary of the check; and that Ribot had approached Cottu's attorneys, asking them to intervene with their client to obtain his assurance that he would not do this. *Le Gaulois* noted the clear implication that Ribot was himself aware of the identity of the famous "X"; and it charged him with impropriety for addressing a request of this nature to a man doing penal servitude.[10]

Ribot, faced with these distressing revelations (and this in the very midst of another cabinet crisis), was obliged to face the Parliament the same day, and to give explanations. "People have approached me from several quarters," he said to the Parliament,

> to tell me that it was persistently rumored that the famous "X" was the representative of a foreign Power, and that tomorrow (this was of course an inept, ridiculous, and abominable calumny) the name of a certain ambassador would be mentioned at the session of the Court of Appeals and that people would try to make it into a scandal. . . .

Ribot went on to say that he had passed the word along that if, as seemed impossible, "one" really intended to stir up a scandal (the reference was obviously to Cottu), one should remember that one was, after all, French. Cottu's attorney, *Le Gaulois* further reported, had replied that he had seen his client and that the latter had no intention of mentioning the name in question, particularly in view of the fact that he had no information whatsoever that the person in question had ever been involved "in this affair."[11]

The effect of all this on the French public can be understood only if it be borne in mind that everyone, by this time, was well aware that

---

*The tone of this communication may be judged from the opening sentences: "Il faut que cela finisse. Il faut que M. Grossier rende gorge. Il faut que Messieurs Franqueville et Rouvier parlent, et parlent haute. Il faut que le gouvernement parle à son tour, et qu'il agisse."

the "ambassador" in question was Mohrenheim. There was never even any question of its being anyone else.

In the formal sense this exchange, including as it did a strong expression of Ribot's abhorrence of the charges relating to Mohrenheim and avoiding as it did any specific mention of Mohrenheim's name, might have been expected to satisfy the Russians. This, however, was far from being the case. Mohrenheim himself promptly appeared once more, greatly excited, in the office of Develle, who was now foreign minister, expressed doubt that Ribot's statement would satisfy the Tsar, and demanded a clearer and more authoritative vindication. Develle protested that the incident had only proven once again how absurd were the charges in which Mohrenheim's name had been mentioned. But Mohrenheim refused to be assuaged.

Indeed, a closer scrutiny of the text of the exchange suggests the reasons for Russian unhappiness. The words describing the insinuations as "inept, ridiculous, and abominable" give an impression of perfunctoriness, if not of direct mockery; and the avoidance, in both statements, of any direct refutation of the truth of the charges strikes the eye, as does the significance of Ribot's appeal to Cottu's patriotism (rather than to his truthfulness) in asking him to avoid mention of the name.

In closing the account of these revelations, it may be noted that only a fortnight after this appearance of Ribot before the Parliament, he, together with his cabinet, fell from office. He was replaced, as noted above, by Charles Dupuy.

. . .

Before taking note of the aftermath of these excitements it will be well to inquire into the extent to which Mohrenheim was or was not guilty of the charges levied against him.

There is of course no direct and absolutely conclusive evidence either way. Public officials who take extensive bribes from the government of another power do not normally leave for posterity documentary evidence confirming such conduct. That Mohrenheim was a venal man, accustomed to cutting corners in taking money from improper sources, is clear from a number of evidences. In the present instance the evidence, while circumstantial and confused, is so formidable in its totality, as well as in the absence of any direct refutation from any quarter, that one can only believe the charge to have been substantially true.

The most detailed account of what really happened, and the one likely to be the closest to the real facts, is that given by Cyon in a highly confidential letter that he addressed, in mid-February 1893, to Pobedonostsev.[12] Cyon was himself a strange character, and of course he hated Mohrenheim; but he had been, at the time when this money was alleged to have passed to Mohrenheim, an agent in Paris of the Russian ministry of finance; he had followed Franco-Russian relations very closely; and he was too much the scientist to be a direct falsifier of statistical information. Beyond which, his letter conveys, in its tone and its detail, a strong impression of verisimilitude.

The check, not for 200,000 but for 500,000 francs, had indeed been extorted, Cyon wrote, from the Panama company. It had been solicited ostensibly for the benefit of the *Moskovskie Vyedomosti*, but Mohrenheim had personally pocketed half the sum. The deal had been negotiated, he thought, by one or both of two agents of the newspaper in Paris (N. V. Shcherban, the regular correspondent, and one Shatokhin, the latter sent expressly for the purpose). The full details had been communicated to the Brisson Commission by the ministers involved, with a view to having the matter hushed up. When he, Cyon, had been asked to testify before the commission, he had professed himself willing to do so, but had insisted that if he were to testify under oath he would have to tell the whole story; whereupon the commission had agreed that it would be better not to hear him.

This was not, Cyon said, the only such subsidy that Mohrenheim had received. At the time of the marriage of his eldest daughter (1891), the French government had given him 300,000 francs through the intermediary of an American Pole by the name of Nachtel, who had founded a society called Les Ambulances Urbaines, of which Mme. Mohrenheim was the president. This money, too, had actually been made available—by Freycinet's arrangement—out of the Panama funds. And finally, Mohrenheim had received another bonanza at the time of the marriage of his second daughter—this time from Hoskier, and in connection with the abortive 3 percent loan of 1891.

The most conclusive evidence of Mohrenheim's guilt will be found in a private letter written by Montebello, from Petersburg, to Ribot on June the 5th, 1893. Here he expressed his anxiety over the possibility that Mohrenheim might be recalled from his Paris post. He obviously feared that if this were done, Mohrenheim might revenge himself on both governments by revealing the full facts of the matter. "Does the Tsar understand, as his Minister does," Montebello asked rhetorically, how dangerous it would be to transfer this ambassador in the near future? I stressed at length this aspect of the question in my talk with Giers, without telling him, incidentally, anything he did not already know. I explained to him the danger of presenting [to Mohrenheim] new pretexts for playing his maleficent game with the help of a yellow press, into the hands of which he has already unduly delivered himself. I did not wish to say all that I thought, but M. de Giers knows his way around, and he understood. It is very unfortunate that we should find ourselves reduced to demanding the maintenance at his post of an ambassador whose activity can only be detrimental to our interests; but unfortunately we cannot fail to recognize that we shall long remain exposed to organized blackmail at his hands. The best we can hope is that this blackmail is not repeated at a moment dangerous to us.[13]

It would seem clear from this curious letter that if the two governments knew a number of things discreditable to Mohrenheim, he also knew some things that, if revealed, would be embarrassing to them. This alone would appear to explain the fact that, although now grievously discredited and taken seriously by no one, he was to remain at his post in Paris for a further five years—until 1898.

.   .   .

There can be no question of Giers' knowledge of Mohrenheim's involvement in these unhappy developments, or of his mortification and disgust over the latter's conduct. He had never trusted the man or approved of his appointment to the Paris position in the first place.

The Tsar's reactions were more complicated. He, too, must have known all the facts. Pobedonostsev would not have failed to pass on to him all that Cyon had reported. But the Russian governmental mind is congenitally preoccupied primarily with appearances and only secondarily with facts. The Tsar considered that even if Mohrenheim were guilty, one must never say so, because Mohrenheim was his, the Tsar's, personal representative, and disrespect for Mohrenheim, publicly stated, would be equivalent to disrespect for his master. This, presumably, accounted for Alexander's fury over what he understood to be the inadequacy of Ribot's statement before the Parliament. The Russian papers were at once forbidden to mention the matter. And Alexander let it be known to the French through Shishkin (on March 29th, the day before the fall of Ribot's cabinet) that he did not find Ribot's statement sufficient to absolve the French government of its duty to remove all stigma from Mohrenheim's name.[14]

Develle, presumably on the receipt of this news, at once wrote to Mohrenheim, formally expressing the French government's regret that his name had been mentioned. Mohrenheim, for some reason, delayed for nearly a month the sending of this letter to Petersburg; but a copy was handed by Montebello to the acting foreign minister, Shishkin; and the latter promptly dispatched it by courier to the Tsar, now in the Crimea.[15]

While they were awaiting the Tsar's reaction, Giers finally returned from his seven-months' stay in Western Europe. By no means fully recovered from his illness, very feeble in body but clear in mind, he received Montebello on the 5th of May, and they discussed the Mohrenheim affair at length. Giers knew, he said, no more than did Shishkin of where the matter now stood. He was harsh in his criticism of Ribot, who, he felt, had let them down. But he feared a strong reaction on the Tsar's part against Mohrenheim, who "had placed them all in a false position." Beyond this, Montebello reported, Giers was significantly silent about Mohrenheim. Nevertheless, Montebello added, one would never have dared to criticize anyone, and above all an ambassador, as Giers had criticized Mohrenheim, if his private life had been irreproachable. "About this one should have no illusions."[16]

In mid-May, the Tsar's reaction to Develle's letter was received in the form of the following brief note: "I find all this entirely insufficient. I consider myself entitled to expect that M. Carnot will himself write to Mohrenheim a letter of regrets and excuses. It is not a matter, here, of Mohrenheim's person, but of Russia herself."[17]

Wired at once to Mohrenheim in Paris, this produced, within two days' time, the desired letter, addressed to him by the French President, Carnot.

"In the desire," the President wrote,

of putting an end to the calumnious allegations made during the course of the Panama affair, the prime minister [the reference was of course to Ribot] thought it necessary to bring before the Parliament the explanations in which your name was involved. The words he used gave rise to a misunderstanding that, unfortunately, one has not been able to clear up to the present day.

I have learned that this incident has produced in Russia an emotional reaction that has not yet been assuaged, and I hasten to express to you my sincere regret.

I feel all the more free to do this because I am confident that in doing so I am responding to the intimate feelings of the country, which shares my high esteem for His Majesty, Emperor Alexander, and which has not forgotten how much Your Excellency has usefully contributed to the strengthening of the bonds that unite Russia and France.[18]

A copy of this letter (the French evidently did not trust Mohrenheim to forward it, and were taking no chances) was sent by special courier to Montebello, in Petersburg. It came with an accompanying note from Develle, explaining that it was not intended that Carnot's letter should be made public. Referring to the rumors, already current, that Mohrenheim was to be withdrawn from his Paris post, Develle went on to say:

> We would not regret his departure. The fury with which he has pursued M. Ribot, the humiliation he has inflicted upon us, the indiscreet statements he has made publicly, and the intrigues he has engaged in, give us the right to wish for his replacement. But I consider, and this is the view of the President of the Republic, that it would have the worst possible effect if he were to be replaced before the October elections.

In addition to this letter, Montebello had already by this time received a copy of a long letter addressed by Ribot to Mohrenheim sometime in May, justifying the conduct as premier for which Mohrenheim had criticized him. Montebello took the two documents to the foreign office on June 1 and left them with Giers for submission to the Tsar. Giers saw the Tsar on the 10th, and was able to report to Montebello, the following day, that the monarch was pleased with Carnot's letter and found it entirely acceptable. He had also approved retaining Mohrenheim, for the time being, at Paris. "Throughout this whole affair," the Tsar had said to Giers, "what I have had in view was not the person of Mohrenheim, which is ridiculous, but the ambassador in his official capacity."[19]

Thus the Mohrenheim affair was finally laid to rest, having, together with Giers' long absence, precluded any further discussion of the military convention over a period of nearly half a year.

. . .

How deeply this matter affected the Tsar's feelings about that convention, and about the French alliance generally, is hard to determine. As Montebello repeatedly pointed out to his Paris principals, so long as Giers was absent, Alexander was dependent upon Mohrenheim's reports, as relayed by *Shishkin* (in whom Montebello had little confidence) for his information about the affair. When Giers returned, the monarch's annoyance was soon dispelled. Montebello considered, in fact, that had Giers been there the whole time, the trouble would never have arisen.

This may well be true; and with Giers' arrival and with the presentation of Carnot's letter the matter seems to have passed entirely out of Alexander's mind. But this circumstance is interesting in itself. The fact that French statesmen—including at least one in particular to whom the Tsar had given his confidence—had bribed his ambassador with a view to promoting conclusion of the alliance appears to have made very little impression on this curious man. He was upset, momentarily, over the effect all this might have on the public; but he evidently attached no serious significance to the charges against Mohrenheim or to the evidences of his guilt.

To what to attribute this? From what little is known about the state of mind (and of body) of the monarch at this time, one has the impression of a real change in his reactions, as compared with those of the 1880s. One notes now a certain detachment, or loss of interest, with relation to matters that, at any earlier date, would have affected him keenly. He was now not only older, but was within less than two years of his death. It is possible that he was already suffering from the incipient stages of the disease that was to lead to it. Rumors to the effect that he was seriously ill were appearing in the foreign press as early as September. He had recently put on much weight. He was spending even more time than usual away from Petersburg. He showed no discomfort over the fact that during his long absences he left Russia, in view of Giers' illness, effectively without a foreign minister. One gains the impression that Alexander, tired and indifferent, had simply come to feel that many complications, including this one, were of little importance.

Montebello sensed something of this. He mentioned it in his account to Develle of his first talk with Giers (May 6) after the latter's return from Europe. "What is very unfortunate at this moment," he wrote,

> is that the Emperor has in his entourage no one who could—if not advise him (which I believe to be very difficult with a character as headstrong as he is)—then at least influence him a little. The Tsar is left to himself and to his own impressions. He is preoccupied with certain intimate problems affecting his second son. He has himself been sick for a time; and his convictions, always very emphatic, are perhaps more so than ever at this moment. Last year he lost a childhood friend in the person of Prince Obolenski, who had always been near to him in the quality of a confidant, well loved, reliable, and full of sympathy for France. Then, some weeks later, death took away another man who was capable of exercising a certain influence over him and who was also one of our friends. Today, I see around him no one on whom he could count or who could replace those whom he has seen disappear and whose loss has affected him profoundly.*[20]

*Montebello might also have mentioned the death, in September 1891, of the grand duchess Alexandra, wife of the Tsar's brother Paul, one of the few people to whom he was said to be deeply,

In so far as they related to the Tsar's isolation, these observations were well taken. When it came, however, to Alexander's political views, and the prospects for completion of the Alliance, Montebello had less to worry about than he supposed. Here, the Tsar's reactions, as the future would soon reveal, flowed from deep-seated emotional trauma relating primarily to the Germans; and he needed no prodding from persons in his entourage to make up his mind about those courses of action the French wished to see him pursue.

. . .

Before leaving this account of the Panama scandal and its effect on Franco-Russian relations, a word is in order, in justice to those in question, about the conduct of the several major French statesmen involved. Of Ribot it may be said at once that at no time was he ever charged with any impropriety; nor is there any reason to suppose that he was guilty of any. If at times he endeavored to quiet the uproar and to repress some of its most sensational manifestations, it was either out of a desire to protect the interests of the Republic as such or to avoid unnecessary damage to France's foreign relations.

As for the three ex-premiers Floquet, Rouvier, and Freycinet, the evidence suggests that all three of them made use of Panama funds but in no instance for the lining of their own pockets—rather, for public purposes that they believed to be worthy. Of these purposes, the least admirable was that with which Floquet was charged: namely, of defeating the Boulangists in the forthcoming elections of 1889. For the rest, it appears to have been, among other things, the cause of a Franco-Russian alliance to which the resources in question were directed; and here, their use appears to have commended itself to the premiers primarily as a means of avoiding the necessity of asking the Parliament for appropriations—a step that could scarcely have failed to leak to the press and thus to vitiate the entire undertaking. Into such bewilderments can statesmen easily wander, particularly when they set about to use money for purposes that they dare not avow.

---

if platonically, attached. (A daughter of the Danish-born King of Greece, she was also a niece of Dagmar.)

Chapter 13

THE CONVENTION ADOPTED

Over the winter and spring of 1893 the question of the ultimate status of the military convention signed the previous August by Boisdeffre and Obruchev remained in limbo. Formally, the situation was that the Tsar was awaiting Giers' judgment with respect to the political implications of the agreement. The French government remained, for its part, committed to the idea of placing before the Russians at some point Freycinet's proposals for amendment of the Boisdeffre-Obruchev draft; but it had not yet taken this step.*

On the Russian side: Giers' illness, and his long absence from Petersburg, precluded his giving any opinion over the winter. There is no evidence that he had as yet seen or had opportunity to study the draft of the convention. He probably would not have wished to give his opinion anyway, even had his health been better, in view of the uncertainties presented by the Panama affair and by Mohrenheim's involvement in it. This last, it will be recalled, was not cleared up until mid-June 1893.

The French, too, did not press the matter over this period. The dramatic domestic-political changes, resulting in the elimination of Freycinet and Ribot from their principal ministerial posts, preoccupied the attention of both the outgoing ministers up to the time of their departure. The new ones, Dupuy and Develle, needed time to orient themselves in their new and unexpected responsibilities.

It was apparently mid-June 1893 before the new French ministers got around to giving attention to the question of the Russian alliance. When they did, their first initiative was to inform Montebello (by letter from Develle of June 22) that they had decided, on Montebello's recommendation, not to press Freycinet's proposed amendments but to continue to ask for final Russian acceptance of the draft convention as already

---

*Whether the French ever formally presented Freycinet's proposals to the Russian government, this writer has not been able to determine. They were evidently under the impression, as of the autumn of 1893, that they had done so; but the writer has been unable to find any evidence that they had.

signed by the two generals. This decision was of course strongly welcomed by Montebello; but Obruchev warned against raising the subject with the Tsar at that juncture.[1] And although Montebello evidently went out more than once to Tsarskoye Selo, some fifteen miles from the capital, to see the ailing Giers, who was installed there for the summer in a species of semiretirement,* the matter appears not to have been mentioned in their meetings.[2]

Moulin, however, was not inclined to give up that easily. On July the 16th, after several months of public controversy and wrangling between crown and Parliament, a new and far-reaching army bill was finally passed by the German Reichstag. It envisaged an increase of some 72,000 men in the German peacetime military establishment and instituted a new system of reserve reinforcements that, when fully implemented, would make it possible for the Germans to mobilize on very short order a force of 520,000 trained men. This was not, actually, a great deal in comparison with the French and Russian standing forces; but, military reactions being what they are, it was enough to excite military leaders in both Petersburg and Paris, to be interpreted by these latter as evidence of aggressive German intentions, and to serve as a stimulus to demands in both capitals for compensating increases in the Russian and French effectives.[3]

Moulin, mindful of the success of the French General Staff memorandum of March 1892 in touching off the first negotiations for a military convention, evidently saw in the passage of this German bill a favorable occasion for repeating the performance. This suggestion was conveyed, in any case, by Moulin to Montebello,[4] who passed it on to General Miribel in a letter of July the 29th.[5] Miribel leapt at the idea. A document responsive to the suggestion was at once drawn up in Paris under his supervision and dispatched to Petersburg on the 8th of August.[6] In this document the new German dispositions were described; and it was pointed out that when they had been completed the German army would constitute "the most formidable offensive force that had ever been organized." No request was made of the Russians for the strengthening of their forces, and nothing was said about the formalization of the military

*With a view, evidently, to avoiding the difficulties of communication involved in his residence at his own dacha in Finland, Giers had been given (no doubt on authorization of the Tsar) quarters in the erstwhile lyceum, attached to the palace at Tsarskoye Selo, where he had himself once been a pupil. Here he no longer held his regular visiting days for the diplomatic chiefs of mission, this duty having been assigned to his deputy Shishkin, at the ministry in Petersburg. But he occasionally received one or the other of the chiefs of the major missions, and kept in touch in this and other ways with the more important matters of foreign office business.

convention. The French, it was stated, were strengthening their own forces. Confidence was expressed that the Russians would do the same.

An interesting feature of Miribel's draft of the memorandum was the wording of the initial sentence. This began with the words: *"En vertu des conventions militaires existant entre la France et la Russie, les Etats-majors des deux armées doivent . . ."** This wording is curious in two respects: first, that it referred to "conventions" in the plural, as though there were more than one of them; and secondly, that it referred to the draft Bois-deffre-Obruchev convention as though it were something already accepted by the two governments and binding on the two staffs. Montebello was quick to notice these abnormalities and changed the sentence to read: *"Par un article du projet de convention militaire arrêtée au mois d'août 1892 entre le général Obroutcheff et le général de Boisdeffre . . .",* thus taking care to respect Giers' insistence that the document was still a draft, not yet formally accepted. But the use of the plural for the word "conventions" remains unclarified. One is reluctant to believe that this could have been a mistake in a document of such importance, or in a volume so meticulously edited as were those of the *Documents diplomatiques français.* One is obliged to wonder, therefore, whether the convention negotiated in 1892 was really the only understanding existing between the two general staffs—whether something more had not been concluded without benefit of the two foreign offices.

By the time this document reached Montebello, in Petersburg, the Tsar had left for his annual vacation in Denmark. Obruchev, too, had left for France. On the 26th of August, Montebello acknowledged the receipt of the document in a letter to Develle and told the latter that it had his general approval; but he explained the difficulty of doing anything effective with it at that moment. Even Giers, he wrote, feeble and exhausted, had suffered a relapse and was expected to remain for some time at Tsarskoye Selo. But he went on to point out in this letter that the situation was not entirely unfavorable. The Tsar, he said, had awaited with impatience the outcome of the first tour of the French elections held in late August and September, which were generally regarded as a test of the ability of the French political system to regain its stability after the shocks of the Panama affair. The results of the first tour of the elections had been reassuring; and the Tsar, Montebello had heard, had been favorably im-

---

*"Pursuant to the military conventions already existing between France and Russia, the general staffs of the two armies must . . ."

pressed.* And as for the military convention, Montebello assured Develle that the Tsar viewed the matter as already completed. The question of the way it was to be finally approved, to which the French attached such importance, scarcely engaged his attention. Of course one had not been able to mention the matter during the Mohrenheim affair; and after that there had still been the uncertainty about the elections. But these impediments were now in the past; and he proposed to pursue the matter when the Tsar returned.[7]

Having reported all this to Paris, Montebello transmitted Miribel's document (September 6) to Giers, who immediately sent it on to Vannovski to get his reaction before sending it on to the Tsar at Copenhagen. Vannovski kept it for a couple of weeks, then returned it (September 23) with a letter for the Tsar. In this letter he associated himself with the French view that the German army bill had been inspired by aggressive intentions. The Russians, he added, had already taken action (July 28) to counter the German move; and he went on to explain what this action consisted of—among other things, the dispatch of two new artillery corps to the western border.

With that, the whole dossier—Miribel's memorandum and letters from the two ministers—was sent off by courier to Copenhagen, where the Tsar received it only in the first days of October.[8]

When Montebello handed Miribel's memorandum to Giers on the 6th of September, he obviously talked with Giers about the existing situation and about the chances for a final regularization of the military convention. In the report he submitted to Paris after this encounter, he did not quote Giers directly, but he made two interesting observations that could only have reflected reactions he had either from Giers or, through Moulin, from Obruchev. First, he pointed out that over the entire past year the Tsar had actually been adhering, in his military dispositions, to the provisions of the convention, and could be expected to continue to do so. But beyond that, Montebello showed himself much more optimistic than he had been a month earlier about the chances for an early resolution of the problem of the status of the convention. "We are thus advancing," he wrote,

*Parliamentary elections had taken place in France on August 20 and on September 3, 1893. As a result of this electoral contest, the existing Opportuniste government gained strength at the expense of the conservative elements; and while it lost some ground to the more radical elements, it emerged generally strengthened from the test. This was generally accepted as a demonstration of the stability of the Republic, and as proof that it had successfully survived the Panama affair.

slowly, perhaps, but nonetheless surely, toward our goal. . . . I am convinced that being now, as we are, relieved of the preoccupation with the proposed amendments to the draft convention . . . and in view of the favorable effect produced by the elections, we will arrive quite naturally next winter at the regularization of the draft, which we may already consider as having been adopted by the Emperor, and for which all that is lacking is simply a question of form.[9]

These words, quite accurately prophetic, as it turned out, would perhaps have been even more cheerful had Montebello known one other thing that had happened just before the Tsar's departure for Denmark at the end of August. Alexander, before leaving, had instructed Giers to examine now, at leisure, the text of the convention and to give his reaction to it. The result of this was that on September the 23rd Vannovski, prior to leaving, himself, for Western Europe, sent to Giers the entire file on the negotiations, together with the actual text of the convention, as agreed upon the previous year by the two generals.[10]

The importance of these dates, from the standpoint of Alexander's motives in finally authorizing the exchange of notes formalizing the convention, cannot be overestimated. He would not have given these instructions to Giers had he not already made up his mind that the time had come to give final governmental sanction to the agreement. The date when the instructions were given can be narrowed down to the period between the 12th and the 23rd of August, when (or so it would appear) the Tsar left for Copenhagen. And one may be reasonably confident that the actual occasion was Giers' final audience, one or two days before the Tsar's departure and just after receipt of the news of the favorable outcome of the French elections.

All of this strongly suggests that Alexander had never really departed from his desire to see the convention regularized as soon as this could safely and conveniently be done. He was unwilling to take the final action so long as Giers remained uncommitted. Should the Alliance, for some reason or other, work out badly, and should it then become known that he had failed to get Giers' favorable opinion, he could later be accused of having rashly entered into an unwise commitment without having consulted his venerable and experienced minister for foreign affairs, or of having ignored the latter's adverse opinion. There had been no use in pressing for this opinion before midsummer in the face of Giers' long illness, the Panama scandal, Mohrenheim's embarrassments, and the uncertain state of France's internal-political life. Now, however, when Giers, if not well, was at least again doing business from his quarters at Tsarskoye Selo, and when these other uncertainties had been removed, Alexander was prepared—supposedly under the needling of Obruchev—to reactivate the question.

From here on, had the French really known it, all was clear sailing. All they needed was patience. For if Giers did not really approve of the convention (and he never did), such were Russian conditions that there were limits to the length of time and the firmness with which he could oppose it in defiance of the strong feelings of his imperial master. From the end of August 1893, the die was really cast.

There were, however, in advance of the final ratification at the end of the year, certain intervening events; and it may be amusing and revealing, if not decisively significant, to take account of them.

. . .

It may first be noted that from the 13th to the 27th of October 1893 a Russian naval squadron paid an official and ceremonial visit to the great French naval port of Toulon, not far from Marseilles. The timing of the visit had no direct connection with the question of the final approval of the military convention. What was involved here was, in the formal sense, merely the normal reciprocation of the visit paid by the French squadron to Cronstadt two years earlier, in 1891. The plans for the event had been agreed upon in principle some three months earlier; but no date was fixed and no announcement made until very shortly before the visit took place.

If the Cronstadt visit was an unprecedented event in Russia, its reciprocation by a Russian fleet at Toulon was no less so in France. The event turned out to be the occasion for a popular demonstration of emotion and enthusiasm such as France too had never seen in the past or would never see in the future. The squadron, commanded by Rear Admiral Theodor Avelan and composed of one battleship-flagship, the *Pamyat Azova,* two battle cruisers, and three smaller vessels, entered the harbor of Toulon on the morning of the 13th. (Its triumphal appearance was only moderately marred by the fact that two of the vessels had collided in open sea en route to Toulon, and the bow of one was embarrassingly disfigured.*) The ceremonial reception of Admiral Avelan on the

---

*The French collaborated loyally with the Russians in concealing from the public the gravity of this accident, which was serious enough to occasion a meeting of the War Council in Petersburg. The French press was successfully appealed to to keep quiet about it. Certain cosmetic improvements to the disfigured vessels were carried out with the help of the French in Toulon; and the visit proceeded normally.

municipal dock was only the first event in an uproarious and continuous round of formalities, receptions, ceremonies, luncheons, dinners, visits, invitations, toasts, and speeches, four full days of which took place in Paris, others in Marseilles—all to the accompaniment of mass popular demonstrations reaching, on many occasions, an intensity that can only be described as delirium. For the onerous hospitality to which French officers had been subjected during their Cronstadt visit, two years before, the unfortunate Russian officers were now made to suffer twofold. Jaded, bewildered, overfed, and exhausted, dragged from event to event amid cheering excited mobs, deluged with flowers, kissed by innumerable enthusiastic women, obliged to embrace an endless procession of wide-eyed and frightened children bearing bouquets, admired, wined, dined, feted, and showered with gifts, these dazed men were shunted about, day after day, until it was only with the most heroic effort that they were able to play their part at all. Their position was not made easier by the fact that only two or three of the more junior ones spoke even passable French.

This entire frenzy was of course grist to the mill of the various French chauvinists, both organizations and individuals; the latter, in fact, were extensively instrumental in creating it. The thousands of gifts heaped upon the visiting Russians included, for example, several hundred bracelets for the wives of the crew members, inscribed on the one side with "Cronstadt 1891" in Russian letters and on the other with "Toulon 1893" in Latin ones, all provided by the efforts of the celebrated French chauvinist-publicist, Juliette Adam, and brought to Toulon (much to the discomfort of the Russian embassy, where she was viewed askance) by that good lady herself, quivering with patriotic emotion.* And when the officers arrived by special train at the gare d'Orléans in Paris and were taken across town through endlessly cheering crowds to the Cercle Militaire—the senior officers' club on the place de l'Opéra—it was none other than General Félix Gustave Saussier, a man long known for his advocacy of the Alliance and repeatedly the object of grateful tributes and gifts from the pro-French Russian nationalists, who, as military commandant of the city of Paris, greeted the Russian admiral, amid wild enthusiasm, at the foot of the staircase of the building. Such examples could be multiplied manifold.

Distance, of course, prevented most of the comparable Russian chauvinists from taking part in this drama, as they would have loved to

---

*The gifts received by Admiral Avelan alone were reputed to have surpassed half a million francs in value.

do. But they were no less excited over the event. It was not without significance that the delegation sent to represent the Russian journalists' association at the various functions attending the visit was headed by none other than Colonel V. V. Komarov, himself an officer, brother of two high-ranking Russian generals, and editor-publisher of the weekly *Svyet*, a strongly nationalistic and Pan-Slavistic paper generally regarded as the mouthpiece of the more nationalistic faction among the senior military officers.*

Leaving aside the Tsar, who was at that time in Copenhagen and of whose reactions more will be said presently, the Russian foreign office and evidently certain others in high position in Petersburg viewed with some apprehension and with a distinct absence of enthusiasm all this demonstrative outpouring of political emotion in France. They were afraid that it would prove provocative to the Germans to the point where it could produce serious political and military complications. For this reason, presumably, Mohrenheim was not sent to Toulon to attend the events and to accompany the Russian officers on their peregrinations, his place being taken by his deputy, Giers' son. It is significant, too, that the choice of Admiral Avelan (and this, again, appears to have been Giers' doing) as commander of the Russian squadron had been strongly influenced by the fact that he spoke no French, the thought being that he, restrained by this handicap, would be less likely to be induced by the enthusiasms of the moment to give, at the various dinners, fulsome toasts—toasts that would appear in the press and that everyone would regret on the following morning. Even more significant was the fact that the Russian minister of the navy, the Tsar's brother, Grand Duke Aleksei Aleksandrovich, whose office would naturally have suggested his participation, was not in attendance, despite the fact that he was no farther away than Biarritz at the time of the visit. He even delayed his departure from Biarritz in order to avoid being present in Paris at the time when the Russian officers visited that city. And the restrained tone of the Tsar's telegram of appreciation to the French president at the end of the visit (again, the product of Giers' influence) was widely noted throughout Europe.

The Russian anxieties concerning the effect of the visit on the Germans were not entirely misplaced. Three weeks before the visit took place Caprivi, the German chancellor, had written, in a secret handwrit-

---

*Komarov had long been the advocate of a close military relationship with France; and it was he who had tendered the dinner in Petersburg for the French poet-chauvinist Paul Déroulède, when the latter visited Russia in 1886.

ten memorandum to the German foreign minister, that he looked forward to the event with anxiety: "It would not take much," he wrote, "for it to produce consequences of the most serious nature." He even went so far as to urge that should it come to a military conflict, the Italians should be encouraged to take the military initiative—this, in the hopes that it would bring England in on the German side.[11]

These gloomy German apprehensions were somewhat—but only somewhat—modified by dispatches received during the visit from the German ambassadors in Paris and Petersburg. Münster, at Paris, reported that while the French of course hoped to regain their former position of preeminence with the help of the Russians, they wanted no early war.[12] And Werder, the new ambassador in Petersburg, wrote that while he saw in this intimate Franco-Russian fraternization a real threat to the peace (with which view the Kaiser expressed himself emphatically in agreement), it was not likely that matters would be carried to an actual initiation of hostilities so long as Giers was in office and Alexander III still on his throne—unless, of course (which he recognized as possible) the Franco-Russian enthusiasm developed a momentum that the Tsar could no longer withstand.[13]

The visit, with its sensational accompanying demonstrations, thus passed off without leading to serious immediate complications. But its effect on public attitudes, and on the popular view of the Franco-Russian relationship in particular, was profound. If the Cronstadt visit had persuaded all of Europe that there already existed something in the way of a political "entente" between the French and Russian governments, the Toulon visit left no doubt in the public mind that the two governments were now in a real state of alliance, whatever might be the nature of the documents or understandings on which that relationship rested. It is, in fact, remarkable how closely the instinctive conclusions of the broad European public coincided with the tenor of the secret understandings actually arrived at around the time of the respective naval visits. From the time of the Toulon visit down to 1914, the Franco-Russian Alliance may be said to have existed as a reality in the eyes of the public, even though the documentary basis for it remained concealed, over all this period, in the deepest recesses of the respective governmental safes.

. . .

Alexander III, meanwhile, had been spending his usual late-summer and autumn vacation in Denmark with his family, at the royal summer palace of Fredensborg, not far from Copenhagen, where the Danish royal family normally provided him with accommodations. He had left Petersburg on or about August the 23rd. Intending to make the passage to Copenhagen in his yacht, he had been detained for two or three days by bad weather at Libau, his port of departure, and had used this time to give formal inauguration to the construction there of what was to become Russia's major ice-free naval base (the Cronstadt base being normally frozen in for much of each winter.)*

The first weeks of the Tsar's Danish vacation passed off peaceably enough, with the succession of luncheons, dinners, picnics, promenades, and hunts to which such periods of royal recreation were customarily devoted. If there was anything out of the ordinary, it was only the reported violence of some of Alexander's reactions when mention was made of the person of the German Kaiser. In early September the Kaiser attended, in company with the Italian crown prince, maneuvers of the German forces in Lorraine, on which occasion he indulged himself, in a speech before the assembled troops, in a few more of the melodramatic and inflammatory forensic outbursts to which he was temperamentally given. The Tsar's verbal reactions on learning of these statements were described as unprintable. And when there was talk in the Danish royal family of the possibility of a visit by the Kaiser to Denmark, Alexander is said to have proclaimed to the assembled family that if William II set foot on Danish soil, he would leave the palace for the duration of the latter's presence there.[14]

It was not long after that episode that the Danish royal family, together with its assembled guests, was racked by painful tensions—all occasioned, in one way or another, by the political emotions and unfortunate conduct of one member of the family: the Orleanist Princess Marie, wife of Prince Valdemar, youngest son of the Danish royal couple. A flaming French patriot, Marie never endeavored to conceal from her Danish in-laws her primary and passionate attachment to the interests of her native France. During this visit of the Russian imperial couple, as during previous ones, she paid assiduous attention to the Russian

---

*The project of constructing this base at Libau had for some time been a hotly contested one in Petersburg; for there was one faction, in which Witte was prominently involved, that favored as an alternative the selection of Murmansk for this purpose, on the grounds that Murmansk, in contrast to Libau, had—in addition to being also ice free—unimpeded access to the world oceans. The final selection of Libau may have been influenced by the recent German acquisition of the island of Helgoland and the construction (in progress since 1887) of the Kiel Canal.

monarch, often accompanying him on walks and other diversions, and losing no opportunity to influence him in the cause of a Franco-Russian alliance.*

Such behavior would have been questionable enough, in any case, for one who had now accepted the status of a member of the Danish royal family; but it was made worse, in this particular summer, by highly imprudent relations that the princess entertained with the French legation at Copenhagen—above all, with the French chargé d'affaires, M. Pasteur, and the military attaché, Captain Beauchamps. The available documents make it abundantly clear that for both of these officials she served, most improperly, as a regular source of information on whatever passed in the Danish royal family circle and in the entourage of the Tsar that might conceivably be of interest to the French.[15]

Such proclivities on the princess's part could hardly fail to lead sooner or later to trouble; and they were not long in doing so. This was the summer of the Siamese crisis—a series of events in which the French government was extensively involved. On one of the days at the end of September 1893, a report was received in Copenhagen, and at once passed along to the King at Fredensborg, to the effect that the French government was demanding of the Siamese government that all foreign advisers to the King of Siam, including certain Danish military officers then in the service of that monarch, be immediately dismissed. This incident led to a lively and painful discussion in the royal family circle. The French action was of course generally resented. The princess Marie, however, leaped at once to the defense of the French government. Tempers rose. Marie's sister-in-law, Alexandra, future Queen of England, reproached her bitterly for lack of loyalty to Denmark. The Tsar, appealed to by the Danish king for support, equivocated and urged patience. All in all, it was an unhappy moment.

And worse was still to come. Somewhere, though certainly not in the Danish government or royal family, the idea had arisen of asking the

---

*The Danish historian Henning Nielsen notes, in his *Dansk udenrigspolitik 1875–1894* (Odense: 1977), that Marie had also been involved, in 1887, in the transmission to the Tsar, at Fredensborg, of the false documents (subsequently known as the Ferdinand Documents) sent to him at that time by the French foreign minister of the day, Emile Flourens. I regret that this detail was not known to me when I wrote about the incident in question—both in the first volume of this present series (Kennan, *Bismarck's European Order*, ch. 19) and in a special study published in the *Jahrbücher für Geschichte Osteuropas* No. 26 (1978) under the title "The Mystery of the Ferdinand Documents." Bismarck, it would appear, was not entirely wrong in his suspicion that the Orleanists, or at least one of them, had a hand in this sordid affair.

French government to send warships to Copenhagen in October, as a gesture of homage to the Tsar at the time of the Toulon visit. That the Tsar actually originated the idea, as was sometimes reported, seems implausible. It was not in his character. But that he in some way connived at it or sanctioned it seems evident, as does the complicity of the French legation at Copenhagen in implementing, if not initiating, the project.

On September the 14th, Pasteur gave a preliminary notice to the Danish foreign office that certain French vessels might soon be making a call at Copenhagen, but gave no date or other details. In preceding years, a French fishing-patrol vessel had occasionally called at Copenhagen, and the Danes at first supposed that something of this nature was involved. Only on the 3rd of October was it made clear to the Danish authorities that the ships in question would actually be arriving the following week. And only at the last minute were the Danes informed that this was to be a naval visit. On the 10th of October, three days before the arrival of the Russian squadron at Toulon, the vessels in question— two French warships, the *Isly* and the *Surcouf*—appeared off the breakwater at Copenhagen.*

The Danes were seriously miffed over this whole procedure. There had been no invitation from the Danish government; nor had that government even been properly consulted. It was clear that the visit was intended as a gesture towards the Tsar. But this was not the Tsar's territory; he was only a guest in Denmark; the sovereign of that country was the Danish king. It was discourteous to send naval vessels to greet the Tsar without the full approval of, indeed, otherwise than at the invitation of, his Danish host.† Beyond that, the Danes, conscious of being a small country in a delicate position on the border of Germany, had no wish to be made a party to Franco-Russian demonstrations, seeing in this a possible complication of their own relations with Germany.

The ships having once arrived, however, it was unthinkable to send them away; and the whole matter now came to a head over the question as to whether the Tsar should visit them. The princess was warmly urging

---

*The *Isly*, a new armored vessel of what would today be called the destroyer class, was very fast by the standards of that day, and was widely admired, even at the British legation, when she appeared in Copenhagen.

†The failure of the French legation to make clear to the Danes what sort of vessels were being sent was all the more offensive because when, in the previous year, the French had proposed to send two naval vessels to Copenhagen to congratulate the King and Queen of Denmark on their golden wedding anniversary, the Danes, fearing political embarrassment, had asked them please not to do so.

that he should do so, and should do so precisely on October 13th, the day of the arrival of the Russian squadron at Toulon. According to the rules of protocol, it should of course have been the King of Denmark who first visited the vessels, received their salute, and allowed his flag to be flown from their mastheads during his presence on board. But King Christian IX, angered at the inconsiderate manner in which the visit had been arranged, had no intention of paying such a visit.* The Tsar, on the other hand, was either inclined or felt himself under obligation to do so.

Once again, severe tension reigned in the Fredensborg palace. Alexander decided, allegedly against the wishes of the King, to include a visit to the French ships in the program for a series of other appearances in Copenhagen (one of them a keel-laying ceremony for a new Russian-imperial yacht to be built at a Danish shipyard) on the day following the arrival of the French vessels. This decision he duly carried out, in the company of two of his sons. Dagmar, the Empress, as a member of the Danish royal family, prudently chose not to accompany him. The French princess desired passionately to be included in the party; but at this point King Christian, who had now had enough, put his foot down and caused the lady to be confined, weeping, to her room in the palace for the remainder of the day.

Alexander, faced with the unhappy situation at the palace, appears to have done what he could to reduce the demonstrational quality of the visit. He made it known that he wished it to be considered as informal, caused the corresponding flag to be flown from his yacht, and changed to what he considered to be the appropriate costume (the uniform of a Russian admiral) for the occasion. But the French ignored these signals, raised the Russian imperial standard on the *Isly,* and gave him the full honors of a visiting head of state, including a 31-gun salute, thus compelling the Russian imperial yacht, the Russian naval vessels escorting it, and other vessels in the harbor, to follow suit as best they could.†

In these circumstances, the visit received wide international public-

---

*The princess told the French legation that the King had received a letter from the Kaiser, begging him not to visit the vessels. The writer knows of no other evidence for this claim.

†This confusion even had a comic-tragic consequence. When the crew of the *Tsarevna,* the Russian torpedo boat that served as naval escort to the Tsar's yacht, attempted, evidently in some haste, to match—or to respond to—the French gun salute, someone forgot to remove the wooden stopper from the muzzle of the gun employed. The detonation of the blank shell popped it out and sent it sailing across the water, with the result that it hit and killed a sailor on another Russian naval vessel then lying in harbor. The Tsar was obliged, a day or two later, to attend a funeral mass for the victim.

ity—so much so that it was sometimes taken to have a symbolic significance scarcely smaller than that of the visit of the Russian fleet to Toulon, which had begun the previous day. This could not fail to have a further unhappy effect on relations between the Tsar and his Danish parents-in-law; and it may not have been wholly coincidental that when, five days later, Alexander took leave of the Danish royal couple and boarded his yacht for the return to Petersburg, he was, whether he knew it or not, completing the last visit he was ever to make to the Danish court.

The fears that the French naval visit might affect Denmark's relations with Germany proved to be not entirely unjustified. The German minister in Copenhagen, Freiherr von den Brinken, saw in it, and so reported to his government, "a highly important event . . . that moves the real center of gravity of the Franco-Russian fraternization, so to speak, from Toulon to Copenhagen." He found it strange that Alexander should not have recognized that this sort of demonstration would quite naturally give offense in Berlin; and he thought (most unjustly) that all this could not have happened without Danish connivance. To which the Kaiser noted, on the margin of the report: "I am entirely in agreement. This is a very good report, which unfortunately only confirms my own impressions."[16]

And not only did the episode affect Denmark's relations with Germany, but it had a most painful aftermath with respect to the French. Some three months later, the Paris *Figaro* came out with an article (February 25, 1894) about the whole affair. This was followed four days later by a similar one in *Le Gaulois*. In each of these articles praise was heaped on both the princess and Captain Beauchamps for their gallant efforts at influencing the Tsar; and it was made clear, with startling candor if not naiveté, that the princess had functioned as a regular informant for the French legation, providing it with information *"sur la pensée, les dispositions, et les impressions de l'Empereur de Russie" (Le Figaro)*. It was then soon revealed that the *Figaro* article had been inspired, if not written, by none other than the French minister at Copenhagen, M. d'Aunay, who, although absent from his post at the time in question, had now risen to applaud in this manner the great patriotic exploits of his subordinates.

The consequences were appalling. All three of those involved—d'Aunay, Pasteur, and Beauchamps—were withdrawn. The careers of the latter two were severely damaged. D'Aunay not only lost his position in the diplomatic service but was placed under indictment and caused to defend his conduct before the Conseil d'Etat. What the effect was on the princess the record does not reveal. When the matter was mentioned to the Empress Dagmar some days later at one of the winter balls in Petersburg, her only comment was, "My poor sister-in-law!"

.   .   .

This episode, obviously, left a bad taste in everyone's mouth. It was, in fact, strangely out of accord with Alexander's earlier behavior. In 1887, in connection with the affair of the Ferdinand Documents (see above), he had shown himself much concerned lest it appear that he had behaved improperly, in his capacity as a guest at the Danish court, in allowing documents of high political significance to be delivered into his hands by agents of the French foreign minister during the course of his visit there. Now, in 1893, he even went so far as to create major embarrassment for his Danish hosts; yet there was, this time, no sign of remorse or concern for this fact on his part. It may well be asked whether one cannot see in this episode another sign of that curious deterioration of Alexander's personality at this time to which reference has already been made.

In the early years of the reign of Alexander III the Danes were still smarting from the humiliation inflicted upon them in the war with Prussia in 1864. The influence of Alexander's Danish wife as well as of her mother, Queen Louise, surely played a significant part at that time in heightening Alexander's congenital dislike of the Germans and in assisting him to get over his distrust of French democracy. But by the 1890s some of the trauma of the 1864 war had begun to wear off at the Danish court. Perhaps the foreign marriages entered into by several of the Danish royal children, bringing with them as they did extensive contacts all over Europe, had the effect, over the course of time, of encouraging at the Copenhagen court a wider view of the complexities of the European scene than that which had prevailed in earlier years. The Danish government, in any case, seeing Europe now dividing into two opposing alliances, showed marked concern for the preservation and protection of its neutrality. The last thing the Danish king wanted at that juncture was to appear in the posture of a virtual ally of the Franco-Russian combination. In these circumstances, the Tsar's presence and behavior in Denmark, seen against the background of the Toulon visit and the general sensationalism of the Franco-Russian "fraternization" of the moment, was understandably a heavy burden for the King and government of a small country in Denmark's position. What surprises is only the Tsar's apparent insensitivity to this situation.

. . .

When Alexander III returned to Petersburg in the final week of October 1893, his mind was made up. It had probably been made up before he went to Denmark; but the intervening impressions had done nothing to weaken his resolve. He had, in the final week of his stay in Denmark, received, at long last, Miribel's memorandum, together with the letter from Vannovski associating himself with Miribel's view that the German army bill reflected aggressive intentions on the part of the Kaiser and his military leaders. Then, he had received abundant reports of the tremendous reception of the Russian fleet at Toulon and was pleased with what he heard. All of this could only support his resolve to see the military convention given governmental approval as soon as this could be conveniently arranged.[17]

Montebello, at the time of the Tsar's return, was away in France on vacation. So was Vannovski. Giers was now almost too ill to be a factor. The Tsar still wanted the latter's reaction to the convention; but this was only for form's sake. His own feelings were strong; and it is unlikely that anything that Giers said, or at any rate anything Giers was likely to say in the circumstances, could have deterred him, at this point, from doing what he wanted to do.

Obruchev, taking advantage of his temporary status as deputy war minister in Vannovski's absence, lost no time seeking an audience with the Tsar. In the very first days of December he was received; and if there were any lingering doubts in Alexander's mind about the need for the step he was proposing to take, Obruchev dispelled them. For this was the occasion on which the general's victory was really won. When the meeting was over, he felt himself in a position to dispatch through Moulin, and did so dispatch, a confidential letter to Boisdeffre telling the latter that all had gone, on this occasion, in accordance with their wishes: when Montebello returned to Petersburg, the exchange of notes would be signed.[18]

Obruchev had evidently already suggested that the French should try their hand, in the meantime, at the drafting of the language of a suitable exchange of this nature, so that Montebello could have such a draft in hand when he returned. The archives of the Quai d'Orsay contain, in any case, three drafts of this nature, one of them in Montebello's hand, all dated simply "November 1893."

In view of the evidence that matters were now rapidly approaching a conclusion, Montebello wanted to advance the date of his return to Russia, already fixed for the beginning of December. Obruchev warned strongly against it. The Tsar, he thought, would see this as an effort on the part of the French to force the pace. Throughout this period, in fact, Obruchev consistently warned the French against taking any initiative of their own in the matter. Things, he felt, were going their way. Everything could be spoiled by signs of overeagerness on their part.

Montebello accepted this advice, and did not return until the 9th of December. He returned, one may suppose, in a state of some anxiety, because on the 25th of November the Dupuy government had fallen, in Paris, the premiership being assumed on December the 3rd by the future president, Jean Casimir-Périer. The question at once arose, in the minds of all the French personalities involved in this question, as to whether this would not once again frighten the Tsar into further postponement of the ratification of the convention. But this anxiety (interestingly enough) proved to be entirely misplaced. No sooner did Montebello arrive than he was received by Giers, who presented him, on the Tsar's behalf, with the Order of Alexander Nevski.[19] Four days later, on the 13th, the ambassador found himself guest of honor at a tremendous dinner, for four hundred guests, tendered to him by an assembly of the marshals of nobility from various parts of the empire— an occasion on which, wearing no doubt his newly conferred Cordon of Alexander Nevski, he was obliged to confront a small mountain of congratulatory telegrams and to respond to a long series of similar toasts. Among the number of the guests, there figured a galaxy of eminent figures of the empire, civilian and military, including all the ministers of the government, with the exception (significantly) of two—Vannovski, who was still abroad, and Giers, who, as we shall see presently, had other reasons for his absence. And three days later (December 16) Montebello found himself received by the Emperor at Gatchina, and this— for the first time in his entire service in Russia—by invitation of the latter, not at his own request.[20]

The Tsar received him with great cordiality, spoke most warmly of the reception given to the Russian squadron on its recent visit to Toulon, and even more warmly of the pleasure he had himself experienced upon visiting the *Isly* at Copenhagen. He was particularly appreciative on the subject of the peaceful disposition of the French government. "I hear talk," Montebello later quoted him as saying, of the ideas of revenge you French are supposed to be entertaining, in which one professes to see such a threat. You would not be good patriots—you would in fact not be French—if you did not cling to the thought that the day would come when you would regain possession of your lost provinces; but between this very natural sentiment and the idea of launching some sort of a provocation with a view to realizing it, in short—the idea of revenge —there is a great distance; and you have shown many times—you have just recently shown it again—that you wish above all for peace and that you know how to await it with dignity.[21]

Even on the occasion of this audience, and despite all the evidence of the favorable direction in which things were moving, Montebello had been advised by Obruchev not to broach with the Tsar the subject of the final approval of the military convention. Twenty times in the course of the audience, Montebello later reported, he had been on the verge of ignoring this advice and bringing up the subject; but he restrained himself each time. (Thus delicately were things done in the Russian capital in 1893.)

This meeting of Montebello with the Tsar took place on the 17th of December. On the following day, Giers capitulated. He had, up to this time, never responded to the Tsar's request for his opinion on the political desirability of the military convention. He had not done so for the reason that he had never wavered in his opposition to seeing the document become an obligation on the Russian government as well as on the General Staff alone, and he knew that as long as he could delay matters by withholding his opinion, the fatal step would not be taken. But the man he served was an absolute ruler, and there were limits to the permissible nature and duration of any opposition to his firmly expressed wishes. One could not, as in a democratic country, simply "make a record" of one's disagreement and resign. At a certain point, if the monarch felt sufficiently strongly about something, there was nothing to do but to swallow one's hesitations and go along. Besides, the Tsar had already taken the bit in his teeth and had advanced the matter to a point where there could be no turning back.

Giers had never concealed from the Tsar his misgivings about the convention or even about the demonstrations of solidarity with France with which the French ambassador had been welcomed back to the Russian capital. Neither he nor any other senior official of the Russian foreign office had attended (he was quick to point this out to the German ambassador) the recent dinner for Montebello. But now, in the wake of Montebello's audience of the 17th with the Tsar, the latter must have conveyed to Giers some message that made further resistance impossible.

Montebello, acting on Obruchev's advice, had evidently never informed the Russian foreign office of the readiness of the French government, conveyed to him six months earlier, to abandon Freycinet's proposed amendments to the convention. Thus Giers now had before him not only the original text of the convention but also the proposed changes. Vannovski, it appears, had accepted those of the proposed amendments that related to military matters, but had deferred to Giers with respect to that which would have modified Article VII, calling for the agreement to be held in strict secrecy. Giers now executed his final and formal surrender. He drew up for presentation to the Tsar (one can imagine with what feelings) a *"notice très secrète"* (as Lamsdorf called it), in which he said that while he found the original wording of Article VII to be preferable to that proposed by Freycinet, in other respects he *"ne verrait point d'inconvénient à l'adoption des clauses stipulés entre les Etats-Majors Russes et Français dans leur forme actuelle qui a été sanctionée par l'approbation principielle de Sa Majesté l'Empereur et n'exclue pas la possibilité de développements ultérieures, si les circonstances les exigeaient par la suite."**[22] He took this piece of paper to Gatchina and presented it to the Tsar the following day (the 19th). Alexander kept it overnight and returned it to him on the 20th with a marginal notation in red pencil, the nature of which is not known to this writer. The next day Obruchev came to see Giers and told him that the French were prepared to abandon their insistence on any or all of the proposed amendments.

Forty-eight hours later the faithful Lamsdorf was put to the drafting of the exchange of notes placing the seal of governmental approval on the convention. Giers took Lamsdorf's draft to the Tsar on the 26th. Then, on the 27th, after conferring once more with his imperial master, he addressed, and signed, his letter to Montebello—the culmination of one and a half years of effort to reach a binding military alliance between the two governments. The note, dated December 27, 1893, read, in English translation, as follows:

---

*In English: With the exception of the proposed amendment to Article VII, Giers "saw no objection to the adoption of the clauses agreed upon between the Russian and French general staffs in their existing form, as sanctioned by the approval in principle of His Majesty the Emperor, this not excluding the possibility of further changes (développements ultérieures), should circumstances demand them." What were conceived to be these possible *"développements ultérieures"* is obscure. There is evidence that in the final stages of the discussions about the military convention the two general staffs were much preoccupied with the question of how they could communicate telegraphically in the event of the outbreak of war with the Germans. The most promising answer was, apparently, via Denmark and England. But this, perhaps, required further exploration and agreement.

Having examined, by order of highest authority, the draft military convention drawn up by the Russian and French general staffs in August 1892, and having submitted to the Emperor my opinion of it, it is my duty to inform your Excellency that the text of this arrangement, as approved in principle by His Majesty and signed by His Majesty's Aide de Camp, General Obruchev, and by General of Division Boisdeffre, may be considered from now on as having been definitely adopted in its present form. The two general staffs will thus have the right to concert their views at any time and to communicate to each other reciprocally whatever information it seems useful to them to communicate.

It was in keeping with the long path that had led to this result, beset as it so often had been with minor obstacles, that even the execution of the order implied in the Tsar's approval of this draft did not proceed without the usual minor hitch. Giers, notwithstanding his illness, had managed to make the short journey to Gatchina to show the draft of the letter to the Tsar and to get his authorization to transmit it. Obruchev, in some way apprised of the final successful termination of this long and patient effort, came at once to tell Montebello the good news: the Tsar, he said, had given his blessing; the signed letter would soon be forthcoming from Giers. Montebello, equally triumphant, and filled with pride over this vindication of his own tactics of patience and restraint, sat down forthwith and got off a letter to Boisdeffre, to be taken by courier, with the momentous tidings. But Giers, laid low once again by the exertion of his journey to Gatchina, was now unable to receive Montebello in order to present the letter to him in person; yet there was, on the other hand, no one else to whom he dared entrust it for transmission. It was not, therefore, until December 30 that Montebello finally received it. He replied to it, on January the 4th, 1894, with a letter simply repeating the language of Giers' communication and confirming that the French government, too, regarded the convention as now being in force.* (The original French texts of both letters are reproduced in appendix III to this account.)

. . .

This brings to an end the tale of how the two documents that originally constituted the written and contractual expression of what has become known as the Franco-Russian Alliance came into existence. This

---

*January the 4th, 1894, was, on the Gregorian calendar used in Russia, the 23rd of December, 1893. This explains the fact that the Alliance, generally described in Western usage as "of 1894," has often been referred to in Russian texts as "of 1893."

is not the proper point for a general appraisal of the significance of this result. But there are a few features of the final action that might well be noted before we leave the subject entirely.

(1) For an alliance of historic significance, destined to play an important part in determining the alignment of forces in the First World War, the two sets of notes exchanged in 1891 and 1893–1894, plus the military convention to which the second set referred, constituted a very flimsy basis. The first merely committed the two governments, through the word of their foreign ministers of the day, to act in concert on all questions involving threats to the peace, and, in case peace should be endangered, to consult on what "immediate and simultaneous measures" might be taken for the protection of their mutual interests. The second recognized a commitment of the two general staffs to the effect that if one of the parties to the Triple Alliance should mobilize, each of them would do likewise; and that if France should be attacked by Germany, or by Italy and Germany together, Russia would come to her assistance; whereas if Russia were to be attacked by Germany, or by Austria and Germany together, France would come to Russia's assistance. Beyond this there was an agreement on the size of the forces that each party would mobilize and employ in the event of war against Germany, and an agreement that these forces should be employed in such a manner as to force the Germans to fight a two-front war—simultaneously, that is, in East and in West. There was a clause about the exchange of military information, and a mutual commitment not to make a separate peace during any war envisaged by the treaty.

This was, in other words, a purely military document. Nothing was said in it about the political objectives for which one might be fighting. The document reflected a world of thought in which only military factors were recognized. Military actions were seen, by implication, as sufficient to all purposes. In this concept, such things as the spirit and ideals of governmental systems, the political purposes that might be served by military action, or the question of peace terms had no place. The document prescribed the circumstances in which military operations were to be put in hand and placed certain strictures on the manner in which they were to be conducted; but it did not treat the question of *why* they were to be conducted in the first place, or to what end.

(2) Neither document bore, on the Russian side, the signature of the Tsar. The second one contained an implicit commitment on his part, in the form of the phrase *d'ordre suprême* (which I have translated as "by

order of the highest authority"); but none of the documents bore his signature.

(3)   While the Russian letter referred to the military convention as having been "definitely adopted," it did not say by whom it was adopted —whether by the governments or by the general staffs. The nearest inference was that it was adopted as an agreement between the staffs, blessed by the governments.

(4)   There is, as noted above, no evidence that Giers ever really approved the adoption of the convention. That he dropped his formal opposition to the final action—dropped it under heavy pressure from Obruchev and the Tsar—is clear. But this could have been a mere yielding to the force of circumstances. One will note that there was nothing in the final wording of the letter he addressed to Montebello to show, or even to suggest, that the letter stood as a reflection of the wishes and views of the man who signed it. Giers, it was here stated, had submitted to the Tsar his opinion of the convention. Yes—but there was nothing to indicate that this opinion was a favorable one. And in informing the French ambassador that the text of the convention was definitely adopted, Giers did not suggest that this action flowed in any way from his own views or motives; on the contrary, he was communicating this information, he wrote, as a matter of duty.

(5)   There were very few people on the Russian side who had any knowledge at all of the signature of this document or of the convention to which it gave a governmental blessing. Giers, Lamsdorf, Obruchev, Vannovski, and Giers' deputy, Shishkin, are the only ones besides the Tsar known to have had knowledge of the negotiations. Shishkin was only partially informed and was never asked for his opinion. Lamsdorf, too, had never been independently consulted, and bore no responsibility for the final decision; he merely did what he was told to do. Vannovski, who had never favored the conclusion of such a convention in the first place, was absent from the country at the time of its final approval and appears to have had no part in this final decision. Giers plainly disapproved, and agreed only with greatest reluctance, and under orders, to play his part in the final formalization of the convention. The entire action must be regarded, then, as the responsibility of two men: the Tsar and Obruchev, overriding the contrary advice of the ministers of both war and foreign affairs.

What a tiny body of expertise and judgment on which to commit, for twenty years to come, the fortunes of a great empire and of the dynasty that headed it! And what a slender pedestal on which to base the future conduct of a great body of Russian officialdom, civilian and military, of whom not one in ten thousand had any knowledge of the document or would ever see it!

(6)   On the French side there was surely a far wider body of persons who had knowledge of the agreement, and even of those (obviously a smaller number) who had actually seen the text. These had at least the comfort of knowing that in concluding such an agreement the French statesmen in question were acting in accord with the compelling emotional commitment of a great body of the French citizenry, including the overwhelming majority of those who constituted its educated classes. There can be no question but that had the 1894 agreement been submitted at the time to the French Parliament, it would have been instantly, and probably unanimously, approved. Those French officials who negotiated the agreement thus not only themselves believed in its desirability but were conscious of acting in response to a powerful trend of public opinion. Whether the decision was a wise one or otherwise is a question —and a very important one—to which a later decade would give the answer. For the French statesmen of the period 1890–1894 it was never a question at all.

Chapter 14

THE AFTERMATH

The relations among nations, in this imperfect world, constitute a fluid substance, always in motion, changing subtly from day to day in ways that are difficult to detect from the myopia of the passing moment, and even difficult to discern from the perspective of the future one. The situation at one particular time is never quite the same as the situation of five years later—indeed it is sometimes very significantly different, even though the stages by which this change came about are seldom visible at the given moment. This is why wise and experienced statesmen usually shy away from commitments likely to constitute limitations on a government's behavior at unknown dates in the future in the face of unpredictable situations. This is also a reason why agreements long in process of negotiation, particularly when negotiated in great secrecy, run the risk of being somewhat out of date before they are ever completed.

With this in mind, it may be interesting to note something of the development of the international situation in the period immediately following upon the final adoption of the Franco-Russian military convention.

·   ·   ·

First, a glance at what was happening in the period from January 1894 to January 1895 with respect to the personalities who had been most prominently involved in the negotiation of the Alliance:

During the year in question, both Alexander III and Giers continued to go rapidly downhill physically, with all the mental, emotional, and practical side effects such a process was bound to carry with it. During the first months of 1894, the Tsar's illnesses were episodic: there were times when he functioned more or less normally (which, in his case, did not mean very actively); at other times he was simply not available for official activity. While he did go, with his family, for the usual yachting cruise in Finnish waters in June and July, there is no evidence that there was even any plan, that summer, for the customary visit to Denmark. (Since he generally profited, physically and in spirit, from his Danish vacations, one is constrained to wonder whether there were not other

238

reasons, connected with the unhappy events of his last visit there, that explained this forbearance.)

There were some days, following Alexander's return from his Finnish cruise, when his health was thought to have improved; and plans were even made for him to attend the annual field maneuvers, scheduled this time to take place in August in the neighborhood of Smolensk. But before the maneuvers could begin, he suffered a serious relapse; and he was packed off, instead, to the Belovyezhskaya Pushcha, a forest and wildlife preserve in Byelorussia, not far from where the maneuvers were to take place, in the hopes that the air there would do him good. The effect of his stay there was, however, just the opposite; and he was soon moved to the Crimea and installed in the Livadia palace, near Yalta, where the famous Yalta "Big Three" conference was to take place a half century later. There he lingered on through the months of September and October; and there he died, only forty-nine years of age, on November the 2nd, of nephritis (and possibly cancer), amid all the tragic and semiromantic family happenings so often and so well described in the various accounts of the life and reign of his son and successor, Nicholas II. He had survived the final adoption of the Franco-Russian military convention by only some ten months.

As for Giers: he was, as we have seen, already at the time when the convention was regularized a man greatly weakened by age and illness—indeed, a shadow of his former self. He should never have been left so long in the position of foreign minister; it was fair neither to him nor to the country. Still less should he have been asked to continue to bear this responsibility over the year (1894) that followed. He was never, in the course of that year, able to reoccupy his office premises in the foreign office building at the Singers' Bridge in Petersburg. Much of the time was spent out at Tsarskoye Selo. The surviving descriptions of his condition during those months are pathetic. "Three days ago," wrote his deputy Shishkin on September the 28th, 1894, to de Staal, the Russian ambassador at London, "he was unable to rise from his chair. It is difficult to fight one's battles, even for the best of causes, when one cannot stand on one's own feet; and discussion becomes more than painful when the balance between the mental and the physical has been so greatly disturbed."[1] The rare visits of foreign ambassadors so obviously tired the foreign minister that the envoys often withdrew, for sheer pity, without having even attempted to broach the main subjects about which they had come to see him.

In the last months of his life, two of his sons, Michael and Constantine, came to be with him and served as his liaison with the world outside his sickroom. Lamsdorf, too, continued to visit him and to tell him what was in the day's mail; but there were days when even this could not be allowed.

Giers survived the Tsar, but not by much. On the 16th of January, 1895, less than two months after Alexander's death, Lamsdorf, summoned urgently to the minister's room, found the two sons weeping over the body of their father, who had just died. What Lamsdorf's own feelings were at that moment the published fragments of his diary do not indicate.[2] They could only have been ones of great and painful profundity. For many years, he had been the man closest to Giers in all the professional and political problems that had engaged the minister's attention. The two men had enjoyed, in this daily collaboration, an intimacy shared with no one else. And there can be no question but that Lamsdorf, while sometimes disapproving of his chief's decisions and usually longing for greater appreciation and praise for his own services than Giers was apt to give him, really loved the old boy, and must have missed him enormously.

Of the two men, Giers, a better balanced personality, was the more experienced and skillful as a political operator. Lamsdorf, however, was really the greater in point of the conceptual grasp of international problems and their implications; he was, in fact, superior to anyone in the Russia of his time or, so far as this writer is aware, anywhere else in Europe, Bismarck excepted. But his effectiveness was restricted by his neurotic shyness, his unsociability, his cultivation of a fastidious privacy, and his utter lack of taste for that peculiar sort of bureaucratic infighting without which no great foreign office, it would seem, can exist, and in the operation of which so many unworthy careers have been established and so many worthy ones broken.

As Giers' physical powers failed, in the final months and years of his life, so did his image, never a very sharp one, in the eyes of the various social circles—bureaucratic, noble, and journalistic—that dominated the Russian capital. It might almost be said that he was, to a large extent, forgotten before he was dead. In the Petersburg paper closest to the foreign office, the *Novoye Vremya*, the news of his death appeared in a four-line item at the bottom of a front-page column, sandwiched in between a story about a lecture, attended by two grand dukes, on the subject of navigation in the Kara Sea, and another one about the refusal of the Turks to admit two English journalists dispatched by Lord Kimberley to study the Armenian problem in Turkey. Thus lightheartedly did Russian officialdom and society inter not only the mortal remains but the very memory of a man who had for fifteen years selflessly and uncomplainingly borne the burden of the conduct of Russian foreign policy, and who, had his wisdom been recognized and respected, could have saved his country from the greatest of disasters.

Giers' body was laid to rest, with a few family members and officials in attendance, at the so-called Sergiyevskaya Pushchina—a monastery retreat on the shores of the Gulf of Finland, along the road to Peterhof, on January 31, 1895. It was a clear, bleak wintry day. It had snowed during the night. A chill wind swept in from across the partially frozen waters of the gulf. The little band of mourners were no doubt glad to get home, after the ceremony, and to inaugurate, with a warming glass of vodka, the process of oblivion that so soon overtakes the memory of statesmen who have labored too modestly and lived too long. The traveler who asks, nearly a century later, to see the grave will be told, with a shocked raising of eyebrows, that the monastery in question is now a police training school where visitors are never admitted; just as he will be told, if he asks to see Giers' office in the erstwhile foreign ministry, that the place is now a police hospital, equally inaccessible.*

Even before Giers' death, the Russian foreign office, lacking any firm directing hand, was in process of partial demoralization and dissolution. Shishkin, the deputy minister, cautious, reserved, and despairingly cynical, was not the man to take any responsibility that could possibly be avoided, or to attempt to exert any very strict authority over a ministry that was not really his. The Asiatic division, in particular, traditionally semiautonomous, paid little attention to Shishkin and went its own nationalistic way with sovereign independence. And as for Lamsdorf: his position had been, for over a decade in the past, that of a true *éminence grise,* his authority resting primarily on the exceptional confidence placed in him by the foreign minister. Now, with Giers gone or almost gone, this authority, too, began to disappear; and he withdrew, nursing bitterly to himself the consciousness of being head and shoulders above his col-

---

*The latter-day Soviet enthusiasm for the preservation of historic monuments is impressive and has produced some remarkable results; but it appears to find its limits when it comes up against the interests of the police establishment. The present disregard for Giers' memory matches ironically that which he was accustomed to experience at the hands of the comparable organs of internal power in the Russia of his day.

leagues in insight and ability, but never dreaming of joining in that jockeying for position that would have been necessary to assure the continuation of his influence.*

From the summer of 1894, therefore, through the remainder of that year and well into 1895, Russian diplomacy was disorganized and semiparalyzed—there being at first only the shadow of a Tsar and of a foreign minister, and then none at all, and no prime minister or organized cabinet (for such did not exist in the Russian governmental system of that day) to hold things together. Each official, whether in the foreign office or at a diplomatic post abroad, did more or less whatever he thought he could get away with. And all of them, with two exceptions (Lamsdorf and Shishkin) did this, be it noted, without any knowledge of the formal military agreements linking their country to France, the coming into existence of which we have just had occasion to observe.

.   .   .

In France, too, the thirteen months following final adoption of the military convention were marked by extensive changes in the governing personnel. The Dupuy government fell, as we have seen, at the end of November 1893 and was replaced by one under the previous president of the National Assembly, Jean Casimir-Périer, who also took upon himself the direction of the Ministry of Foreign Affairs. Casimir-Périer, in the tradition of democratic politicians, had had no significant previous experience with foreign affairs. Upon taking office in early December 1893, he was startled to learn that a Franco-Russian military convention had actually been negotiated more than a year before, but that the Russians had not yet been willing to give it governmental sanction. This so upset him that his first impulse was to give the Russian government an ultimatum: either approve the convention at once or France would give up the entire entente with Russia and seek other ways of assuring her security. This impulse overtook him precisely at the time when, it will be recalled, success was finally at hand after many months of skillful and quiet diplomacy. All that was needed was only another fortnight of restraint on the French side to permit the sensitive Tsar to do things in his own way. Fortunately for the success of the enterprise, Casimir-Périer was dissuaded by frightened underlings from proceeding with this undertaking, which

*Despite all this, Lamsdorf was to become, briefly and unhappily, Russia's foreign minister some years hence.

would certainly have killed the entire project at least for the remainder of the reign of Alexander III.

The Casimir-Périer government lasted only to the 27th of May, 1894, when the usual parliamentary shuffling made it necessary for him to yield the premiership once again to Charles Dupuy. The foreign affairs portfolio was now taken over, for the first time, by Gabriel Hanotaux. Hanotaux, as it happened, was a man excellently qualified, intellectually and otherwise, for this position. A firm partisan of the Russian alliance, he was also well equipped to review and to understand the processes by which the exchange of notes of 1891 and the military convention of 1892 had come into being.

These qualities on Hanotaux' part went some distance to compensate for the blow that fell only four weeks after the change of government just mentioned: namely, the assassination of the President, Sadi Carnot, in Lyons, on June the 24th, 1894, by an Italian anarchist. This removed from the scene of active political life, at least for the time being, the last of the three French figures who had been leaders in the negotiation of the Alliance. It must have occasioned considerable inner uneasiness on the part of both Giers and the Tsar to be made to realize that the direction of foreign and military affairs in a government with which they had just secretly allied themselves was now entirely in the hands of new people, about whom they knew very little. But there was nothing they could do about it; and even if there had been, weariness and poor health would hardly have permitted them to take advantage of the opportunity.

Casimir-Périer, upon the death of Carnot, took over the presidency, turning over the premiership once more to his rival, Dupuy, but leaving Hanotaux as minister for foreign affairs. His tenure as president, however, was brief. After little more than six months in office, disgusted with the opposition he was receiving from both the left and the right wings of the political spectrum, and keenly resentful of the efforts of Dupuy to deprive the presidency of its traditional prerogatives, he resigned in January 1895, one day after Giers' death. He was succeeded in the presidency by Félix Faure, who was to hold the office down to the end of the century.

This series of changes in occupancy of the leading positions of the French government was indeed an extensive one; but it did not occasion so sharp a break in continuity as that which occurred in Russia at the same time; for this last change in the presidency, just mentioned, brought back into the premiership, at least for a few months, Alexander Ribot. With him at the head of the government and with Hanotaux at the foreign ministry, the custody of the Alliance, if so it may be termed, was again in competent hands.

. . .

It was not just in terms of the rapid turnover in personalities that the Alliance seemed to be slipping rapidly into the past before it had been fairly negotiated. The years 1894–1895 introduced a whole series of new issues and situations, so compelling that they tended quite to obliterate from the consciousness of the responsible officials on both sides any awareness they might have had of the Alliance just concluded, or indeed any preoccupation with the problems to which it had been addressed.

These new issues and situations were of both domestic-political and international significance. We have already had occasion to note the disarray into which the Russian government was thrown by the death of Alexander III and the consequent succession to the throne of a young man, Nicholas II, whose dreadful deficiencies, from the standpoint of the powers and responsibilities now being thrust upon him, were to lead to the most tragic consequences in the years to come. And in France, too, the year 1894 witnessed the onset of another domestic-political crisis— one destined, this time, to shake the French political community to its foundations even more violently than the Panama scandal had done, and to preempt the attention of both politicians and public down to the final years of the century.

This was, of course, the Dreyfus case—"l'affaire Dreyfus." It was, after all, in late September 1894 that Major Henry brought the famous bordereau to the attention of his senior military superiors, including Boisdeffre and the new minister of war, General Mercier. It was on the first of November, the day before the death of Alexander III, that the name of Captain Alfred Dreyfus, as the suspected culprit, was revealed to the French public. And it was in late January 1895, when Giers lay on his deathbed and the French presidency was passing from Casimir-Périer to Félix Faure, that Dreyfus, having already been convicted in camera of treason and publicly degraded, was awaiting his deportation to Devil's Island. From this time on, far more attention would be given publicly to the treatment and fate of this single man than to the millions of young men now faithfully training for the war that the military convention envisaged.

In foreign affairs, too, the year 1894 brought new problems—problems envisaged only faintly, if at all, by the men who had concluded the Alliance. For France, these were largely the problems of overseas colonialism: rivalries with the British and the Germans in Africa; the sharp conflict with the government of Siam and the attendant complications with the British, which preoccupied the respective foreign offices over much of the summer of 1894; new developments in the perennial Egyptian problem; and new frictions with Italy arising out of the presence of Italian workers in French mines and the killing of a number of them at Aigues-Mortes in a fracas with their French fellow workers.

The Russians, too, had new things to think about. For one thing, there was a somewhat changed situation in their relations with Germany. The summer of 1893 had witnessed, as already noted (see chap. 8), the deterioration of Russo-German trade relations into a full-fledged tariff war. In October of that year, a Russian delegation was sent to Berlin to undertake negotiations with the Germans for a settlement of the conflict. For some weeks little progress was made; but in the early winter of 1894 both emperors appear to have brought pressure to bear upon their respective negotiators to make concessions; and in mid-February the draft of a new, and in many respects far-reaching, commercial treaty was agreed upon by the negotiators. There still remained the problem of ratification by the Reichstag; and this took some time, for there was strong opposition to the treaty on the part of the German estate owners, who continued to fear the competition of Russian grain. But the Kaiser threw himself into the battle; and on March the 16th, 1894, the treaty was ratified.

The German negotiators were of the opinion that it was the Russians who, in order to assure the final success of the negotiations, had made the greatest last-minute concessions. However that may be, the final Russian agreement would not have been forthcoming without the consent of Alexander III. While he generally tended to deny that such mundane matters as tariff wars and commercial treaties were of any importance from the standpoint of the political relations between great powers, and while he appears to have reiterated this view to Giers as late as the summer of 1893,[3] it does seem probable that he saw in the conclusion of the commercial treaty with Germany in that winter of 1894 a means of balancing off the conclusion of the military convention with France— this, at least, in the sense that if there should be leaks to the press about the military convention (and the possibility of this sort of thing could never be wholly excluded), the conclusion of the commercial treaty with Germany would serve to absorb some of the shock, and to keep the Germans from seeing in the acceptance of the military convention an act of unmitigated hostility to Germany.

Actually, the news of the conclusion of the Russo-German commercial treaty was a major sensation in Europe. To many people (including most of the officials of the Russian and French governments) ignorant of the existence of the military convention and unaware that Russia had not retained her full freedom of action in European policy, the commercial treaty appeared as a sign of a significant German-Russian rapprochement. Even the Kaiser was inclined to believe that it could be of real importance in this respect. And the impression of a significant incipient shift in the interrelations of the European great powers was heightened by the fact that the Kaiser appeared, in just that year of 1894, to be making efforts to improve Germany's relations with France as well. He was, after all, a man capable of being as warm and charming on some occasions as he could be offensive on others. Thus his reaction to the news of Carnot's assassination (the warm words with which he accompanied the wreath he sent for the grave, and his action in pardoning two French officers imprisoned in Germany for espionage, as a gesture to the French in a moment of grief) produced genuine appreciation in France both in the government and among the public.

To the extent, then, that reports of the demonstratively favorable treatment accorded to Montebello upon his return to Russia in December 1893 might have encouraged the impression that Franco-Russian relations had reached some new and important turning point, the evidences of reduced tension between both of those countries and Germany tended to obliterate the effect of this reaction.

Finally, there was—as a major new claim on the attentions of the Russian foreign office and to some extent on those of the French one as well—the emerging situation in the Far East. That part of the world had scarcely entered into the concerns and calculations of the men who inaugurated and conducted the negotiations for the Franco-Russian Alliance. But by 1894 the construction of the Trans-Siberian Railway was well under way. It had drawn the attention of the Russian government increasingly to developments in the Manchurian-Korean region. And now, with the emergence of complications between Japan and China over Korea in the first months of 1894, and then with the outbreak of war between those two powers on the 3rd of August of that year, Russia could not remain indifferent to what was happening in that region, particularly because the initial Japanese military successes gave rise to Chinese appeals for joint intervention of the European powers to protect the diplomatic corps in Peking. This appeal stimulated new suspicions, but also in some instances brought to light previously undiscovered common interests among the powers to which it was addressed. And the reactions to these events, as the near future would show, once again cut across the pattern of relationships that the Franco-Russian Alliance had reflected, even bringing France, Germany, and Russia together in a joint action from which the British were excluded.

All of these developments tended to confuse not only a European public unaware of the conclusion of the Alliance but even an officialdom in the various capitals equally in ignorance of what had taken place in Petersburg and Paris at the turn of the years 1893–1894. Since the military convention now required no further treatment or attention at the political levels of the two governments, and since most of those who were now responsible for formulating policy in the two governments were aware only dimly, if at all, of its existence, it ceased for some years to be a significant factor even in the unfolding of their mutual relations. Only in the closely concealed, deeply buried inner web of the respective general staffs did it remain an active factor in determining the realities of the last years of the century.

. . .

The final act in the negotiation of the Franco-Russian Alliance was not, then, a great event in the consciousness of the peoples of Europe, who were generally under the impression that something of this sort had long existed; nor was it the real turning point in the international relations of the time. The real "event," in the eyes of the European public, had been the combination of the Cronstadt and Toulon naval visits—spectacular, suggestive, but not conclusive. And as for the turning point: it did indeed take place just at the time—namely, the onset of the year 1894—when the Alliance was being formalized, but for quite other reasons. It took place because the more prominent personalities of recent years just happened at that time to be rapidly fading from the scene, and because new problems were emerging to claim the attention of the various European chanceries.

The Alliance was, in reality, an arrangement conceived as a response to various events of the 1870s and 1880s: the Franco-Prussian War, the Russo-Turkish War, the domination of European diplomacy by Bismarck, the Austro-Prussian Alliance of 1879, the Triple Alliance, the frustrations experienced in Russia's Balkan policies. It was, if you will, a delayed response to all these situations. So much was it delayed that it was, by the time it was formalized, already backward-looking. It envisaged a world that was partially disappearing—a world the concerns of which still seemed important to those few persons who shaped the Alliance but were far less immediate in the minds of a general European public that had passed on to other things. Thus the work of its authors was partly deprived of its meaning by the time it was completed.

But only partly deprived, after all—because for the two general staffs the Alliance retained its entire validity down through the years to come. If, in the case of the diplomats, it was an arrangement directed to the past, for the military establishments it was one directed to the future—to the future war, the overwhelming probability of which they assumed, and the inevitability of which they assured by virtue of this very assumption. Here, no explicit sanction of public opinion—indeed, not even any complete awareness on the part of public opinion of what was up—was necessary. The workings of the two great military machines had found their public sanction—uncritical and implicit sanction—in advance; found it in the fever of nationalism by which the educated portion of the public in each country was overcome. In France there was, to be sure, an occasional obstacle to be surmounted in the form of a military appropriations bill— in Russia, scarcely even that. Beyond these minor obstacles the military had, essentially, a free hand. For the masters of the two great military machines it was largely inconsequential whether civilian statesmen came or went, whether changes occurred in the moods of public opinion, whether new diplomatic problems did or did not emerge on the horizons of the various foreign offices. What was important for them was only that they, the military staffs and commands, were permitted to indulge their own inner compulsions in their accustomed way, and that their energies were never too sharply diverted from the major undertakings, such as those embodied in the Franco-Russian Alliance, to which they had become dedicated. These military machines constituted, in reality, an irresistible force, and the determining one. The excitements of public policy and journalism were only froth, visible on the surface of those deep, powerful currents that military thinking engendered, and upon which the nations were carried, unaware and unsuspecting, to the tragedies of 1914–1918.

EPILOGUE

We have had occasion to observe in the above narrative the processes by which the two parties arrived at what is generally known as the Franco-Russian Alliance of 1894. Certain of the conclusions to which this spectacle leads, particularly those relating to questions of historical fact, have been brought forward in the narrative itself. There are, however, certain broader reflections to which the account gives rise; and these, too, deserve a word of mention before it is brought to an end and permitted to take its modest place among the multitude of studies devoted to recent diplomatic history.

It will be well to begin by recalling that of the four great powers most immediately affected by the Franco-Russian Alliance—France, Russia, Germany, and Austria-Hungary—the only two that had what might be called clear expansionist motives were the two parties to the Alliance—France and Russia.

In the case of the French the objectives in question—the recovery of Alsace-Lorraine and possibly a little something beyond that—were latent rather than active ones. Most influential French figures naturally hoped strongly for the ultimate achievement of these objectives; but they did not contemplate, in the circumstances then foreseeable, launching an aggressive war for this purpose. Any such undertaking would have had internal-political implications that none of them would at that time have wished to confront. If war were to develop from other causes, then, certainly, it was for such objectives, in the first instance, that the French would have fought. But deliberately to unleash a war for such purposes was not within the intentions of the French statesmen of that day.

In the case of the Russians, things were a bit different. There were, of course, serious differences of opinion within the tiny circle of persons involved on the Russian side in the preparation of the Alliance. Giers and Lamsdorf consistently denied the necessity or desirability of any expansionist undertakings and vigorously opposed all decisions that pointed in that direction. But they were largely helpless. It was the contrary views

249

—those of the military as represented by Obruchev, of the civilian chauvinists, and of the Tsar himself—that prevailed; and here things were not so simple. One wanted to acquire for Russia the Austrian portion of the divided Poland. One wanted to establish a position at the Turkish Straits that would bar foreign warships from entering the Black Sea. Alexander III, in particular, would very much have liked to achieve a position with relation to Bulgaria that would have made of that country an effective military-political satellite of Russia. Nothing in the available record suggests that the Russian military, had they felt themselves equal in the technical-military sense to the conduct of a successful war against Austria, and had they seen some way to prevent the Germans from participating in or profiting from the conflict, would have shrunk from provoking, if not initiating, the war in question. Their principal objective in their dealings with their French counterparts was to find some way, even if this involved Russia's going to war with Germany as well as with Austria, to keep the Germans from deriving profit from a Russian-Austrian war and from emerging at the end of it in an improved position with relation to both those powers.

With these reflections in mind, it may be useful to glance once more at the wording of the military convention, as finally agreed upon, and at the circumstances surrounding its conclusion.

Plainly, the heart of this document lay in the second article, relating to mobilization. Bearing in mind that both the general staffs not only viewed mobilization as an outright act of war but insisted that all normal operational decisions be based on that assumption, it is clear that this article effectively eclipsed the first one, addressed to the contingency of an attack; for there was unlikely to be any attack without some form of preceding mobilization. It also largely eclipsed the terms of the exchange of notes of 1891. These latter had called for consultation in the case of a threat to the peace of Europe or danger of military aggression. Here, however, by the terms of the military convention, the Franco-Russian response, in the event of mobilization by any of the parties to the Triple Alliance, was to be the immediate inauguration of hostilities against all of them—inauguration of hostilities "at the first announcement of the event and without necessity of any previous concerting of policy between them." Nothing could have been clearer than this; and it is no wonder that poor Giers saw in this provision the destruction of his last great effort to confine the Franco-Russian rapprochement to limits within which Russia would retain some flexibility of decision in the face of contingencies then impossible to foresee.

Beyond that, the text of the convention required France and Russia to respond in this way—that is, by entering immediately into a war with Germany along with the others—to a mobilization by any of the parties to the Triple Alliance, even a mobilization with which Germany might be in no way associated. And it was not just a *general* mobilization by one or another of those parties to which the French and the Russians bound themselves to react, but a partial one as well. A curious feature of that crucial Article II is that while it made it incumbent upon the two contracting parties to respond by an immediate *general* mobilization—by the mobilization *"de la totalité de leurs forces"*—to any mobilizational move by members of the Triplice, it applied no such criterion when it came to the hostile mobilization to which they would presumably be reacting. If we are to take the wording of the convention at its face value, any sort of mobilization by any of the parties to the Triplice, even a partial one by Italy or Austria acting alone, would suffice to trigger a general mobilization on the Franco-Russian side and thus to assure the inauguration of hostilities against Germany as well as the others. Nor did the document even prescribe that the mobilization to which the contracting parties thus bound themselves to react should be one directed against either of them: it could just as well have been one directed against a third party. A partial Austrian mobilization against Serbia, for example (and one has only to recall the events of 1914 to understand the potential significance of this circumstance), could alone become the occasion for the launching of a general European war.

Freycinet, be it said to his credit, at once spotted certain of these weaknesses and protested against them, demanding changes in the wording of the article. But so intense was the desire of the other French statesmen to get on with the conclusion of the Alliance that his objections, as we have seen, were never pressed, and were eventually swept aside.

This particular point—the failure to specify that the mobilization to which the parties bound themselves to react should be a general, not a partial, one, and one conducted by the members of the Triplice as a whole—was of great potential importance; for it would not have been difficult for the Russians to provoke a partial Austrian mobilization whenever it might suit them to do so. A certain amount of serious military pressure on the Bulgarians could easily have sufficed for this purpose; because the Austrians and Hungarians, well aware of the dangers of Russian and

Pan-Slav influence on the restless Slavic nationalities within the Austro-Hungarian empire, were extremely sensitive to any developments among the southern-Balkan Slavs that could serve to heighten that restlessness; and this would assuredly have been the effect of any clear incorporation of Bulgaria into a Russian sphere of influence. It is true that the central entity of the Russian foreign office (the so-called Grand Chancery—the Velikaya Kantselyariya) could never have been had, particularly under Giers' direction, for any enterprise of this nature. But the same could not be said of the Asiatic division of the ministry, which was responsible for Balkan affairs and was only imperfectly under the foreign minister's control. This division, like the military and secret-intelligence authorities with which it extensively collaborated, was accustomed to dabbling independently in various forms of Balkan intrigue; and none of these circles was known for its scruples, its discrimination, or its breadth of view.

. . .

Plainly, then, the final text of the Franco-Russian military convention had some strange and disturbing features, placing largely in Russian hands, as it did, the power to unleash a major European war whenever this might suit Russian purposes—and this in undefined future situations, then impossible to envisage. No wonder Giers would never give it his approval. But even more fateful, individually or in combination with these explicit deficiencies, were certain omissions—certain things that the document failed to mention at all.

The convention was addressed, as we have seen, to two specific contingencies: (a) a mobilization by any of the powers of the Triple Alliance; and (b) an attack on France or Russia by Germany alone, or by Germany in combination with one or another of the other parties to the Triple Alliance. But one searches in vain, not only in the text of the document but in the record of the various exchanges that led to its conclusion, for evidence of any serious examination of the plausibility of these contingencies in the first place, or any exploration of the circumstances in which they might be conceived to arise.

The German Kaiser William II had, of course, no lack of faults. But his bark was known to be worse than his bite, as the French and Russian ambassadors in Berlin would have confirmed; and the Bismarckian principles, which precluded an unprovoked German attack on either France or Russia as well as German support for any such move by other members of the Triplice, were still strongly persuasive among the men around the

Kaiser, even when they were not themselves fully aware of that fact and would have been disinclined to admit it. It is difficult for the historian to picture, in retrospect, any circumstances in which Germany, under the conditions then prevailing, could have been brought to depart from those principles. Germany was, after all, a satiated power, so far as Europe itself was concerned, and stood to gain little from a major war on the Continent. This was clearly visible to Bismarck, and it must have been reasonably so to his successors. This is not to say that these successors could not perceive the possibility of such circumstances arising in the more distant future. But situations of that nature were not then visible, or even fully imaginable. The question thus arises as to whether, if the purposes of the two parties to the Franco-Russian military convention were really defensive, it was wise for them to bind their own hands and those of their successors to a given action—and an extremely far-reaching and fateful one at that—predicated on the realization of these improbable hypothetical contingencies.

This, throughout, was precisely Giers' point. It was because he realized that the future could never be foreseen clearly and in all its aspects —that it never looked exactly the way you might have thought it would look—that he tried to limit Russia's obligation vis-à-vis France to an agreement to confer when the moment came, rather than to see her bind herself, possibly many years before the actual event, to launch a major European war, automatically and without further consultation, in a situation that no one, at the moment, could foresee or picture.

The second question *not* treated in the convention itself and only casually mentioned in the negotiations was that of the objectives for which, if war developed, one would conceive oneself to be fighting. To be sure, Alexander had once mentioned—but to Giers, not to the French —his idea that a successful war against Germany should bring about the breakup of the German empire. And Obruchev, talking with Boisdeffre in the Dordogne, had spoken of Russian aspirations for the acquisition of Galician Poland and of a "key" to the Turkish Straits. He had even tried to draw out Boisdeffre on the subject of the corresponding French aims. But Boisdeffre, aside from the obvious reference to Alsace-Lorraine, had been vague, and had only said, "Let us begin by beating them; after that it will all be easy." And the two men had then dropped the subject, agreeing that these were really questions to be handled on the political-diplomatic level (which they never were).

Today's reader might well be inclined to ask: Why did the two powers need to agree in advance on any specific war aims? Why, indeed, should either of them even have had need to clarify its own mind on this subject at that stage of the game? Both, albeit for different reasons, wanted to defeat Germany, to break up that country to one extent or another, or in any case to weaken and humble it. The Russians, in addition, had certain aims respecting Austria-Hungary, and possibly Turkey, which did not greatly concern the French. Was this not enough to sustain an effective military partnership in the general European war they were envisaging? Where was the need for aims more specific than these, and for preliminary agreement upon them between the parties to the Alliance? Do we of this generation not have before us, it might be asked, in the examples of the two great European wars of this century, the evidence that in the modern era one does not fight wars, anyway, for specific aims? That the immediate issues that occasioned the opening of hostilities, such things as Sarajevo, Danzig, or Pearl Harbor, are soon forgotten once hostilities develop—swallowed up in the wider effort to bring the adversary to total defeat, unconditional surrender, complete submission to the will of the victor? Only after all that has been achieved comes the question of the uses one wishes to make of one's victory. After that, supposedly, "it will all be easy."

This view was the reflection, then as now, of a profound and highly significant change in the prevailing attitudes towards military conflict. At the risk of some repetition (for this was mentioned in chap. 10, above), we must note, once again, the nature of this change.

As late as the eighteenth century, wars, being conducted in the name of dynastic rulers rather than entire nations, were generally fought for specific limited purposes. The amount of force was made, if possible, commensurate to the purpose at hand—no more, no less. When the immediate objective had been obtained, or had proven unobtainable, one desisted. One did not try to carry hostilities to the point of the total destruction of the adversary's armed power and his complete humiliation and political emasculation. For that, there was too keen an awareness of the ultimate community of fate of all dynasties, even those with which one might, at the moment, be contending.

The virtues of this limitation of armed conflict were not unperceived by contemporaries. Edward Gibbon, ruminating on the causes of the decline and fall of the Roman Empire, found it possible to congratulate himself and his readers on the fact that the European armies of his day were, as he put it, "exercised only in temperate and undecisive contests," and to see in this fact one of the sources of reassurance that Europe would not be faced with the disasters that eventually befell ancient Rome.

The change, of course, was a gradual one. Signs of it were visible as early as the Napoleonic wars. But in the negotiations described in this book it comes through with great clarity. One has only to consider Obruchev's memorandum of May 1892. War, in the first place, was not to be localized—not to be limited in the number of the contestants. It was not, in his view, even desirable from Russia's standpoint that it should be. "Powers remaining initially on the sidelines" must sooner or later become "participants in the conflict." Why? Because the war he had in mind was to be a war *à outrance*—a war in which everything would be at stake and by which the ultimate fortunes of all of Europe would be determined. "In the face of the readiness of entire armed peoples to go to war," he wrote, "no other sort of war can be envisaged than the most decisive sort—a war that would determine for long into the future the relative political position of the European powers. . . ." And even this language did not convey the full meaning of what he was saying; for the war he was envisaging implied, whether or not he was aware of this, the destruction of both the German and the Austro-Hungarian empires—the obliteration, in other words, of both of Russia's prospective opponents as political entities.

May we ask: Whence came this change? What had occasioned it? The true answer would be, no doubt: many factors, no single one. But two of these factors deserve special mention here.

The industrial revolution and the rapid rise in populations that accompanied it had played a major part in making possible the maintenance in peacetime of great standing armies. These armies were not only numerically greater than anything known in the preindustrial era, but they were rapidly acquiring technological capabilities, particularly in point of firepower and mobility, that gave them the possibility not just of inflicting massive and devastating damage on the armed forces of another country but also of threatening the integrity of its political system, and sometimes even its very identity as a sovereign member of the family of nations. And along with these developments went the rise of a new military professionalism accompanied (in a manner not unknown in other professions as well) by a narrowing rather than a broadening of the field of vision. Precisely because of the higher degree of specialization and professional concentration to which he was subject, the senior military figure of the new era tended to have his eyes riveted more exclusively on the technical-military aspects of his dedication than were those of his counterparts of earlier ages, and to be less familiar and less involved with the wider political interests military forces were supposed to serve.

For the statesman and the military leader these new and unprecedented possibilities stimulated, of course, a new order of ambitions and a new order of anxieties. Of these, the anxieties were often the more dangerous; for they could lead to defensive reactions, or what were conceived as such, even more savage, open-ended, and destructive than the ones inspired by ambition. And to both of these impulses the military leaders, and particularly the military planners, were especially vulnerable, compelled as they were to deal with hypothetical military contests divorced from any and all political background, charged as they were with the responsibility for figuring out how wars could be "won"—not how they could be avoided—compelled as they were to postulate the prospective adversary's total hostility and to ignore the political restraints that might affect his behavior.

All this—the combined effect of industrialization, population growth, and increased military specialization—was one major factor in the rise of a new view of warfare. And a second, of equal if not greater importance, was the growing power—the stormy, sweeping, unwithstandable power—of modern nationalism over the minds and emotions of men. In part, this could be seen as a product of democracy—of the spreading of the decision-taking power from crowned heads and their personal aides to parliamentary bodies and the constituencies they represented. But it was more than this. It could be seen and felt even in Russia, where there was no democracy at all. It was, and is, a fever of the time and one so virulent that its power has not been broken to the present day, nearly a century after the events described in this book. And it had a profound effect on attitudes towards war.

The nation, as distinct from the dynastic ruler of earlier times, is—even in theory—a secular force. Ready as it is to invoke the blessing of the Almighty on its military ventures, it cannot claim the divine right of kings or recognize the moral limitations that right once implied. And it is outstandingly self-righteous—sometimes to the point of self-adoration and self-idealization—in its attitudes towards any country that appears to oppose its purposes or threaten its security. The kings and princes of earlier times were usually cynical, indeed; but their cynicism often related, in a disillusioned way, to themselves as well as to their rivals. The nation-state is cynical, too, sometimes pathologically so, but only in relation to opposing military-political force. In the view it takes of itself it is admiring to the point of narcissism. *Its* symbols always require the highest reverence; *its* cause deserves the highest sacrifice; *its* interests are sacrosanct. The symbols, causes, and interests of its international rivals are, by contrast, unworthy, disreputable, expendable. Once involved in a war, regardless of the specific circumstances that gave rise to the involvement in the first place, the nation-state fights for vague, emotional, essentially punitive purposes. *They*, the opponents, must be punished, made to regret their recalcitrance, made to be sorry. *We*, on the other hand, must be vindicated by victory; the justice of our cause must be confirmed (as though this proved something) by its very military triumph; *our* admirableness must be documented by *their* ultimate recognition of our superiority.

These, as will readily be seen, are anything else but limited aims. And it is not difficult to see how beautifully they dovetail with the hopes and anxieties of military men charged with the planning or pursuing of sweeping military victories over hypothetical opponents in essentially purposeless wars. The nationalistic euphoria provides the moral-political justification for those visions of all-out military effort and of total military victory that unavoidably command the imagination, and shape the efforts, of the military planner. And between the two of them they tend to obliterate, in minds of both statesmen and popular masses, all consciousness of that essential community of fate that links, in reality, all great nations of the modern world and renders the destruction of any one of them the ultimate destruction, too, of the country that destroyed it.

. . .

In the history of the negotiation of the Franco-Russian Alliance one can witness the growth of a whole series of those aberrations, misunderstandings, and bewilderments that have played so tragic and fateful a part in the development of Western civilization over the subsequent decades. One sees how the unjustified assumption of war's likelihood could become the cause of its final inevitability. One sees the growth of military-technological capabilities to levels that exceed man's capacity for making any rational and intelligent use of them. One sees how the myopia induced by indulgence in the mass emotional compulsions of modern nationalism destroys the power to form any coherent, realistic view of true national interest. One sees, finally, the inability of otherwise intelligent men to perceive the inherently self-destructive quality of warfare among the great industrial powers of the modern age.

The governments that negotiated the Franco-Russian Alliance were, as we have seen, largely unable to discern and resist these tendencies; and the sufferings the two great European wars of the following century visited upon their children and grandchildren were in part the terrible penalty for this limitation of vision. But those wars, let us note, were fought with conventional weapons; and while not all that was valuable in the old Europe survived them, some of it did. The lives and potential contributions of the fifteen to twenty million young men—the cream of Europe's youth—who fell in those contests could of course never be restored or made good; and the genetic loss alone was one that could be absorbed only through generations. But the physical infrastructure of European life could be, for the most part, restored; and the immense cultural achievements of European civilization were, in the main, not lost to the generations that followed. The weapons with which men fought in those two great conflagrations were, in other words, only partially, not totally, self-destructive. There could be, and was, another day.

For us of the late twentieth century these background realities no longer prevail. The nuclear weapon has changed all that. If, today, governments are still unable to recognize that modern nationalism and modern militarism are, in combination, self-destructive forces, and totally so; if they are incapable of looking clearly at those forces, discerning their true nature, and bringing them under some sort of control; if they continue, whether for reasons of fear or of ambition, to cultivate those forces and to try to use them as instruments for self-serving competitive purposes—if they do these things, they will be preparing, this time, a catastrophe from which there can be no recovery and no return.

Obruchev and Boisdeffre were blind, admittedly, to these realities. They had some reason to be that way; for they lacked those lessons of experiences that are available to the statesmen of this present age; and they had a greater margin, whether they knew it or not, in which to make mistakes. We of this generation can claim neither of these mitigating circumstances. If we cannot overcome our blind spots and learn to look reality in the face, our failure will be final—for ourselves and for all future generations.

APPENDIX I

(See chap. 7, p. 108)

Exchange of letters, Foreign Minister N. K. Giers to Ambassador A. Mohrenheim, 9/21 August, 1891; Mohrenheim to French Foreign Minister Alexandre Ribot, 15/27 August, 1891; and reply of Ribot to Mohrenheim, August 27, 1891.*

Source: DDF, vol. 8, no. 514, pp. 683–684, and no. 517, pp. 686–687.

M. de Giers, Ministre des Affaires Etrangères de Russie, à M. de Mohrenheim, Ambassadeur de Russie à Paris

L.   *Saint-Pétersbourg, 9/21 août 1891*
La situation créée en Europe par le renouvellement manifeste de la Triple Alliance et l'adhésion plus ou moins probable de la Grande-Bretagne aux visées politiques que cette alliance poursuit a motivé entre l'ancien Ambassadeur de France et moi un échange d'idées tendant à définir l'attitude qui, dans les conjonctures actuelles et en presence de certaines éventualités, pourrait le mieux convenir à nos Gouvernements respectifs, lesquels, restés en dehors de toute ligue, n'en sont pas moins sincèrement désireux d'entourer le maintien de la paix des garanties les plus efficaces.

C'est ainsi que nous avons été amenés à formuler les deux points ci-dessous:

1° Afin de définir et de consacrer l'entente cordiale qui les unit et désireux de contribuer d'un commun accord au maintien de la paix qui forme l'objet de leurs voeux les plus sincères, les deux Gouvernements déclarent qu'ils se concerteront sur toute question de nature à mettre la paix générale en cause.

2° Dans le cas où cette paix serait effectivement en danger et spécialement pour celui où l'une des deux parties serait menacée d'une agression, les deux parties conviennent de s'entendre sur les mesures dont la réalisation de cette éventualité imposerait l'adoption immédiate et simultanée aux deux Gouvernements.

En vous faisant part de ces dispositions souveraines, je vous prie de vouloir bien les porter à la connaissance du Gouvernement français et de me communiquer les résolutions auxquelles, pour sa part, il pourrait s'arrêter.

M. de Mohrenheim, Ambassadeur de Russie à Paris, à M. Ribot, Ministre des Affaires Etrangères

L. Secret.   *Paris, 15/27 août 1891*
Durant mon récent séjour à Saint-Pétersbourg, où j'ai été mandé d'ordre de mon auguste Souverain, il a plu à l'Empereur de me

munir d'instructions spéciales, consignées dans la lettre ci-jointe en copie que m'a adressée Son Excellence M. de Giers, Ministre des Affaires étrangères, et dont Sa Majesté a daigné me prescrire de donner communication au Gouvernement de la République.

En exécution de cet ordre suprême, je me fais un devoir de porter cette pièce à la connaissance de Votre Excellence, dans le ferme espoir que son contenu, préalablement concerté et formulé d'un commun accord entre nos deux Cabinets, rencontrera le plein suffrage du Gouvernement français et que vous voudrez bien, M. le Ministre, conformément au voeu exprimé par M. de Giers, m'honorer d'une réponse témoignant du parfait accord heureusement établi désormais entre nos deux Gouvernements.

Les développements ultérieurs dont les deux points ainsi convenus sont non seulement susceptibles, mais qui en formeront le complément nécessaire, pourront faire l'objet de pourparlers confidentiels et intimes à tel moment, jugé opportun par l'un ou l'autre Cabinet, où ils estimeront pouvoir y procéder en temps utile.

Me tenant à cet effet à l'entière disposition de Votre Excellence, je suis heureux de pouvoir me prévaloir d'une occasion pareille pour la prier de vouloir bien agréer l'hommage, etc.

M. Ribot, Ministre des Affaires Etrangères, à M. de Mohrenheim, Ambassadeur de Russie à Paris

L. Secret.   *Paris, 27 août 1891*

Vous avez bien voulu, d'ordre de votre Gouvernement, me communiquer le texte de la lettre du Ministre des Affaires étrangères de l'Empire où sont consignées les instructions spéciales dont l'Empereur Alexandre a decidé de vous munir, à la suite du dernier échange d'idées auquel la situation générale de l'Europe a donné lieu entre M. de Giers et l'Ambassadeur de la République française à Saint-Pétersbourg.

Votre excellence était chargée d'exprimer en même temps l'espoir que le contenu de cette pièce, préalablement concerté et formulé d'un commun accord entre les deux Cabinets, rencontrerait le plein suffrage du Gouvernement français.

Je m'empresse de remercier Votre Excellence de cette communication.

Le Gouvernement de la République ne pouvait qu'envisager comme le Gouvernement impérial la situation créée en Europe par les conditions dans lesquelles s'est produit le renouvellement de la Triple Alliance et il estime avec lui que le moment est venu de définir l'attitude qui, dans les conjonctures actuelles et en présence de certaines éventualités, pourrait le mieux convenir aux deux Gouvernements, également désireux d'assurer au maintien de la paix les garanties qui résultent de l'équilibre entre les forces européennes.

Je suis heureux en conséquence de faire savoir à Votre Excellence que le Gouvernement de la République donne son entière adhésion aux deux points qui font l'objet de la communication de M. de Giers et qui sont ainsi formulés:

1° Afin de définir et de consacrer l'entente cordiale qui les unit et désireux de contribuer d'un commun accord au maintien de la paix qui forme l'objet de leurs voeux les plus sincères, les deux Gouvernements déclarent qu'ils se concerteront sur toute question de nature à mettre la paix générale en cause.

2° Dans le cas où cette paix serait effectivement en danger et spécialement pour celui où l'une des deux parties serait menacée d'une agression, les deux parties conviennent de s'entendre sur les mesures dont la réalisation de cette éventualité imposerait l'adoption immédiate et simultanée aux deux Gouvernements.

Je me tiens d'ailleurs à votre disposition pour examiner toutes les questions qui, dans l'état actuel de la politique générale, s'imposent plus particulièrement à l'attention des deux Gouvernements.

D'autre part, le Gouvernement impérial se rendra compte sans doute, comme nous, de l'intérêt qu'il y aurait à confier à des délégués spéciaux, qui seraient désignés le plus tôt possible, l'étude pratique des mesures destinées à parer aux éventualités prévues par le second point de l'accord.

En vous priant de porter à la connaissance du Gouvernement de Sa Majesté la réponse du Gouvernement français, je tiens à marquer combien il m'a été précieux de pouvoir concourir, en ce qui me concerne, à la consécration d'une entente qui a été constamment l'objet de nos communs efforts.

APPENDIX II

(See chap. 10, pp. 161ff.)

Memorandum of General N. N. Obruchev, enclosed
with letter of Minister of War P. S. Vannovski to
Foreign Minister N. K. Giers, May 7/19, 1892
(translated from the Russian).*

Source: Arkhiv vneshnei politiki, Moscow. Sekretny arkhiv, Delo 373.

Obruchev Memorandum sent with Letter, Vannovski to Giers, May 7/19, 1892

Sincerely esteemed Nikolai Karlovich:
    . . . In connection with the proposal for the conclusion of a military convention with France, it is necessary to have in mind, first of all, the following circumstances.
    (1) The armaments of the European countries have now been developed to extreme limits, while their preparedness for mobilization is now measured not in weeks but in days and hours. Success on the battlefield now depends (other things being equal) on the most rapid possible deployment of the greatest possible mass of troops and on beating the enemy to the punch. Whoever first concentrates his forces and strikes against a still unprepared enemy has assured himself of the highest probability of having the first victory, which facilitates the successful conduct of the entire campaign. The undertaking of mobilization can no longer be considered as a peaceful act; on the contrary, it represents the most decisive act of war.
    This leads to the conclusion that today, in the light of the unavoidable approach of war, mobilization on the two sides has to take place as far as possible simultaneously, to the extent possible at the same hour, because the side that delays for even as much as twenty-four hours can pay for this bitterly. The term "mobilization" must now signify the inauguration of military operations themselves, at least by the advance detachments, which on both sides will endeavor to assure the mobilization and concentration of their own forces while hindering the similar operations of the enemy.
    The impossibility of delaying the actual opening of war means that at the moment of the declaration of mobilization no further diplomatic hesitation is permissible. All diplomatic decisions must be taken in advance on the basis of an entirely clear recognition of the military-political side of the struggle.
    (2) In order that at the moment of mobilization our diplomacy may be able to establish just who it is against whom we are launching the war, the following must be borne in mind:
    Given the present state of extreme military tension in Europe, marked by the buildup of armies of millions with all

their necessary equipment, it is hard to conceive that any war beginning on the Continent could be limited to an isolated struggle between any two states. Powers remaining initially on the sidelines would become sooner or later participants in the conflict: one in terms of open force, another in terms of political influence.

In any case, the conflict will end with a general congress; and at that congress the party that at the moment represents the strongest force will carry the greatest weight. The peace treaty will be written not so much by the victor, if the latter has exhausted his forces, as by the side that has preserved its forces and can threaten to launch a new war under conditions advantageous to itself.

Less than any other can our diplomacy count on an isolated conflict of Russia, for example, with Germany, or Austria, or Turkey alone. The Congress of Berlin was lesson enough for us in this connection, and it taught us whom we should regard as our most dangerous enemy—the one who fights with us directly or the one who waits for our weakening and then dictates the terms of peace?

For this reason, even though the treaty binding together the members of the Triple Alliance contains a clause recognizing the possibility of independent and separate actions by one or the other of the parties at its own risk and relieving the other parties in this case of responsibility for the consequences of the launching of war, nevertheless we should not attach serious significance to this clause, because the essence of the Triple Alliance with respect to Russia remains always the same, and the clause only provides for our neighbors a convenient means of masking the real extent of their compact at the very moment of the break.

At the outset of every European war there is always a great temptation for the diplomats to localize the conflict and to limit its effects as far as possible. But in the present armed and agitated condition of continental Europe, Russia must regard any such localization of the war with particular skepticism, because this could unduly strengthen the possibilities not only for those of our enemies who are hesitating and have not come out into the open, but also for vacillating allies.

Applying these considerations to the wishes concerning the conclusion of a military convention that have been put forward from the French side, the following becomes clear:

(1) The French are talking not about a treaty of alliance but only about a military convention that would provide for simultaneous mobilization of the French and Russian armies and for a plan of their operations, agreed upon in advance.

This procedure seems advantageous to them, because the conclusion of a treaty of alliance, like a declaration of war, requires parliamentary ratification, whereas the mobilization of the army can be declared by the President of the Republic, bypassing the Parliament, not wasting time on the debates of the Parliament, which, instead, will have to deal with an accomplished fact.

This way of looking at the question seems entirely reasonable. By having to deal only with the French government we protect the agreement from the influence of the political parties, the squabbling of which is given free rein in the Parliament. For this reason, casting our agreement in the form of a military convention is quite acceptable.

(2) As far as concerns the *simultaneity* of the mobilization of the armies: this entirely rational provision not only can but must be placed at the very foundation of the convention; but here one has to define the occasion for mobilization itself.

The French view Germany, almost exclusively, as their immediate enemy; they attach only secondary importance to Italy; and for Austria they even feel a certain sympathy, continuing to see in it the historical opponent of Germany.

To a certain extent this state of affairs is mutually advantageous for us; but we have to note that it is considerably more advantageous for France than for us. Having secured for herself a guarantee against her most dangerous enemy, France, in the event of a war between Russia and Austria, and even one arising at the orders of Germany, could remain disengaged and could await the development of events, which could have for us the most disastrous consequences. Given the extremely peace-loving disposition of the mass of the French people and the cleverness of German diplomacy, quite capable of restraining France from breaking entirely (if only temporarily, by offering her certain concessions), we could be left to our own devices and then, of course, could be compelled to fight not only with Austria but with the larger part of the German forces, and very possibly even with those of other German allies.

It would be extremely disadvantageous for us to venture alone onto the theater of war. Our isolation will always have an encouraging effect on all our opponents. But effective as may be the formidable combined forces of Russia and France in restraining others from getting into the conflict, with equal ease there could grow up a coalition against Russia, which would then be forced to defend herself from all sides.

For this reason it would scarcely be agreeable to us to conclude the convention exclusively with a view to a war with Germany. We are confronted with a Triple Alliance closely knit together in the military sense. Under no circumstances may we envisage separate actions against us by Austria or Germany. For this reason, we have to provide in the convention for simultaneous mobilization of the French and Russian armies in the case of an attack against them not of Germany but *of any of the powers of the Triple Alliance*, considering them to be solidly and inseparably united.

From the diplomatic point of view one can of course criticize the obligation on us that would flow from these considerations: i.e., to go to war immediately on our western border in case of a conflict between Italy and France; but only by the acceptance of such an obligation could we balance out the obligation laid upon France to mobilize and to go to war in case of an attack on us if only by Austria alone. This provision alone will remove all ambiguity, ensure to us the protection of an unvacillating ally under any and all circumstances, and limit the extent of the coalition formed against us.

(3) After that, the question of agreeing on the military operations of the two contracting parties can be decided in different ways.

The parties to the Triple Alliance, so far as is known, have agreed to deploy under certain circumstances a certain number of units. For example: in the most probable eventuality—that of a war between Austria and Russia—two auxiliary German armies (six–seven corps) and two Italian corps are to be attached to the

Austrian forces. Similarly, in the case of the conclusion by Russia of a convention with France, there can be a proposal to define their mutual participation in the struggle in terms of a certain number of corps. It would seem, however, that such a determination would not be suitable from our standpoint.

Once we have been drawn into a war, we cannot conduct that war otherwise than with all our forces, and against both our neighbors. In the face of the readiness of entire armed peoples to go to war, no other sort of war can be envisaged than the most decisive sort—a war that would determine for long into the future the relative political positions of the European powers, and especially of Russia and Germany. Entering upon military operations along our entire western border, we cannot bind ourselves by an obligation to deploy so and so many corps or 150,000 men against Germany and so and so many against Austria. We must retain full freedom to distribute our forces in such a way as to deliver a decisive blow at the armies of the Triple Alliance. It might be that for the achievement of this purpose we would find ourselves obliged to deploy our main forces against Germany, as the most dangerous and strongest opponent; but it might turn out to be even more advantageous to smash the Austrians as soon as possible, in order then to cope with an isolated Germany.

We have to retain for ourselves an absolute freedom of action, and for this reason it will be best, in questions of joint action with the French, to bind ourselves only by the general obligation: in case of an attack upon France by one of the parties to the Triple Alliance, to mobilize our army immediately and to begin military operations against the nearest to us of the powers of that alliance—Germany or Austria—while demanding a similar obligation of the French.

Adjutant General Obruchev

Upon the above paper, the Tsar made the notation: "I have read it. I would like this memorandum to be given to N. K. Giers, to be read by him, and to get his opinion on its political aspects."

APPENDIX III

Exchange of notes: Foreign Minister N. K. Giers to French Ambassador Montebello, 15/27 December, 1893; reply of Montebello, December 24, 1893/January 4, 1894; and text of military convention signed in August 1892 by generals N. N. Obruchev and Raoul le Mouton de Boisdeffre.*

*Sources: For letter of Giers to Montebello, December 15/27, 1893, *DDF*, vol. 10, no. 488, p. 712; for letter of Montebello to Giers, December 24, 1893/January 4, 1894, *DDF*, vol. 11, no. 7, p. 9; for text of military convention, signed in August 1892 between the two generals mentioned above, *DDF*, vol. 9, no. 444, pp. 643–644, as modified by ibid., vol. 9, no. 461, p. 682.

M. de Giers, Ministre des Affaires Etrangères, à M. de Montebello, Ambassadeur de France à Saint-Pétersbourg

L. Très secret.   Saint-Pétersbourg, 15/27 décembre 1893

Après avoir examiné, d'ordre suprême, le projet de convention militaire élaboré par les États-majors russe et français en août 1892 et en avoir soumis mon appréciation à l'Empereur, je me fais un devoir d'informer Votre Excellence que le texte de cet arrangement, tel qu'il a été approuvé en principe par Sa Majesté et signé par MM. l'aide de camp général Obroutcheff et le général de division Boisdeffre, peut être considéré désormais comme ayant été definitivement adopté dans sa forme actuelle. Les deux États-majors auront ainsi la faculté de se concerter en tout temps et de se communiquer réciproquement tous les renseignements qui pourraient leur être utiles.

M. de Montebello, Ambassadeur de France à Saint-Pétersbourg, à M. de Giers, Ministre des Affaires Etrangères de Russie

L. Secret.   Saint-Pétersbourg, 24 décembre 1893/4 janvier 1894

J'ai reçu la lettre que Votre Excellence m'a fait l'honneur de m'adresser le 15/27 décembre 1893, par laquelle elle m'annonce qu'après avoir, par ordre suprême, examiné le projet de convention militaire élabore par les États-majors russe et français et soumis ses appréciations à l'Empereur, elle se fait un devoir de m'aviser que cet arrangement, tel qu'il a été approuvé, en principe, par Sa Majesté et signé en août 1892 par M. l'aide de camp général Obroutcheff et le général de division de Boisdeffre, délégués tous deux à cet effet par leurs Gouvernements respectifs, peut être considéré désormais comme définitivement adopté.

Je me suis empressé de faire part de cette determination à mon Gouvernement et je suis autorisé à déclarer à Votre Excellence, en la priant de porter cette résolution à la connaissance de Sa Majesté l'Empereur, que le Président de la République et le Gouvernement français considèrent également ladite convention militaire, dont le texte est approuvé de part et d'autre, comme désormais exécutoire.

En conséquence de cet accord, les deux États-majors auront,

dès à présent, la faculté de se concerter en tout temps et de se communiquer réciproquement tous les renseignements qui pourraient leur être utiles.

Convention Militaire Signé en Août 1892 par M. L'Aide de Camp Général Obroutcheff et le Général de Division de Boisdeffre

1° Si la France est attaquée par l'Allemagne ou par l'Italie soutenue par l'Allemagne, la Russie emploiera toutes ses forces disponibles pour attaquer l'Allemagne.

Si la Russie est attaquée par l'Allemagne ou par l'Autriche soutenue par l'Allemagne, la France emploiera toutes ses forces disponibles pour combattre l'Allemagne;

2° Dans le cas où les forces de la Triple Alliance ou d'une des Puissances qui en font partie viendraient à se mobiliser, la France et la Russie, à la première annonce de l'événement et sans qu'il soit besoin d'un concert préalable, mobiliseront immédiatement et simultanément la totalité de leurs forces et les porteront le plus près possible de leurs frontières;

3° Les forces disponibles qui doivent être employées contre l'Allemagne seront, du côté de la France, de 1,300,000 hommes, du côté de la Russie, de 7 à 800,000 hommes.

Ces forces s'engageront à fond et en toute diligence, de manière que l'Allemagne ait à lutter à la fois à l'Est et à l'Ouest;

4° Les États-majors des armements des deux pays se concerteront en tout temps pour préparer et faciliter l'exécution des mesures prévues ci-dessus.

Ils se communiqueront, dès le temps de paix, tous les renseignements relatifs aux armements de la Triple Alliance qui sont ou parviendront à leur connaissance.

Les voies et moyens de correspondre en temps de guerre seront étudiés et prévus d'avance.

5° La France et la Russie ne concluront pas la paix séparément.

6° La présente convention aura la même durée que la Triple Alliance.

7° Toutes les clauses énumérées ci-dessus seront tenues rigoureusement secrètes.

NOTES

For a list of abbreviations of titles frequently referred to in these notes, see page xii.

Chapter 3
THE NARVA MANEUVERS

1. *Grosse Politik*, vol. 7, no. 1370, p. 14. Dispatch of Schweinitz, April 3, 1890, reporting his talk with Giers of March 31.
2. Ibid., no. 1372, p. 18. Report of talk with Giers of May 14, 1890.
3. Ibid.
4. Austrian archives, P.A. X, box 92. Russland, Berichte 1890. Dispatch, Aehrenthal to foreign office, September 10, 1890.
5. *Grosse Politik*, no. 1612, pp. 352–353.
6. Serge Goriainov, "The End of the Alliance of the Emperors," *American Historical Review* 23 (January 1918): 324–349. Goriainov was, prior to the Revolution, archivist of the Imperial Foreign Ministry; he prepared this article on the basis of materials from those archives.
7. *DDF*, vol. 8, no. 165, pp. 234–240. Excerpts from communication, Boisdeffre to Freycinet, August 15/27, 1890.
8. Boris Nolde, *L'Alliance franco-russe: Les Origines du système diplomatique d'avant-guerre* (Paris: Droz, 1936).

Chapter 4
THE "ENTENTE CORDIALE"

1. *DDF*, vol. 8, no. 165, pp. 234–240. Excerpts from communication, Boisdeffre to Freycinet, August 15/27, 1890.
2. Pierre de Boisdeffre, "Le général de Boisdeffre et l'alliance franco-russe (1890–1892)," *Hommes et Mondes* 9 (October 1954): 368–387.

3. *DDF*, vol. 8, no. 179, pp. 257–258. Dispatch, Laboulaye to Ribot, October 9, 1890.
4. Lamsdorf diary, February 19–March 3, 1891.
5. *DDF*, vol. 8, no. 304, pp. 419–420. Telegram, Ribot to Laboulaye, March 10, 1891.
6. French military archives. Dispatch of Briois, January 24, 1891.
7. The episode of the false documents is described in chapter 19 of this writer's *Bismarck's European Order*, and, in greater detail, in his article entitled "The Mystery of the Ferdinand Documents," *Jahrbücher für Geschichte Osteuropas* (Wiesbaden: Franz Steiner Verlag GmbH, 1978) 26:321–352.
8. *DDF*, vol. 8, no. 306, pp. 421–422. Telegram, Ribot to Laboulaye, March 12, 1891.
9. Alexandre Ribot, "L'alliance franco-russe," *Revue d'Histoire de la Guerre Mondiale* 15 (July 1937): 201–228.

Chapter 5
PRIVATE STIRRINGS

1. *La Nouvelle Revue* 69 (April 1891): 449–460.
2. Ibid.
3. René Girault, *Emprunts russes et investissements français en Russie, 1887–1914* (Paris: Publications de la Sorbonne. Librairie Armand Colin, 1973), pp. 191–193.
4. Austrian archives, P.A. IX, box 126. Frankreich, Berichte 1891 VII–XII. Varia, 1891.
5. *New York Times*, May 24, 1891, p. 2. (AP story with Berlin dateline.)
6. Lamsdorf diary, May 13/25, 1891.

Chapter 6
THE DISCUSSIONS RESUMED

1. Lamsdorf diary, May 28/June 9, 1891.
2. Ibid.
3. Ibid., July 3/15, 1891.
4. Ibid., July 6/18, 1891.
5. Ibid., June 22/July 4, 1891.

6. *DDF*, vol. 8, no. 415, pp. 556–558. Dispatch, Vauvineux to Ribot, July 9, 1891.
7. Ibid., no. 483, p. 645. Telegram, Laboulaye to Ribot, August 10, 1891.
8. Austrian archives, P.A. X, box 95. Russland, Berichte 1891 X–XII. Varia, 1891. Letter, Aehrenthal to Kálnocky, June 25/July 7, 1891.
9. *DDF*, vol. 8, no. 415, pp. 556–558. Dispatch, Vauvineux to Ribot, July 9, 1891.
10. Letter, Vlangali to Giers, July 2/14, 1891, box 4. Giers Family Papers, New York Public Library, New York, N.Y.
11. *DDF*, vol. 8, no. 427, p. 582. Telegram, Laboulaye to Ribot, July 18, 1891.
12. Ibid., no. 429, pp. 586–589. Letter, Laboulaye to Ribot, July 19, 1891; and no. 430, pp. 589–591. Letter, Laboulaye to Ribot, July 20, 1891.
13. This account of the Boisdeffre-Obruchev talks is drawn from Bois-deffre's report to General Miribel, as reproduced (apparently in full) in *DDF*, vol. 8, no. 424, pp. 576–580.

Chapter 7
CRONSTADT

1. *Grosse Politik*, vol. 7, no. 1514, p. 227. Giers related these details to the Germans when passing through Berlin later that year.
2. Austrian archives, P.A. X, box 95. Russland, Berichte 1891 X–XII. Varia, 1891. Letter, Wolkenstein to Kálnocky, August 9/21, 1891.
3. · Hans Lothar von Schweinitz, *Denkwürdigkeiten des Botschafters General von Schweinitz* (Berlin: Verlag von Reimar Hobbing, 1927), vol. 2, pp. 427–428.
4. Ribot mss., French archives. These data, concerning the reactions of Freycinet and Ribot to Giers' initiative, are taken from a long undated memorandum, drawn up at some later date by Ribot, summarizing the course of the negotiations for an alliance.
5. The simplified account given in this chapter of the various relevant exchanges of the days from August 5 to 10 is drawn from the confusing welter of communications reproduced, or described, in *DDF*, vol. 8, in some 15 of the items numbered from 457 to 483, pp. 618–645; and personal communications exchanged between

Ribot and Laboulaye, and also between Ribot and Freycinet and Carnot, as contained in French archives, vol. 30.

So complex is this body of material that attempts to relate individual statements in this account to individual items in the source material would only compound the confusion.

6. Russian archives, Delo 373. This contains the original of Mohrenheim's letter to Giers, reporting his transmission to the French of Giers' official letter to him. A Russian translation of it also appears in Lamsdorf's diary, August 18/30, 1891.

7. The letter just mentioned in note 6 above, with which Mohrenheim reported to Giers his exchange of communications with Ribot, does not include among its enclosures a copy of the covering letter with which he had forwarded to Ribot Giers' official communication, and which contained the unauthorized paragraph. A copy of that covering letter is indeed present in the Russian file, but not as an enclosure to Mohrenheim's communication; on the contrary, typed on a wholly different sort of paper, it is evidently of other provenance.

8. French archives, vol. 30. Ribot cited these statements of Mohrenheim in a letter he addressed to Carnot on the day (August 27) of the exchange of communications.

9. Lamsdorf diary, August 19/31, 1891.

10. The authentic text of this letter is found in the Russian archives, Delo 373. It is also reproduced in full in Lamsdorf's diary, August 23/September 4, 1891.

11. Lamsdorf diary, August 23/September 4, 1891.

12. Russian archives, Delo 373.

13. Jules Hansen, *Ambassade à Paris du Baron de Mohrenheim,* 2nd ed. (Paris: Flammarion, 1907), pp. 131–136. The account of this episode is found in Hansen's book.

14. Lamsdorf diary, September 4/16, 1891.

Chapter 9
THE MILITARY CONVENTION I

1. *DDF,* vol. 9, no. 76, pp. 111–114. Memorandum by Ribot of his talk with Giers of November 21, 1891, in Paris.

2. For the account of these interviews see: ibid., nos 74 and 76, pp. 109–114; and Ribot's memorandum on the negotiations in the

Ribot mss., French archives. A letter from Vlangali to Giers of October 31/November 12, 1891 (Giers Family Papers, New York Public Library), makes it evident that this visit was not the result of Giers' initiative but was arranged at the insistence of Mohrenheim, who claimed to feel that it was necessary for the purpose of supporting the political positions of Freycinet and Ribot.

3. *DDF*, vol. 9, no. 104, pp. 161–164. Letter, Montebello to Ribot, December 11, 1891. One is all the more puzzled over Giers' professed satisfaction with this discussion because reports, for which there was presumably some substance, were soon heard in diplomatic circles that Freycinet had shown himself anything but satisfied with Giers' statements, charging that Giers had spoken vaguely and superficially, professing dedication to the idea of preservation of the status quo, but failing to explain what he meant by that term. (Austrian archives, P.A. X, box 95. Russland, Berichte 1891 X–XII. Varia, 1891. Dispatch, Wolkenstein to foreign office, November 27/December 9, 1891.)

4. Accounts of Giers' visit to Berlin, from the pens of the German chancellor, Caprivi, and the minister for foreign affairs, von Marschall, are found in *Grosse Politik*, vol. 7, nos. 1513, 1514, and 1515, pp. 226–231. The details cited here are drawn chiefly from these documents.

5. Lamsdorf diary, November 19/December 1, 1891.

6. *DDF*, vol. 9, no. 90, p. 138. Telegram, Montebello to Ribot, December 5, 1891.

7. Ibid., no. 102, pp. 159–161. Dispatch, Montebello to Ribot, December 10, 1891; and no. 104, pp. 161–164. Letter, Montebello to Ribot, December 11, 1891.

8. Lamsdorf diary, January 9/21, 1892.

9. Ibid., November 15/27, 1891.

10. *DDF*, vol. 9, no. 134, pp. 199–202. Letter, Montebello to Ribot, January 9, 1892, enclosing paper prepared by Moulin.

11. The two drafts of this paper appear in *DDF*, vol. 9, no. 182, pp. 263–267, February 4, 1892, and no. 218, pp. 317–320, February 29, 1892.

12. These figures are culled from reports of May 29, June 10, and December 13, 1890, and December 30, 1891, from Moulin, as found in French military archives at Vincennes. The figures on the number of Russian reservists *de première ligne* are confusing, and

make it very difficult to estimate the number that could conceivably have been brought up to the European front sufficiently promptly to affect the initial stages of a war against Germany and Austria. As is evident, the French General Staff appears to have estimated these reserves at approximately 1,124,000 (1,600,000 minus the 476,000 already in line along the western border). These would have had to be drawn out of a total of 1,950,000 *"reservistes appelés au 1er tour,"* as mentioned by Moulin in his report of May 29, 1890, of which number it may be calculated that only some 1,600,000 might have been available for combat duty. This, however, would have been the figure for the empire as a whole. Not all, presumably, would have been available for the western front. Only about one-half of the peacetime standing army was normally stationed there.

13. Austrian archives, P.A. X, box 127. Frankreich, Berichte 1892. Dispatch, Hoyos, March 10, 1892.

14. Lamsdorf diary, February 8/20, 1892.

15. Ibid., February 25/March 9, 1892.

16. Ibid. This entire account of Giers' visit of March 8 to the Tsar and of Lamsdorf's reaction to it is taken from the latter's diary entry.

17. French military archives. Report of Moulin, February 21, 1892.

18. *DDF*, vol. 9, no. 231, p. 341. Telegram, Montebello to Ribot, March 16, 1892.

Chapter 10
THE PRELUDE TO NEGOTIATION

1. Ribot mss., French archives. Letter, Ribot to Montebello, April 12, 1892. (Montebello's reply suggests that this letter was actually dated the 14th.)

2. *DDF*, vol. 9, no. 285, pp. 413–415. Personal letter, Montebello to Ribot, April 22, 1892.

3. Ribot mss., French archives. Personal letter, Ribot to Montebello, April 28, 1892.

4. *DDF*, vol. 9, no. 296, p. 428. Telegram, Montebello to Ribot, May 4, 1892; and no. 300, pp. 434–436. Personal letter, Montebello to Ribot, May 6, 1892.

5. French archives, vol. 30. Telegram, Montebello to Ribot, May 23, 1892.

6. *DDF*, vol. 9, no. 318, p. 453. Personal letter, Ribot to Montebello, May 25, 1892.

7. Russian archives, Delo 373. The Russian original from which this translation is drawn is the copy sent to Giers by Vannovski, on the Tsar's orders, on May 7/19, 1892. The translation is my own. The text was also reproduced in Lamsdorf's diary, May 31/June 12, 1892.

8. Russian archives, Delo 373. Letter, Giers to Vannovski, May 13/25, 1892.

9. Jules Hansen, *L'Alliance franco-russe* (Paris: Ernest Flammarion, 1897), p. 90.

10. *Grosse Politik*, vol. 7, no. 1588, pp. 326–329. Dispatch, Münster to Caprivi, June 8, 1892. Ribot told the Austrian ambassador that Mohrenheim had inquired of the Tsar at Copenhagen and had obtained the latter's permission. If so, this was surely known to Giers.

11. Lamsdorf diary, June 4/16, 1892.

12. Ibid., March 30/April 12, 1892.

13. Ibid., April 27/May 9, 1892.

Chapter 11
THE MILITARY CONVENTION II

1. *DDF*, vol. 9, no. 366, pp. 522–524. Personal letter, Ribot to Montebello, June 23, 1892.

2. Letters, Shishkin to Giers, June 17/29 and July 2/14, 1892, Giers Family Papers, New York Public Library, New York, N.Y.

3. French archives, vol 31. Personal letter, Montebello to Ribot, July 16, 1892.

4. *DDF*, vol. 9, no. 421, pp. 614–616. Personal letter, Ribot to Montebello, July 28, 1892.

5. Ibid.

6. In this account of Boisdeffre's negotiations I am following, where not otherwise indicated, the long and detailed report, dated August 10, 1892, that he himself rendered to Freycinet, as reproduced in *DDF*, vol. 9, no. 447, pp. 647–663.

7. Pierre de Boisdeffre, "Le général de Boisdeffre et l'Alliance franco-russe (1890–1892)," *Hommes et Mondes* 9 (October 1954):368–387.

8. Lamsdorf diary, July 1892. (There were no actual diary entries for July. The copy of this letter, dictated by Giers but written in the hand of his son, was simply inserted among the pages of the diary.)

9. *DDF*, vol. 9, no. 444, pp. 643–644. Telegram, Montebello to Ribot, August 10, 1892.

10. Ibid., no. 461, pp. 672–682. Supplemental report by Boisdeffre to Freycinet, dated August 18, 1892.

11. Ibid., no. 447, pp. 647–663. See note 6 above.

12. Ibid., no. 444, pp. 643–644. Telegram, Montebello to Ribot, August 10, 1892.

13. Ibid., no. 449, pp. 663–664. Personal letter, Ribot to Freycinet, August 12, 1892.

14. Ibid., no. 458, pp. 669–670. Personal letter, Ribot to Montebello, August 17, 1892.

15. Lamsdorf diary, pp. 347–348 (date not given).

16. *DDF*, vol. 9, no. 457, p. 669. Telegram, Montebello to Ribot, August 17, 1892.

17. Lamsdorf diary, August 7/19, 1892.

18. Ibid., August 8/20, 1892.

19. *DDF*, vol. 9, no. 461, pp. 672–682. See both Boisdeffre's final report to Freycinet of August 18, and Montebello's letter of August 19, 1892, transmitting that report.

20. Ribot mss., French archives. Notes on events of September 1, 1892.

21. *DDF*, vol. 10, no. 7, pp. 9–10. Letter, Freycinet to Ribot, August 26, 1892; and ibid., no. 9, pp. 11–13. Letter, Ribot to Montebello, August 27, 1892.

22. Ribot mss., French archives. Notes for September 1, 1892.

23. Ibid. Letter, Ribot to Montebello, recorded under the date of September 7, 1892.

Chapter 12
PANAMA AND MOHRENHEIM

1. Austrian archives, P.A. IX, box 127. Frankreich, Berichte 1892. Dispatch, Hoyos to foreign office, November 17, 1892.

2. Ribot mss., French archives. Letter, Ribot to Montebello, January 14, 1892.

3. Lamsdorf diary, April 27/May 9, 1892.

4. Elie de Cyon, *Histoire de l'entente franco-russe, 1886–1894: documents et souvenirs,* 3rd ed. (Paris: Librairie A. Charles, 1895), pp. 441–443.

5. In the Ribot mss., French archives, there is a letter from Mohrenheim to Ribot, of highly agitated content, dated simply *"lundi"* but evidently from either the 13th or the 27th of March 1893, to which is attached a document entitled "Communication de l'Agence Dalriel," and dated *"Budapest, 21 janvier."* It contains the verbatim text of a statement by Szekely, from which the details mentioned in my account are taken.

6. Cyon, *Histoire,* p. 446.

7. *DDF,* vol. 10, no. 115, pp. 169–170. Telegram, Montebello to Develle, January 19, 1893.

8. Ibid., no. 120, pp. 177–178. Footnote to telegram, Develle to Montebello, January 21, 1893.

9. This is the letter referred to in note 5 above.

10. *Le Gaulois,* March 16, 1893, as cited in Adrien Dansette, *Les Affaires de Panama* (Paris: Perrin, 1934), pp. 164–219.

11. *DDF,* vol. 10, no. 186, p. 271. Footnote to telegram, Develle to Montebello, March 17, 1893.

12. K. P. Pobedonostsev, *K. P. Pobedonostsev i ego Korrespondenty,* vol. I (Moscow: Gosudarstvennoe Izdatelstvo, 1923), part 2, pp. 984–986. Letter, Cyon to Pobedonostsev, dated merely February 1893, received February 7.

13. Ribot mss., French archives. Private letter, Montebello to Ribot, June 5, 1893.

14. *DDF,* vol. 10, no. 195, p. 283. Telegram, Vauvineux to Develle, March 29, 1893.

15. Ibid., no. 212, pp. 308–310. Personal letter, Montebello to Develle, April 21, 1893.

16. Ibid., no. 229, pp. 334–338. Personal letter, Montebello to Develle, May 6, 1893.

17. Ibid., no. 241, p. 352. Note by Shishkin, May 16, 1893, transmitted by Mohrenheim to the French foreign office.

18. Ibid., no. 243, p. 354. Letter, Carnot to Mohrenheim, May 18, 1893.

19. Ibid., no. 264, pp. 388–390. Personal letter, Montebello to Develle, June 11, 1893. (Ribot's letter, referred to therein, appears as no. 253, pp. 365–368.)

20. Ibid., no. 229, pp. 334–338. Personal letter, Montebello to Develle, May 6, 1893.

Chapter 13
THE CONVENTION ADOPTED

1. Peter Jakobs, *Das Werden des französisch-russischen Zweibundes 1890–1894* (Wiesbaden: Otto Harrassowitz, 1968), pp. 153–154. In the preparation of this excellent work, Professor Jakobs was able to have more extensive access than was this writer to both the Boisdeffre mss. and the French military archives at Vincennes. So scrupulous was his use of these materials in his treatise on the negotiation of the Alliance that I have not hesitated to rely on his work for indications of the contents of documents I myself was unable to see.

2. See Montebello's confidential letters to Develle in *DDF*, vol. 10, no. 290, pp. 425–427, July 11, 1893; and in French archives, vol. 31, August 26, 1893.

3. The Miribel memorandum, as transmitted by Montebello to Giers on September 6, 1893 (*DDF*, vol. 10, no. 362, pp. 521–524. Letter, Montebello to Develle, September 7, 1893) gives a good summary of the contents of this bill, as finally approved by the Reichstag.

4. Jakobs, *Das werden*, p. 156.

5. *DDF*, vol. 10, no. 331, footnote 2, p. 484. Letter, Miribel to Develle, August 8, 1893.

6. Ibid.

7. French archives, vol. 31. Letter, Montebello to Develle, August 26, 1893.

8. Russian archives, Delo 373. Unsigned and undated memorandum, evidently placed in the file by Lamsdorf.

9. *DDF*, vol. 10, no. 362, pp. 521–524. Letter, Montebello to Develle, September 7, 1893.

10. Russian archives, Delo 373. Further undated memorandum in Russian, this time definitely written by Lamsdorf. The first paragraph of this memorandum reads as follows, in translation: "In the summer of 1893 His Majesty directed . . . Giers to reexamine the draft military convention held in the files of the General Staff but, while awaiting the reaction of the minister for foreign affairs,

not yet confirmed." The remaining contents of this document strongly suggest that these orders were given to Giers by the Tsar shortly before the latter's departure for Denmark, on or about August 23.

11. *Grosse Politik,* vol. 7, no. 1530, p. 247. Excerpt of letter, Caprivi to Marschall, September 24, 1893.

12. Ibid., no. 1533, pp. 250–253. Dispatch, Münster to Caprivi, October 30, 1893.

13. Ibid., no. 1534, pp. 253–254. Dispatch, Werder to Caprivi, November 27, 1893.

14. Jakobs, *Das Werden,* p. 162.

15. The data on the tensions within the royal party at Fredensborg and on the Tsar's visit to the French warship are taken from several sources, including H. Nielsen, *Dansk udenrigspolitik 1875–1894* (Odense: 1977); the so-called *Taffeljournaler* (record of those present at meals attended by the King and Queen of Denmark); and the similar *Dagjournaler,* in which the daily activities of the royal couples were recounted. Danish national archives, Overhofmarskallatets arkiv, Q. I. 13. *Dagjournaler,* Q. III. 9. *Taffeljournaler;* documents from the archives of the Danish foreign office, notably: note of October 10, 1893, Pasteur to foreign office, and dispatches of March 1, 2, and 3, 1894, from the Danish minister at Paris; Pasteur's various agitated reports in *DDF,* vol. 10, nos. 374, 376, 381, of October 1, 2, and 8, 1893, respectively, and above all, no. 400, pp. 583–586, of October 20; clippings from French newspapers of the period, included with the Danish foreign office documents; dispatches from Sir F. Denys, British minister at Copenhagen, of September 4, 9, 12, 14, 23, and October 17, 18, and 29, 1893, Public Record Office, London.

16. *Grosse Politik,* vol. 7, no. 1531, pp. 247–248. Dispatch, von Brincken to Caprivi, October 13, 1893.

17. Russian archives, Delo 373. Memo by Lamsdorf, dated only "1893," in French, describing disposition made by Giers of the Miribel memorandum.

18. Jakobs, *Das Werden,* p. 164.

19. Ibid., p. 166. Also, *DDF,* vol. 10, no. 475, pp. 692–695. Footnote on p. 694 in Dispatch, Montebello to Casimir-Périer, December 17, 1893.

20. *DDF,* vol. 10, no. 466, p. 682. Telegram, Montebello to Casimir-

Périer, December 13, 1893; ibid., no. 475, pp. 692–695. Dispatch, Montebello to Casimir-Périer, December 17, 1893.

21. Ibid., no. 475, pp. 692–695. Dispatch, Montebello to Casimir-Périer, December 17, 1893.

22. Russian archives, Delo 373. Further undated memo by Lamsdorf, in French, giving text of Giers' "Notice très secrète" of December 6, 1893, and describing events following upon its presentation.

Chapter 14
THE AFTERMATH

1. M. de Staal, *Correspondance Diplomatique de M. de Staal (1884–1900)*, vol. 2 (Paris: Publiée par le Baron A. Meyendorff, Librairie des Sciences Politiques et Sociales, 1929), p. 229.

2. Beyond the two volumes of Lamsdorf's diaries (*Dnevnik*, vol. 1 [Moscow: Gosizdat, 1926] and vol. 2 [Moscow: Akademia, 1934]), another fragment from the period around the deaths of Alexander III and Giers appeared in the series *Krasny arkhiv*, vol. 46.

3. *Grosse Politik*, vol. 7, no. 1663, pp. 445–446. Dispatch, Werder to Caprivi, July 28, 1893.

INDEX

Abdul-Hamid II, Sultan of Turkey, 127, 129–30, 131, 141

Adam, Juliette (French publisher), 69, 70, 72, 221

Aehrenthal, Count Lexa (Austrian chargé in Russia), 42, 86n., 103n., 111–12n.

Afghanistan, 126

Africa, 22, 119, 245. *See also* Egypt; Tunisia

Aigue-Mortes riots (1894), 245

Aix-les-Bains (France), 187, 189

Alaska, 133

Aleksei, Grand Duke (Russian naval minister), 40, 222

Alexander, prince of Battenberg and Bulgaria, 131

Alexander, King of Serbia, 133

Alexander II, Tsar of Russia, 5, 7, 8, 14, 16, 48, 141, 142, 148; assassination, 6, 18, 75

Alexander III, Tsar of Russia, xviii, 29, 31, 102n., 121, 171, 203, 223, 243

    DOMESTIC POLICY: anti-Semitic ukaz, 73–4, 74n., 77 and n., 145n., 174n.; famine and financial crisis, 144–6; nationalism, 9, 11, 20–1, 36, 74; railroad ukaz, 78, 134; reactionary attitudes, 5, 6, 74–5

    FOREIGN POLICY: 5, 6, 8–9; and Appert, recall of, 26, 65; Austrian relations, 8–9; Bulgarian policy, 8, 19, 41, 124, 128, 130–1, 132, 190,

250, 252; and diplomatic corps, 64 and n.; and Dreikaiserbund, 8–9, 18–19; and Ferdinand Documents, 60–1, 225n., 229; and French parliamentary crisis, 151–2, 200, 217–18; on French revanchism, 231–3; and German commercial treaty, 122–3, 245–6; German relations and attitude towards William II, 7–11, 32n., 39–41, 43–4, 50, 116, 120–1, 124, 136, 139, 140, 153–4, 164, 169, 174, 253 (*see also* Reinsurance Treaty; William II); and Giers, 5, 9–11, 35–6, 82, 88–9, 135, 140–1, 232; on Great Britain and Triple Alliance, 86; ministers and advisers, 6–7; and Narva maneuvers, 39–40, 43–6, 50–1, 68; on Panama scandal and Mohrenheim, 205–6, 210, 211–13; and Reinsurance Treaty renewal, 19, 20–1, 34, 35, 37, 41, 120; Turkish policy, 9, 34, 38, 39

    AND FRANCO-RUSSIAN ALLIANCE: and Empress Victoria episode (Feb. 1891), 56–7; decorates French officials (March 1891), 57–8, 58n., 67, 79; meetings with Flourens (1891, 1892), 60–1, 61n., 79 and n., 160 and n.; diplomatic initiatives (March–June 1891), 67–8, 87–9, 93, 94n.; and

285

Baku oil fields, 77

Balkans, 94 and *n.*, 132–3, 175, 187; and Austrian imperialism, 8, 37, 251–2; and military convention, 251–2; Russian policies toward, 9, 34–5, 130, 132–3, 190, 247, 252. *See also* Bulgaria; Serbia

Balzac, Honoré de, xvii

banks, bankers: French loans to Italy, 55; French loans to Russia, 32–3, 75–8, 80*n.*, 144–5, 159, 201 and *n.*, 202; German loans to Russia, 75, 122, 159

Banque de Paris et Pay-Bas (Paribas), 76, 144

Barrès, Maurice, xvii, 27

Beauchamps, Capt. (French attaché in Denmark), 225, 228

Belovyezhskaya Pushcha maneuvers, 239

Berlin, 75; Alexander III's 1889 visit, 39–40

Berlin, Congress and Treaty of (1878), 8, 95, 128, 265

Bialystok, 47, 148

Bismarck, Prince Otto von (German chancellor), xiii, xv, 7, 37, 43, 44, 119, 121, 124, 165, 225*n.*, 240, 247; and Ferdinand Documents, 60; and Reinsurance Treaty, 19, 20, 21–2, 34, 35; retirement, 11, 19, 20, 22, 33, 34; Russian opinion of, 8, 33; and Triple Alliance, 116, 119, 120, 252–3; on war with Russia, 156

Black Sea, 9, 83, 95, 127, 129, 130. *See also* Straits

Boisdeffre, Gen. Raoul le Mouton de (chief of French General Staff), 59, 88, 142, 147, 148, 157, 164, 230, 244, 258; character and life, 11–13, 16–17; report on talks with Russian officials (Aug. 1890), 45–9, 53–4, 65, 68, 142*n.*; audiences with Russian and German emperors (Aug. 1890), 49–50, 51; talks with Obruchev (June–July 1891), 88, 91–6, 142*n.*, 163, 253; military convention document (with Obruchev, July–Aug. 1892), 171, 173, 175–92, 234; on

need for publicity of Franco-Russian Alliance, 186, 193

Borodin, Alexander, xviii

Boulanger, Gen. Georges (French war minister), 3, 25, 69–70, 195

Boulangist movement, 3, 118, 195, 204, 214

Brinken, Freiherr von den (German ambassador to Denmark), 228

Briois, Col. (French attaché in Russia), 59

Brisson Commission, 198, 203, 205, 209

Bulgaria: Alexander III's policies toward, 8, 19, 41, 60, 124, 128, 130–1, 132, 190, 250, 251, 252; German, French, and Turkish policies toward, 131, 137; Giers-Ribot talks on, 137; Prince Ferdinand's regime, 41–2, 131–2

Caprivi, Gen. George Leo von (German chancellor), 93, 121; and Reinsurance Treaty renewal (1890), 19–20, 38–9; on a Franco-Russian alliance, 38, 39; at Narva (Aug. 1890), 41, 42, 45, 50; Muraviev interview (Sept. 1890), 43–4; Giers' visit to (fall 1891), 140; memo to Marschall (Sept. 1893), 222–3

Carnot, Sadi (French president), 59, 102, 103, 137, 151, 152, 168, 200; personality and political views, 29; decorated by Alexander III (1891), 57–8, 67; and Boisdeffre-Obruchev document (Aug. 1892), 180, 183, 186, 187, 188, 189; letter to Mohrenheim on Panama scandal (May 1983), 211–12; assassination (June 1894), 243, 246

Casimir-Périer, Jean (French premier and president), 231, 242–3

central Asia, 21, 35, 126

Chanzy, Gen. Antoine (French ambassador to Russia), 11–12

Chanzy, Mme. Antoine, 70

Charmes, Francis (French foreign-office official), 174*n.*

288
INDEX

Chatellerault munitions plant, 32, 59–60, 62

Chekhov, Anton, xviii

Chernyshevski, Nikolai Gavrilovich (Russian publicist and philosopher), 14, 165

Chikachev, Adm. (Russian deputy naval minister), 146

China, 105, 134, 135, 246–7

cholera epidemic (1892), 186

Christian IX, King of Denmark, 7, 60, 227 and n., 229; golden wedding anniversary, 157n., 226n.

cigarette smoking, xvi, 10

Claudel, Paul, xvii

Clemenceau, Georges, 151n.

Compagnie Universelle du Canal Interocéanique, 196–7

Constans, Jean-Antoine-Ernest (French interior minister), 31–2

Copenhagen, 98; French naval visit, 225–6, 226n., 227–9, 231; Hansen's mission to 112–15, 136, 138, 139

Cottu (Panama company director), 207, 208

Crenholm mills (Narva, Russia), 40

Crimean War, 34, 75, 96

Crispi, Francesco (Italian premier), 55

Cronstadt naval base, 40, 49, 224; French naval visit, 65–6, 88, 97–100, 103–4, 220, 223; political impact, 99–100, 106, 137, 140, 143, 145, 147, 202, 223, 247

Cyon, Elie de (I. F. Tsion; scientist, journalist, historian), 203 and n., 204, 205 and n., 209

Dagmar, Empress of Russia (Mariya Fyodorovna, wife of Alexander III), 8, 80, 178, 227, 229; character, 7; and Mohrenheim, 58, 107, 201

Danzig, 254

Dardanelles. See Straits

Dautresme, Auguste-Lucien (manager of French exposition), 79

de Staal (Russian ambassador to Great Britain), 239

Débats, Les (newspaper), 174

Decembrist uprising (1825), 98–9

Delahaye, Jacques (French editor), 203

democracies, 4, 256

Denis, Maurice, xvii

Denmark (see also Copenhagen): Alexander III in, 60, 110, 112–14, 136, 140, 217, 223–9; and Franco-Russian Alliance, 229–30; war with Prussia (1864), 7, 8, 229

Déroulède, Paul (French poet), 56, 69, 70, 222n.

Detaille, Edouard (French artist), 56

Develle, Charles-Paul (French foreign minister), 199, 208, 213, 215, 217–18; and Panama scandal, 210–11, 212

diseases, xvi–xvii, 186

Documents diplomatiques français, 12, 46, 217

Dolgorukov, Prince V. A. (governor general of Moscow), 71, 72, 73, 74 and n., 78

Dordogne region (France), 14, 16, 186; Boisdeffre-Obruchev talks, 88, 91–6, 142n., 163, 253

Dragomirov, Gen. Mikhail Ivanovich (Russian official at Kiev), 147n., 155

drama, xviii

Dreikaiserbund (Three Emperors' League), 101, 121, 165; and Alexander III, 8–9, 18–19. See also Reinsurance Treaty

Dreyfus affair, 12, 13, 244

Drumont, Edouard (French editor and publicist), 198

Dupuy, Charles (French premier), 199, 208, 215, 231, 242, 243

Durnovo, "Missi" (wife of Russian interior minister), 98

East Prussia, 47, 148

Egypt, 28, 105, 125, 128, 131, 137, 245

World War I, xiii–xiv, xx, 16, 166, 235;
casualties, xx; inevitability, acceptance
of, 30, 156, 163, 248, 257; as modern
war, 164, 166
World War II, 166, 254, 258

Zanzibar Treaty, 22. *See also* Helgoland
Zita, Empress of Austria, 132*n*.
Zola, Emile, xvii, 13